Creating and Managing the
Literate Classroom

Creating and Managing the Literate Classroom

SUZANNE I. BARCHERS

Illustrated by
Leann Mullineaux

TEACHER IDEAS PRESS
A Division of
Libraries Unlimited, Inc.
Englewood, Colorado
1990

TEACHER IDEAS PRESS
A Division of
Libraries Unlimited, Inc.
P.O. Box 3988
Englewood, CO 80155-3988

Library of Congress Cataloging-in-Publication Data

Barchers, Suzanne I.
    Creating and managing the literate classroom / Suzanne I. Barchers
; illustrated by Leann Mullineaux.
    xv, 187 p. 22x28 cm.
    Includes bibliographical references.
    ISBN 0-87287-705-1
    1. Language arts (Elementary) 2. Teaching. 3. Activity programs
in education. 4. Reading (Elementary) 5. Classroom management.
I. Title.
LB1576.B294   1990
372.6'044--dc20   89-48229
                                                   CIP

Dedicated to my mother, Inez, and the memory of my father, Charles Dumville, who together created my first literate environment.

Contents

8—MANAGEMENT OF THE WRITING PROGRAM (*continued*)

9—MAKING THE READING AND WRITING CONNECTION 121

Preface

Underlying my creation and management of a literate classroom is a philosophy of teaching and learning drawn in part from the writings of Jeannette Veatch, Donald Graves, Frank Smith, Dan Kirby and Tom Liner, Jim Trelease, and Susan Ohanian, editor for *Learning* magazine. Their publications are cited throughout this book. This philosophy was also influenced by college professors such as Virginia Westerberg, a children's literature professor, and Miles Olson, my thesis advisor, who both treated me like an independent learner and encouraged me to search for answers to teaching in the areas of literature and writing. It has evolved through fifteen years of teaching in public and private schools in small towns, inner cities, and suburbs across the United States.

Creating and Managing the Literate Classroom is grounded in the belief that a literate, interdisciplinary, library-centered classroom can exist, and it provides the "how-tos" of the management of alternative programs. It is written in the hope that it will inspire other teachers, librarians, and administrators to take some risks and become true participants in the education of our children. The activities or projects were used with my recent classes of grades three through five. Interested primary teachers tested projects such as the research reports, and my past years of teaching kindergarten and first grade using language experience techniques complete the background upon which I have drawn.

Creating and Managing a Literate Classroom provides guidance for finding inexpensive and effective materials, in addition to management techniques, lesson ideas, structured projects, and immediately usable reproducible pages for implementation of the many ideas that are described. It is ideal for both inexperienced or seasoned teachers who want to explore alternative techniques while continuing with the traditional program. It is also designed to offer support to those teachers, librarians, parents, and administrators who want to begin a collaborative transition from manual-driven curricula to alternative programs.

Chapters 1 through 5 assist with the utilization of resources such as your libraries and the nuts and bolts of organization. Chapters 6 through 10 deal with the program in process—reading, researching, writing. Chapter 11 provides my first choices for books for the literate classroom, and the appendixes provide parent handouts, a unit on mice, and a bibliography of alphabet books.

As you read through the chapters, keep in mind that all teachers develop their own individual styles. Keep an open mind, selecting, rejecting, or adapting practices or units that suit your style and needs. Copy the reproducible pages for student use and alter or use them as provided.

Participatory education involves not just the students, teachers, and administrators, but includes parents, community members, legislators, and school staff such as custodians, secretaries, and paraprofessionals. As you begin to expand your program to include more participants, remember that just as the students need time to learn and grow, so do teachers. And that although success is important, failure is also part of the learning process. Good luck with creating and managing your own literate classroom! And don't forget to have fun!

SUZANNE I. BARCHERS, Ed.D.

Acknowledgments

Appreciation for support is due many people: my former principal Bill Branch, who gave me the freedom to create and teach in a literate classroom, the many professional friends and associates, whose names are sprinkled throughout this book, editor David Loertscher, and my readers: fellow educator Carolyn Alfredson, educator/illustrator Leann Mullineaux, and friend Dick Scott. I especially want to thank educators Marla Jacobson and Charla Pfeffinger (also my sister) who not only read and responded, but who painstakingly edited my drafts.

My husband Dan deserves a special award for keeping me functional on the computer and for claiming he didn't mind getting up at 5:00 a.m. to fix something I destroyed. Thanks also goes to my sister Connie Mantarro for her support and the presumptuous and pretentious tee shirt. Finally, my boys, Jeff and Josh, are given my appreciation for a summer of no altercations during which I could write.

Chapter 1

Introduction to
the Literate Classroom

The use of alternative language arts programs, especially whole language or literature based, seems to be the 1990s answer for the eternal question of how to teach reading and writing. Universities are offering classes, school districts are holding regular inservices, and teachers are either embracing new techniques with enthusiasm or nervously struggling to understand how to manage in light of these latest trends.

Using the whole language or literature based approach is basically a philosophical orientation which depends on teachers developing the skills needed to teach from their heads rather than from manuals. There is no package system to support the instruction. Yet, historically, most districts have fostered the profession's lack of confidence by investing heavily in basal readers rather than in teacher skills or credibility. Now the rules are changing. Professionals who have been taught largely with basal readers are being given the directive to buy into what they secretly suspected all along—that children learn best by actually reading and writing, not by doing endless exercises. Yet teachers are being expected to implement these processes with little, if any, administrative support, and those who were totally indoctrinated by the use of the package system are legitimately overwhelmed by district demands to become autonomous—bereft of the comfortable and supportive basal readers.

JUST WHAT IS A
WHOLE LANGUAGE PROGRAM?

A whole language program is a philosophical perspective that recognizes the need to use reading and writing in a meaningful manner, not as isolated skills. Readers strive for understanding through all available cueing systems. Writers endeavor to create comprehensible expressions of their thoughts. Mastery of the language arts occurs through the purposeful use of a variety of pertinent materials that might include trade books, reference materials, journals, signs, charts, letters, newspapers, and student published works. It does not mean that skills or phonics are never taught; instead, they are taught in the context of need rather than in the order of a prescribed system such as a basal reader.

Whole language is difficult to characterize because it is a framework that has choices. Thus any group of whole language teachers may have shaped a program differently to best meet the needs of the children and utilizing the skills of the individual teacher. Jane Thomas, a whole language teacher in Denver, describes whole language as a continuum of activities ranging from teacher directed to student directed. A teacher who selects a novel for a group to read and guides the discussions is on one end of the continuum, while the teacher who allows students to choose their books and respond to them as they please might be on the other end of the continuum. In the middle of the continuum is the teacher who uses activities such as the Student Implemented Book Guides described in chapter 6. All of these activities are acceptable and a teacher might find a niche that works especially well for everyone or shift positions on the continuum throughout the year. (For a succinct overview of whole language, consult Ken Goodman's *What's Whole in Whole Language?* and for an in-depth discussion of a literature based program, see Jeannette Veatch's *Reading in the Elementary School*.)

I strongly advocate either a whole language or literature based program and have been using these techniques for many years. I believe that most children learn best using these methods because they serve a variety of learning styles and develop the students' thinking skills. Yet, I also believe that the worst thing that could happen to whole language is for districts to *mandate* its usage in individual schools, or worse, entire districts. It takes study, change, and hard work for a teacher to manage the complexity of such a program. For whole language or literature based programs to be successful, they depend not only on teacher internalization of a new philosophy, but on student investment from the bottom up.

Just as I believe that children learn most effectively through having choices, teachers teach best when they are in control of the classroom. All over the United States, teachers are studying Donald Graves and Ken Goodman and beginning to make the transition on their own. These professionals have either become inspired through their own desires to meet the needs of their students or by courses, professional reading, or coworkers. They have chosen to face the challenge of learning a new way. They were not directed to learn it. Thus dictating administratively that whole language is now the answer not only challenges the basic principles on which such programs have been developed, it almost guarantees failure.

WHY CREATE A LITERATE CLASSROOM?

District policies and philosophies aside, few experts would argue with the need to provide students with a literate environment. Any classroom would benefit from having its own internal library and a teacher who keeps current in the area of children's literature. Providing a literate classroom could be accomplished easily with unlimited money, space, and time, but a modest beginning is not only wise, it is nearly always dictated by economics.

However, even with support, making the transition to an alternative program can be challenging. Though good teachers have been using many whole language or literature based techniques regularly, it seems unreasonable to expect them to become an expert in any alternative program with one or two workshops. Yet teachers are rarely allowed the luxury of time to assimilate an entirely new approach—critical to the success of teaching an alternative program.

Creating and Managing the Literate Classroom provides support for those teachers who want to begin to explore new ways to think and teach. It is not an instruction manual for teaching a whole language or literature based program, although it has the same basic philosophies. I have tried to concentrate on techniques of management and implementation. Through my years in the classroom and the workshops I have presented I am well aware that while teachers need an understanding of the philosophy, they also want help with getting started. They want to be able to go to class Monday morning eager to try something because it fits with the needs of their students.

CREATING THE LITERATE CLASSROOM

Physical Setting

The physical setting of my classroom in Park Hill Elementary had a strong influence on my program. The eighty-year-old-school in Denver has a newer wing that houses the library and primary classrooms. However, I was fortunate to have a large airy room with high ceilings and three walls of built in oak bookshelves that had been the old library. I filled the room with hundreds of books I had acquired over the years. For the first time I could have all my books housed in my classroom, reducing the amount of time and effort spent hauling them to and from school.

Teaching in the atmosphere of a library helped me fulfill a fantasy of spending my professional life introducing children to good literature. I didn't want to become a librarian, because I never wanted the burden of cataloguing, shelving, and ordering. Rather I wanted to be surrounded by the beloved books I would share with the children. As I refined my program I began to think of it as library centered, in part because of the setting but also because the library—classroom, school, professional, or public—became my first source when preparing to teach a unit. Often the library was the setting for the initial stages of research the students undertook.

A literate classroom has structure, although at first it may appear chaotic. It is full of books and materials that are available for students. If it is a primary classroom everything has labels at the children's eye level. There are projects in progress, and artwork or writing on every available wall, hanging from wires, and propped on shelves. There are areas that invite reading, writing, creating, contemplation, or isolation. There may be centers with materials for learning organized by subject matter or theme.

There are many books from a variety of sources. There are fiction and nonfiction titles, dictionaries, thesauri, atlases, perhaps a set of encyclopedias, and textbooks. Magazines and newspapers are available. Everything has labels so students know how to find them.

There is audiovisual equipment available for student and teacher use. If space allows, it may be permanently arranged for independent use. If space is limited it may be used with units of study and then stored until another time. Maps, globes, and basic equipment such as microscopes for spontaneous study are accessible for immediate needs.

Supplies for communication and creation need not be in abundance, but needs are met with variety and creativity. All sorts of paper are used for different projects: used computer paper, scraps of construction paper, notebooks, etc. Students never lack paper or pencils.

Underlying the books and materials is the order of the classroom. Desks maximize learning, allowing for small work groups, movement, and gathering of large groups. Being able to meet as a group is important to the atmosphere. (For more information regarding recent research related to the arrangement of a room, refer to *Supporting Literacy: Developing Effective Learning Environments*.) However, no matter what the constraints regarding space, materials, supplies, and student and/or administrative needs, creating a literate classroom is as much a state of mind as a state of being. With creativity and the utilization of an array of resources, you can expand the classroom walls to include as large a community of teachers and learners as you wish.

The Teacher

A successful alternative program demands a teacher with a strong sense of the program and a degree of confidence. At my son's recent Back to School Night, the teachers carefully explained how they handled the diversity in the reading classes. They used three different basals for the three different groups of learners, but all the basals were at the same grade level! These teachers were very pleased that they met differing needs, oblivious to the apparent irony. Granting that their suburban neighborhood was more homogeneous than the urban school in which I taught, perhaps three similar grade-level basals really covered everyone's needs. But I doubt it.

Not once during this Back to School Night did anyone mention thinking skills or that critical word "process." Their *entire* presentation consisted of showing the textbooks used. Of course, accountability is more difficult in an alternative program because you can't point to a stack of textbooks and say, "That's what I teach." It requires intimate knowledge of the students—who they are, what they know and don't know, what they are doing, and where they are going—without a stack of papers to validate their assessment. An approach that develops literacy requires a broad knowledge of existing materials and supplies, plus the energy to acquire or borrow them.

Once the program is in place, organization must be apparent to all users, even if it isn't obvious to a casual visitor. With the open-ended activities, many teachers might flounder unless they are convinced the students are truly following through with their assignments. For example, many teachers prefer to work in a relatively quiet room although such an atmosphere is counterproductive in certain instances. It is necessary to teach your expectations carefully and rehearse appropriate behaviors with the students (chapter 4 discusses these skills in more depth).

The Oxford dictionary defines listening as "hearing attentively." We never outgrow the need to have someone give us his or her undivided attention. We know when someone has tuned us out—the eyes glaze over or the body becomes fidgety. I had to encourage my students to come to me for help—the willingness to seek help often gets squelched (or isn't needed) in a prescriptive program. But one student noted, quite accurately, that when she requested help in math I would get cranky. I told her that was true because she didn't listen when I was giving direct instruction and I was tired of giving her private lessons. We struck a deal: she would be more attentive and I would be less irritable when she really needed help. Our frankness with each other was possible because she felt she could tell me exactly what she thought without reprisals and that I would be willing to listen. Build trust and give your students the attention you would like when communicating and it becomes easier to insist upon their reciprocation.

A successful program also requires a teacher with an attitude of collegiality, a willingness to cooperate and facilitate collaboration for the education of the children. A teacher of such a program cannot retreat behind the classroom doors, gather together the children, and ignore the rest of the school or world. Success requires the willingness to recruit help among administration, staff, and parents. One of the sources of knowledge most often ignored is the students' parents. Teachers are often threatened by the parents, envisioning them as adversaries. When teachers insulate themselves from parents until conference time, they miss an opportunity to build the base for a collaborative effort. Once parents are equally invested in the program, they become allies. Obtaining parental involvement needs to be an integral part of the program, and not just lip service to what we know is best.

Creating the literate classroom also requires an active involvement with or appreciation of music, art, current events, books, films, magazines, the community, and the world of the children. If the resident faculty resists such cooperation, the conscientious teacher proceeds with the program, generating support gradually through demonstration of enthusiasm and success.

Flexibility is another key attribute of the teacher in a literate classroom. In the middle of a science lesson about the solar system, this teacher will remember a favorite poem about the stars and will reach for the poetry collection kept available for those very moments. The teacher in the literate classroom will share his or her talents or passions with the children: musical instruments, biking, photography, hiking, writing poetry, or reading. Conversely, student and parent sharing is encouraged and incorporated into the program whenever appropriate.

In sum, successful programs require teachers who carefully structure the routine, actively teach their expectations, and rehearse appropriate behaviors. These teachers listen to the students through journals, conversation, or letters, demonstrating that what students have to say is important, and then respond through journals, letters, notes, or conversation. Also, these teachers listen to the parents, seek help from other professionals, and participate in the educational process, serving as mentors, coaches, managers, critics, facilitators, and educators.

An Interdisciplinary Approach

Developing literate learners in a classroom of diverse students requires a program that draws upon every possible resource. No one approach reaches every learner. My son, who had reading problems, was in essentially a literature based program and his progress was minimal. Since he had been diagnosed as being reading disabled and was in a private school with outstanding teachers, I trusted that it all would work out eventually. And it did, but not until he was in a public school in fifth grade using a basal reader! Was it his age, the basal, the teacher, some changes in his brain? No one knows why students who are disabled readers suddenly become successful. I believe that the literature based program maintained my son's love of books, and that this love might have been lost with the structure of a basal reader. Even though I truly believe the remedial students are the ones who most desperately need to be charmed into reading books, I am always alert to the fact that it is not easy to predict what will work for each child.

There is no single best way to manage a successful program. Although some teachers find no value whatsoever in the basal readers, some use favorite stories from the basal. Some teachers reorganize the skill sheets to teach skills as students need them. A teacher might choose some stories, skipping most and then spending an extensive amount of time on others. Other teachers might spend a month in a basal with one group while reading novels with another group and then spend a month with the whole class reading and writing fairy tales. One group could be reading one novel while another reads a different novel. An entire class might read the same novel together, using paired reading or other cooperative techniques. Sometimes everyone might read different books of their own or the groups choosing. The astute teacher will judge what will work by watching, listening, sometimes eavesdropping, and thinking about where each student is and what that student is doing. Sometimes student activities are simply for pleasure.

If you are in a district that has the luxury of art and music teachers, keep them advised of your program and work towards integrating the curriculum. Some special teachers do not have the flexibility to adjust their programs, especially given the preparation time involved. However, if you ask the teachers what their plans are, you might discover that they are working on similar activities or can easily adapt to a unit of study you have in mind. A bit of diplomacy will help in this instance.

If you have to teach your special classes by yourself, you will need to have an even greater knowledge of the library's resources. I am lucky to have training in music, a piano in my classroom, and a passable singing voice. But many teachers have received only the rudiments of music during their undergraduate work. Developing a knowledge of picture books with related records, such as *Peter and the Wolf* by Sergei Prokofiev, can aid the teacher who must teach music and art. Several weeks of music classes can be spent studying Russian music, Prokofiev, instrumentation, illustrations, and viewing the film (see end of chapter 3 for other ideas for integrated units for music and art).

Groupings

Over the past few years I have become more and more disenchanted with grouping students, finding groups artificial and restrictive. It has always been difficult to assign students to groups; and, with the recent emphasis on mainstreaming special education students, the absurdity of groups becomes even more apparent. When other teachers are involved, grouping students becomes additionally constraining as their needs are often at odds with yours. I have observed that students learn best when interacting with students of different abilities. What could be more stultifying than being a poor reader and listening to a group of other poor readers stumble through the reading and discussion of a book? Also, the gifted students who learn through the open-ended activities described in this book have their own internalized personal and academic challenges. Developing a community of learners means recognizing that all children are contributors and that collaboration is not only acceptable but is supported by the program.

Although I gather students into groups for instruction, for example, separating twenty-five students reading the same novel into smaller groups, I group students for specific reasons, not because it is routine. The teaching of skills is best done in small groups made up of the children who need to learn that particular skill. Assemble groups as needed, not just because grouping has been the normal pattern of teaching reading in the past.

The techniques in this book generally cut across all groupings. They were tested with all levels of learners, including the mainstreamed mentally retarded, learning disabled, remedial, average, and gifted. Other teachers' priorities can dictate your groupings, and the reading and writing program can accommodate a diverse population. Expectations should vary with different levels of ability or achievement, but every sincere effort by a student should be considered worthy and validated, no matter how basic or exploratory the result.

The Students

Elementary students are probably going to become even more diverse over the next few years. Special education teachers may become more rare as tax dollars dwindle, or instead they may be coming into the classroom to collaborate on the teaching of all kinds of students. As mentioned in the discussion of groupings, a teacher's job is to develop students who will rely on class members and/or themselves for much of their learning. They will talk, read books, and read their writing to each other. They will learn the skills to support and coach each other with tact and grace. They will be like a sports team that groans at the goofs and cheers at the successes. You will have a group of truly collaborative learners. They will make mistakes, goof off, and sometimes escape. But in time they will stretch, succeed, coach, praise, critique, learn, and become literate.

The students in an alternative program will have more freedom than ever before. This is sometimes difficult for students who have always been told every move to make. All students need to be coached so they know that help is available from anyone who is in the room, regardless of age or function. Many thrive on the options, others will take shortcuts and have to experience lower grades before they accept the program; and a few will be intensely uncomfortable with the alternatives, feeling as if they are "drowning." Those few will need coaching and directing to become successful managing the more open-ended aspects of their own learning. (Often it is the brighter students who struggle the most with choices, possibly because they know that now the burden to perform truly rests on their shoulders.)

One of the most irritating questions a student can ask is, "How long should it be?" There are certainly some projects that require a minimum number of pages, but when someone is writing a fairy tale or poem, it is presumptuous to dictate length for such an individually creative process. A typical response of mine is, "Write what it takes to tell the story (or make the poem effective). If you have extra time, write another." After hearing this response for a month or two, the students give up and become good judges of what is appropriate; they learn to make their own choices.

It is tempting to organize the work for those dependent learners, but help should be minimal, perhaps in the form of a checklist that provides the learner a reminder of general requirements. Living successfully in today's world requires a vast number of decisions, and schools do a disservice to students and to society by not incorporating choices into the daily routine. With a steady diet of step-by-step instruction, children are ill equipped to deal with an increasingly demanding society. Learning to make choices and accept the consequences is best accomplished in an environment that supports taking risks.

In a workshop about teaching research reports, I was once asked, "But what about the student who doesn't do the research or does a poor job?" My answer was that during the process you monitor, cajole, nag, and perhaps bribe. If students are capable and still do not follow through, they suffer the consequences and earn a grade that corresponds to the effort expended. The student has in effect chosen the grade. Of course, the individual who struggles against a learning disability or low achievement to complete only a portion of the assignment must be evaluated with some compassion.

When students receive grades they don't say "Whadja' earn?" They say "Whadja' get?" But teachers and students need to remember teachers don't *give* the grades; students *earn* them through their choices. The management of whole language or literature based programs requires a greater degree of student responsibility. This does not mean that students are given the assignments and are then left to flounder. Rather, the effort is collaborative, with students being coached to take responsibility for their learning as well as self-evaluation.

Time

Teachers never feel as if they have adequate time to teach everything. All too often they try to fill every moment with "busyness," even to the extent of putting problems on the board for students to tackle while they complete the day's preliminary tasks. One child wrote eloquently in her journal about these activities assigned by another teacher: "Every day we do these papers, and we never have time to finish them. They are piled up in my desk. What do you think I should do, Mrs. Barchers?" She clearly recognized that these worksheets must not be significant, because they were never collected or evaluated. My mother, a teacher for over thirty years, said, "Sometimes it would be 9:30 before I could start teaching—there would be so many things to do first. I didn't try to be a magician and have a perfect situation every second. You could have a nervous fit if you tried to keep everything working perfectly all the time." My preference is to have students write in their journals during the morning rituals. It gives them a chance to communicate with you even if you can't read the journals till later, and they can take time to ease into the business of learning.

Once teachers have accepted that making choices is an important feature of an alternative program, it becomes essential to provide the time to make responsible choices. When we encourage students to experiment and take risks, they need the liberty to sample, dabble, suspend, meditate, stretch, and sometimes quit. It takes maturity to recognize that a certain book may not be quite right, and students should be allowed the dignity to bail out in midstream. I have had students who are struggling with a project or open-ended assignment come up to me and ask, "But what do *you* want me to do?" I tell them I want them to think and decide what is right for them. They know what the general expectations are and they know I respect any work if it represents a sincere effort. They also know that I won't dictate to them.

If students are to think about their options, they need the time to do so. Writing in journals takes some degree of contemplation, or the entries are rote or frivolous. Finding the right words for a poem can be one of the most time-consuming tasks a student faces, especially when the finished product, by definition, is compact. Deciding which books are appropriate for research is especially taxing. Consider how many hours we spend in a library or bookstore, sampling a paragraph or page of many books before deciding to invest time and money, or both, in one single title. We all want our choices to be suitable ones, and we devote time to such decisions routinely. Students deserve the same privilege.

Bringing the Larger Community of Resources and Learners Together

Teachers who want to open the world to their students cannot do it alone. Few of us have mastered all the subjects that are taught in the elementary classroom; yet, depending on the resources of our district, we might be expected to teach math, reading, social studies, economics, geography, history, art, music, physical education, writing, grammar, spelling, health, sex education, affective education, and social skills, plus whatever new gimmick might come down the pike. We also might be expected to provide remediation for low achievers and enrichment for the gifted students, while turning out disciplined, responsible future citizens. And yet, all those subjects are not what children remember. My mother said, "The main thing is to treat the kids with love and respect and give them some interesting things to do so they love you back. I know that from going to the fiftieth reunion of students I taught in Allendale, Michigan. No one talked much about subjects, but they remembered the extra activities and the things we did for fun."

Teachers need to quit trying to do it all alone and need to open the classroom doors to all the resources available to them. Some districts have a community resources service that recruits specialists in the arts, sciences, and businesses who are willing to donate time to the classroom. Through our program this year my class hosted (among others) a watercolor artist, a physician from China, a retired science teacher who presented demonstrations on electricity, and the head of a blood bank who gave a presentation on blood and the circulatory system.

An alternative way to bring the world to the classroom is to recruit presenters during Back to School Night. Parents can be asked to list their vocations and avocations. This information can be filed and added to from year to year. Often just one visit from an expert will provide you with a start for related topics. For example, after the visit of the watercolor artist, I could help the students paint watercolors of the planets during our study of the solar system. One student was so taken by the process that he began painting at home and during Teacher Appreciation Week he proudly brought me a lovely framed watercolor of Saturn. Another student's painting won inclusion in the district's art exhibit.

Don't sell your parents short, even in the poorest district. Make it clear that you will work *with* any volunteer and you do not expect one person to create an entire program. Even if recruiting parents does require extra work and is not always totally successful, always be open to ideas. Last fall I received a note from a parent who wanted to know if she could help out in my reading program. I was not sure how to respond since my students were quite independent and most of my assignments were *not* worksheets that could be taught or graded by anyone. Further, I felt it was important that I be in charge of the individual reading and writing conferences to establish the level of trust so necessary to the success of my program. Finally, I suggested she talk with me after hearing the presentation about the program at Back to School Night. Perhaps this would give us ideas of how she could help out.

When we met, I was delighted to learn that Ruth Cambier was a former reading teacher who wanted to take small groups of students to the library once a week to work on short- and long-range research topics. She had materials and a direction, yet was willing to adjust her plans for projects such as our New York City research (see *The Cricket in Times Square* research project in chapter 7). There were occasions when she was unable to come, but since she was taking small groups while our program continued, I was able to adjust. The students' research skills improved dramatically, which was evidenced on both criterion- and norm-referenced tests, and I was able to concentrate on other aspects of the program. The following year she returned to teach speech and debate to groups of students.

Another parent, Mary Lee Chin, asked me if I would like her help in celebrating the Chinese New Year in the classroom. Due to her Chinese heritage, she had several suggestions including a speaker, cooking, a slide show, a presentation on Chinese objects she had collected, and use of a dragon she had made for a previous class. Coincidentally, *Classmate* (see bibliography in chapter 3) had several worksheets on Chinese characters, geography, art, and the language. The issue also included several appropriate art projects. Other references included Ms. Chin's Chinese books; some books I had bought at Epcot Center, and collections I found in the library. We planned a two-week period of immersion in the Chinese culture. Students did a short research project with teacher-directed questions. The class spent an afternoon of preparing, cooking, and eating Chinese food with chopsticks. Our study culminated with the entire class winding its way through the school under a magnificent dragon. Ms. Chin, a nutritionist by profession, later was helpful with a unit on nutrition.

It is necessary to be flexible when using parent and professional volunteers. They are donating their time and teachers need to be willing to adjust to emergencies. Our China unit was postponed for two weeks because Ms. Chin's child got the chicken pox.

In school districts where there are no art teachers, formal programs of recruiting parent volunteers to provide art appreciation have evolved. Various names for this program have existed, and "The Picture Lady" has been replaced in most areas by "Friends of the Arts." In some cases the Parent Teacher Association (PTA) acquires a set of prints, and parents research the artist, period, technique, and history of a print before presenting it to a class. The presentation is basically art appreciation, but if the parent is comfortable with a related hands-on art lesson this is also offered.

If your school has no art program, consider suggesting to the PTA that they undertake such a project. Many libraries already have a print file and the project could begin by researching the available resources. If you are near an art museum there may be a program available or your school may be able to collaborate with the museum on a program.

Music appreciation may be offered by a volunteer in a similar fashion. A parent may provide music for listening, along with a brief presentation on the composer's life, period of history, style, the instrumentation of the music, and other appropriate information. With a bit of luck, the PTA might be able to find two or more volunteers who could coordinate the music and art presentations to be drawn from the same historical period.

Fremont Elementary School in Arvada, Colorado, uses a coupon book to recruit volunteers for general and specific programs. Each year parents receive a packet of coupons that request help for a variety of needs. They decide which requests they can fulfill and return the appropriate coupons. In essence, they are allowed to plan their volunteerism for the year, donating services in their areas of expertise or comfort, or simply when convenient.

In addition to parents, don't forget to have your colleagues help with special classes. Often a teacher is willing to trade the teaching of art for the teaching of music or physical education. If you are in a school where there are no paraprofessionals for recess duty, consider trading that chore. Classes can be combined relatively easily for music if space is available, but hands-on art is more complicated although art appreciation can be presented with larger groups.

Often some of your finest resources are right under your nose. Gloria Palomino is a fourth-grade teacher who also teaches art lessons. She has graciously "loaned" students who have mastered a process to other teachers. While I was teaching a lesson on perspective (that I had learned from observing another guest artist), I noticed one of my fourth graders, who has had art lessons, creating a far more sophisticated rendering than any I could accomplish.

CONCLUSION

A literate classroom has a physical setting that promotes learning, a teacher who participates in the learning process and elicits help from professionals and volunteers, and students who assume some responsibility for their education. It is built on trust, curiosity, and fascination with learning. It defies total definition because it is never static.

REFERENCES

Goodman, Ken. *What's Whole in Whole Language?* Portsmouth, N.H.: Heinemann Educational Books, 1986.

Loughlin, Catherine E., and Mavis D. Martin. *Supporting Literacy: Developing Effective Learning Environments.* New York: Teachers College Press, 1987.

Veatch, Jeannette. *Reading in the Elementary School.* 2nd ed. New York: John Wiley and Sons, 1978.

Chapter 2

Letting Your Library
Work for You

Despite the move by many districts to develop programs that are more dependent on books, one of the first places money is often cut is in library funding. Librarians who once managed one elementary school may be required to manage two. In some districts there are only one or two librarians who serve primarily as administrators, supervising many paraprofessionals who merely maintain the collections in several school libraries.

The growing diversity of a librarian's job is reflected in the tendency to call libraries instructional media centers and to call librarians media specialists. The bespectacled Marion the librarian who checked out books to eager readers has been replaced by a professional who must manage the library environment, the acquisition and processing of materials, the circulation of collections, computer operations, and the budget. The librarian may organize and maintain in working order the bibliographic information, a wide variety of equipment, and the collections of books, films, and computer software. Further, the librarian must serve as an educator to students, teachers, and parents, while actively promoting the library program.

The growth of alternative programs coupled with restricted budgets means that today's librarian can not wait passively for customers. These specialists must take the program to the teachers and students, collaborate with them, and serve them, making their services indispensable. Today's librarian may have to work closely with the parents and/or PTA to obtain the funds needed to expand the collection.

The library program must be flexible enough to allow for the provision of these services. The job is complex enough that any elementary school of 500 students that uses whole language or literature based programs legitimately could keep two library specialists busy. Districts must recognize that the librarian is an integral and essential member of the educational team. And, librarians who are not actively becoming part of the team risk relegation to custodial work such as supervising several libraries rather than collaborating with other professionals in the development and enhancement of the educational program.

THE SCHOOL LIBRARY

Lucie Lawson, the librarian at Park Hill School in Denver, works hard at getting teachers into her library. Many schools, like Park Hill, have their routine faculty meetings in the library. Mrs. Lawson loves to cook and often shares her creations at these faculty meetings, especially during the fall when many teachers are new and meetings are frequent. Her coffee and freshly baked coffee cake make the library an especially inviting environment for teachers and staff. Of course, every school librarian finds a way to encourage users, but the combination of food and books is certainly one of the most powerful enticements.

Throughout the year Mrs. Lawson consciously continues to be supportive of teachers. A great amount of informal planning occurs during the lunch hour and she regularly eats lunch in the faculty room so she is available for discussions about books, programs in progress, rescheduling needs, and future units of study. She never forgets a request for help with a topic, even if it is made on the run.

Her library is also inviting because of her efforts to create an environment that goes beyond books. Pillows and bolsters are available for individual or shared reading. Displays involve a variety of materials, with aesthetic touches such as plants and dried flowers.

Mrs. Lawson doesn't stop with coffee cakes, lunch hours, and an inviting setting. She will help pull together collections on specific topics, providing filmstrips or tapes from the library collection for classroom use (sometimes from just overhearing a comment about a topic under study), and will contact the district's professional library for additional materials.

She carefully acquaints the teachers and students with her library in the fall, providing an organization that allows for maximum independence for her clients. She makes her planbook available, posts calendars for VCRs, and checks out equipment as needed. All materials are as accessible as possible. To expedite delivery of materials and films, she uses older students as assistants, relieving the teachers of the need to return films.

Centers, areas with a variety of materials on a specific topic, are available for drop-in groups, and teachers receive a monthly update on what is happening in the library and what is appropriate for different grade levels. Often the centers relate to a special or historical event. Because Mrs. Lawson expects the students to manage the centers themselves, they foster independent learning or research. However, she is always available if someone has a problem.

She recognizes that no one can predict how quickly or slowly a student reads a book, and she wants to keep the books circulating. Rather than requiring students to check out and return books on a strict schedule, she encourages students to drop in regularly throughout the week to check out new books. She also offers help and advice when she is not instructing a scheduled class.

Mrs. Lawson will adjust her program to a teacher's needs with alacrity. When she overheard a teacher mention that a class was doing a mystery unit, she provided a set of very effective mystery kits that included a filmstrip about Sherlock Holmes, multiple copies of unsolved crimes, a tape of audio clues, and an envelope of visual clues. Students worked through the kits in groups, solving the mysteries and defending their choices through skits, pantomimes, and juries. The unit would not have been half as successful had Mrs. Lawson not volunteered these materials.

Mrs. Lawson involves the faculty with decisions regarding the collection. Periodicals are a very large portion of the budget and she seeks faculty input regarding which subscriptions to renew. If teachers and students aren't using a certain magazine, she cancels the subscription and uses that money for other materials. Acquisition is a slow process in a big district, but she has a certain amount of money available through PTA and other sources for the occasional purchase that requires immediate attention.

When it is time for housecleaning, Mrs. Lawson invites teachers to examine materials for use in their classrooms. During the period when there was money for a reading lab, many supplementary materials were purchased. When these funds were no longer allocated, the library housed the materials and teachers ignored them. Over the years an abundance of other materials accumulated and collected dust. Then Mrs. Lawson organized and made them available for classroom teachers. The teachers were more than happy to take the materials, and the library ended up with more shelf space.

One Halloween Mrs. Lawson held a contest in which pumpkins were decorated as literary characters. Nearly 100 famous pumpkin figures, such as Pippi Longstocking, Garfield, and Charlie Brown, filled the library. Pictures were taken, parents viewed the pumpkins, and small prizes were given to the winners.

Her library is open for other special occasions. It hosts the monthly citizenship awards that are presented by a local police officer. The Reading Is Fundamental (RIF) distribution takes place in the library. (The science fair and the book fair are scheduled for the same week, and the book fair takes place in the library also.)

All these special events are disruptive to the library schedule and require extra energy and effort. Often portions of the library program must be suspended. But the trade-off is worth the effort: teachers, students, and volunteer parents who help with RIF and the book fair regard the library as a focal point of the building.

THE PROFESSIONAL LIBRARY

Alicia Sabatine, librarian at the Professional Library Media Center (PLMC) for Jefferson County Public Schools in Colorado, is also committed to selling not just the library's services, but the benefits from using those services. Ms. Sabatine is actively involved in educating teachers and staff about what the library can do for and with them. She believes it is easy to tell teachers that the library has online information retrieval systems, but unless teachers know how these systems can benefit their programs, the knowledge that the service exists is superfluous. Her goal is to convince educators that the PLMC can make their job both more exciting and easier.

PLMC activities are organized to recruit potential users. Knowing that it is difficult to get teachers to cross town to attend a session on library use after school, staff members will take the program to the teachers and school librarians, even if it means transporting computers and modems for a session on retrieval systems. Through these programs staff members can demonstrate how access to a database can assist teachers, convincing them that the PLMC can be an integral part of the educational process.

In addition to having access to over 600 commercial databases, the PLMC maintains ERIC documents on microfiche and a collection of education journals and periodicals. It provides inter-library loan services, with searches extending to the national level if necessary. The staff also devotes time to answering requests for information, even if it means traveling in person to other area libraries.

Copies of audiovisual materials and computer software are made available for review, allowing librarians and teachers to sample materials before investing in school copies. Newspapers, curriculum guides, professional books, art books, art prints, records, and sheet music complete the offerings to the county.

The PLMC maintains an ongoing commitment to acquainting teachers with new materials. Inservices or workshops are designed to suit the needs of the teachers and are taken directly to them. Regular presentations on professional resources are given. Staff members talk with teachers to find out what their demands are, and then find resources that fit current needs. For the popular resources, Ms. Sabatine tries to keep multiple copies available.

A major goal of the PLMC is keeping users abreast of recent acquisitions and events. A quarterly publication lists new books and audiovisual materials acquired by the PLMC. Two newsletters which keep school-based and central staff aware of new activities in the library and trends in information science are published. This information reaches district staff in printed form and as an electronic newsletter via the district electronic messaging system. With the current emphasis on trade books, the PLMC offers teachers guidance on fair use of copyright materials, recognizing the temptation to copy such materials.

Although any taxpayer has access to the PLMC, few citizens take advantage of it. Having experienced major funding cutbacks, Ms. Sabatine welcomes and promotes use by the public, hoping that by building a broad base of users, the PLMC will be regarded by the taxpayers as an integral and critical part of the community.

THE PUBLIC LIBRARY

"Reading is just listening with your eyes." Judith Volc, the children's librarian, educator, and self-described facilitator at the Boulder Public Library, loves to talk about her young users who make such profound observations. Knowing she can't reach every child in the area, she dedicates herself to reaching as many as possible through the teachers and the community. She ensures success by carefully orchestrating all programs for maximum coverage and efficiency.

Her library resembles a maze, with bookcases creating areas for a wide range of activities. It has computers placed strategically to encourage interaction among users. A puppet theater invites participation by children, and pillows provide comfortable reading areas. Children can watch videos on the televisions and see filmstrips. The library houses 50,000 books, 500 video tapes, 1,000 audio tapes, 500 records, plus a variety of magazines, posters, and art prints.

It is a "no rule" library. Because the room absorbs noise, children can talk, interact, and move freely, short of running. There are no limits on the number of books and materials a child can check out, and there are no fines for overdue books. Ms. Volc points out that this library is probably the only place where a child may use library materials with no restrictions.

Believing that the library exists to serve the public, including public and private schools, preschools, and day-care centers, Ms. Volc makes her programs available in a variety of ways. One goal is to provide assistance with acquisition decisions to financially limited school libraries. She has recruited groups of ten to fifteen student readers from six area schools to help preview new books. These students may be the best readers who welcome extra reading materials, or they may be struggling readers who need the boost that comes from participation. She also uses adult professionals in related fields for help in selecting nonfiction titles. Once a month she holds an acquisition meeting for area school librarians, parents, and teachers at which she gives a synopsis of the new books plus reactions from her many readers. Participants have the option of checking out the new books or trusting the reviews before making their decisions.

Teachers can borrow sets of thirty to sixty books on any topic with an eye to future acquisitions or for occasional curricular use. Sets of fiction titles can also be borrowed to supplement the school library's titles. Teachers can keep the sets for sixty days with no overdue charges. Ms. Volc says that in the busy periods she may pull up to six classroom sets of books per day, demonstrating the success of this program.

She regularly invites classes to the library for research, special programs, or collaborative teaching efforts. When fifth graders studying the Civil War come in, Ms. Volc may suggest they look up the day and month of their birth on the microfiche records of the newspapers of that era. Many students will opt to spend a dime to obtain a copy of the front page, fascinated with this historical link to their lives. The library devotes fifteen to twenty hours per week to direct contact with students and teachers during the traditional school year, with summer use continuing for private schools, preschools, and day-care centers.

Ms. Volc is continually searching for ways to develop literate learners. Concerned with those intermediate students who were not fluent readers, she developed a program to train older students to read aloud to the younger ones. These students choose from a carefully selected group of easy-to-read picture books. Ms. Volc models the process, explaining what it takes to be a good storyteller and reader, or both. She takes students through an analysis of the plot, characterization, and setting of each book, guaranteeing a thorough understanding that transfers to their own grade level reading. The readers then practice reading the book aloud with a tape recorder and later with a video, listening to and observing the results. Students are gently coached and allowed to continue their rehearsal until they are ready to read to younger students. Then they are paired with other students to present their stories in sessions of moderate length. For the student who is still reluctant to share books, Ms. Volc goes through the same process using filmstrips. The student can read the filmstrip aloud to the class, comfortably sheltered behind the projector in a semidarkened room. Some students are so successful that they go on to write and share their own books.

Like Ms. Sabatine, Ms. Volc takes programs to the teachers. She will take new books and curriculum ideas to PTAs, teachers' meetings, workshops, and conventions. She will shape the offering to meet any needs: computer software, videos, filmstrips, books, reference materials, retrieval systems, etc. Knowing that any diversion on a Friday afternoon is welcome, she will use that time to go into a teacher's class and give a book talk. She encourages classes to leave Legacy Lists, annotated lists of their favorite library books, for the succeeding class.

All the above is just part of the program. A typical summer of special events includes quiet reading periods during which students can earn free paperback books, a week of movies based on books, a nonfiction week featuring movies, a poetry writing workshop, a puppet-making workshop, a storytelling week, and the annual birthday party with children invited to attend as their favorite book character.

Ms. Volc also believes that children and the community need to be brought together. Sunday Specials include visits from specialists in the area who are willing to share time with children and adults: opera buffs, bear handlers (bear included), weavers, model train aficionados, and computer specialists.

In addition, the library maintains regular story hours, puppet shows, a display case reserved for classroom and/or individual projects, plus whatever activities Judith Volc can dream up to lure children through the doors of the Boulder Public Library.

WHAT DO YOU DO IF YOU DON'T HAVE A LUCIE LAWSON, ALICIA SABATINE, OR JUDITH VOLC?

The above programs are exemplary and with dwindling tax money, they may become nearly extinct. This leaves the classroom teacher with the challenge of collecting materials and planning units with little support. Most teachers are in a situation somewhere between the above examples and no library support whatsoever.

Before school or early in the year, conscientiously devote an hour or two to familiarizing your-self with your school library. Librarians periodically spend time in "shelf reading"—checking for misplaced or damaged books. As a classroom teacher, take a notebook and work along the shelves, scanning the titles, to get a general idea of what is in the library. Spend more time with the nonfic-tion section, noting which areas have especially large collections. I look for a large collection of fairy tales because I use them for a writing unit. If there is a section which is not well stocked, you may want to choose an alternative research topic once the year has begun.

As you browse, inevitably you will find some sections or even individual titles that will inspire a thematic unit, research project, or just a short writing assignment. Make note of these ideas for later in the year when you are ready to use them. You will also run across books that you want to have available in the classroom. Most librarians allow long-term checkout privileges for teachers, and this is a good time to begin assembling your classroom collection.

Spend time with the audiovisual materials section and you may find unexpected treasures such as the previously mentioned mystery kits. If there is a large selection of materials in one area and it fits with your curriculum, consider building a thematic unit around them. A mystery unit can also include a filmstrip of an Encyclopedia Brown story and a tape of Jack Prelutsky's scary poems.

Later when you have the time go through the professional library with your notebook. Note if there are multiple copies of a novel in the event you wish to teach the novel to a group. It is more practical to see which novels are available before you make a decision—if the collection of novels is adequate, money can be used for other books.

Don't forget your public library. Most public libraries will check books out to teachers on a long-term basis or will waive overdue charges. Take time to find out what is on those shelves, especially in the record and audiovisual collections. Check into the interlibrary loan, particularly if you intend to teach novels to groups. Often the public libraries keep useful booklists. If you establish a rapport with your public librarian as well as your school and professional librarians, you can benefit from the expertise of several professionals.

USING OTHER RESOURCES

Having a broad knowledge of children's literature is an important part of the management of a literate classroom. Chapter 3 recommends how to become familiar with many books, but no one has time to read every deserving title. Your school or public librarian can help you by referring you to book reviews in professional journals (see end of chapter 3 for a list of suggested journals). Some periodicals discuss only books or their use in the classroom; others, such as *Language Arts*, a journal of the National Council of Teachers of English, have a regular column on children's books. Besides helping you become familiar with what is new, they will allow you to select more knowledgeably the books you wish to read. I strongly recommend that you read or skim any book before giving it to children, no matter who recommends it.

USING AUDIOVISUAL MATERIAL

If your district has a centralized media center, take the catalog home one evening and skim through it as you would a Sears catalog. I once spotted a film on sun art and ordered it with no knowledge about it other than the short description. It was a magnificent film integrating mythology, art, folktales, and literature. We then created our own sun art with several related picture books such as Gerald McDermott's *Arrow to the Sun*, additional sun myths, and a sun batik I happened to own.

I especially like to use films when teaching subjects in which I am relatively insecure, such as art. I once ordered a film on watercolors that was so old the colors had faded. We still watched it, in fact twice, because the instruction on drawing a tree was fascinating. We were able to use the techniques, even though the film quality was poor. When a guest instructor came to teach a lesson on watercolors, the students had a head start on the terminology and process.

If you can borrow films at no cost, take some risks when ordering. I have had a few surprises, such as a film on wind that I thought would fit with my science unit. Instead of being scientific, it was a fanciful, wordless, animated film of the wind blowing around a variety of children, etc. It didn't fit my plans, but it was a refreshing ten-minute interlude.

Keep a record of what films you order. Some districts have carbon order forms and you can save the copies in a file folder. Otherwise keep a notebook or folder on films that you have ordered, and note if they were successful. This will help with the next selection process and prevent unnecessary ordering.

The advent of the VCR has given teachers a wonderfully convenient teaching tool. Our school receives a bulletin by the public broadcasting station that describes the programs in more detail than the newspaper. Knowing that teachers will be interested in tapes of shows, the bulletin also provides information regarding copyright restrictions. Often the cassette rental stores have excellent videos that will augment a unit of study.

Again, preview a tape before using it in the classroom.

A WORD ABOUT CENSORSHIP

While on the subject of using a variety of literature and media in the classroom, it is necessary to broach the difficult subject of censorship. During a children's literature course we examined certain books to discover why each title was the subject of controversy. A few examples were William Steig's *Sylvester and the Magic Pebble* (the policemen were pigs), Maurice Sendak's *Where the Wild Things Are* (scary monsters) and *Into the Night Kitchen* (the nudity). Recently a book of folktales collected and retold by Alvin Schwartz, *In a Dark, Dark Room*, has become a subject of controversy because one of the tales (about a girl whose head, tied on by a ribbon, rolls off upon her death) gave a child nightmares. Parent groups have also tried to prohibit the use of Robert Peck's *A Day No Pigs Would Die* because of the graphic writing and language.

If your students make their own choices of books from the school library or from books that you have previewed for the classroom library, you are entrusting the student with selecting appropriate materials. Districts are becoming more and more sensitive to the issue of censorship and most school libraries follow the policies set forth by the district.

When you assign a novel for a group to read, you need to be certain you will not be facing a challenge of your selection. This is partly why I repeatedly emphasize the need to preview materials. Since there are so many excellent books available at the elementary level, if I know a book is controversial I simply avoid it. This is not so easy at the junior high or high school level when some of the best writing, such as books by Robert Cormier, deals with provocative issues. But even at the elementary level, one never knows what will be offensive to an individual or a special interest group. Attending conferences, reading the journals, and talking with librarians will help you know which books are potentially controversial.

To prevent any problems, in the fall I send out a list of titles our students *might* be reading during the year, giving parents an opportunity to preview the books. To date, no one has had any objections, but if a parent would object to a book I would allow that child to read another selection. The key point is that I prefer this be an issue between the parent and child, not the teacher and student or the teacher and parent. Each teacher must decide how to handle this issue, but in a program that advocates choice and responsibility, it seems inconsistent not to respect the wishes of a parent. Though having an open library is certainly an important issue on a school or public level, for my classroom library it simply is not worth jeopardizing my entire reading program to fight for the assignment of an individual title.

CONCLUSION

Your first step in the creation of a literate classroom is to unearth the resources lurking on the shelves and behind the desks of all the libraries available to you. This will save you countless hours and you possibly will discover wonderful human resources in the form of librarians who are willing to assist with many aspects of your program. Your biggest problem will be finding time to sample all the wonderful books and materials you will discover.

REFERENCES

McDermott, Gerald. *Arrow to the Sun*. New York: The Viking Press, 1974.

Peck, Robert Newton. *A Day No Pigs Would Die*. New York: Dell Publishing Company, Inc., 1972.

Schwartz, Alvin. *In a Dark, Dark Room and Other Scary Stories*. New York: Harper and Row, Publishers, 1987.

Sendak, Maurice. *Into the Night Kitchen*. New York: Harper and Row, Publishers, 1970.

_____. *Where the Wild Things Are*. New York: Harper and Row, Publishers, 1963.

Steig, William. *Sylvester and the Magic Pebble*. New York: Simon and Schuster, Inc., 1969.

Chapter 3

How to Implement Your Program from 3:30 p.m. to 9:00 a.m. and in June, July, and August

Most teachers routinely bring in supplementary materials, especially primary teachers who are responsible for a variety of experiential activities. This chapter discusses suggestions that should decrease rather than increase your workload, although it will seem the other way around at first. Some ideas you already will be using and some will not fit your lifestyle or needs. Choose what will work for you, incorporating a few at a time into your routine, expanding when you are ready.

Creating a literate classroom cannot be accomplished during the hours the students are in class. It need not take an inordinate amount of time outside of your classroom, but it does require a shift in your thinking. Though you can still leave the building, you will be actively planning or preparing for your program during your "free" time. This is necessary simply because a major feature of your program is bringing a wide range of resources to your classroom, often temporarily. Once you have established your routine and have acquired a core of materials, your job will be easier. But in the meantime, you need to become alert to how you can use odd moments to your advantage and minimize the time you spend getting ready to teach.

Most teachers already do their creative planning outside the hours of their regular school day. It takes time to think, evaluate, dream, and implement, and rarely does a teacher have time during the regular teaching day to think about anything besides what is happening in the classroom let alone explore a new resource.

HOW TO FIND, SCROUNGE, BEG, AND SOMETIMES BUY YOUR MATERIALS

The central focus of a literate classroom is the collection of books that are available to the children. Once you have used some of the ideas in this book to develop a broad background in children's literature, you will be ready to build your classroom collection. Chapter 11, "Books to Savor," offers my favorites for instruction, sharing, and general reference. But you will also need to begin acquiring a variety of titles for silent reading, reading aloud, browsing, and research. This chapter discusses several ways to enlarge your collection economically.

Building a useful collection requires some discrimination. Just having hundreds of books on the shelves does not mean you have provided a literate environment. Among the bargains, you will find many titles that you will need to reject. Fortunately, with the popularity of quality paperbacks, you will be able to find many excellent titles at quite reasonable costs. But if you come across a questionable title, don't invest even a quarter in it. And, don't assume that just because you recognize an author's name you can trust the title. I was once browsing through the shelves in a chain bookstore and was stunned that a bawdy adult novel by Judy Blume was parked by her children's books. The manager paled when I told him what I had found—a new clerk had made an innocent mistake. You want to be certain that what you place in the hands of children deserves such placement.

Garage Sales

A large portion of my collection came from years of buying books at garage sales at the rate of 25 to 50 cents each. I nearly always find a handful of terrific paperbacks at a garage sale and I don't worry if I already have a copy of a certain title (if it is cheap), because these help build the classroom sets I use when teaching a novel to a group. Garage sales are also terrific sources for yarn, wallpaper samples, or other usable materials for art projects.

Library Sales

Libraries often have public sales of books that have low circulation or have become outdated. Just because the public library has discarded a book doesn't mean it won't be useful. Often these copies have library binding that is more durable and is thus more costly than you would normally expect. Other books are ones people have donated to the libraries to sell with its discards. Sometimes libraries will let teachers buy books the afternoon before the sale opens to the public, which provides an excellent opportunity to expand a collection.

This is also a good way to find an economical set of encyclopedias. Joe Bauwens, a principal in Peoria, Illinois, believes that having a current set of reference books in every classroom is critical, and he has set up a schedule annually providing new encyclopedias for a specific number of classrooms. With the help of his PTA, he is able to keep every classroom's collection reasonably current.

For those of us who teach in schools where provision of reference materials has a lower priority, we must compromise. Much research can occur with an older set of encyclopedias and it is convenient to have such a set for spontaneous reference.

New Book Stores

Some bookstores will offer a 10 percent discount to teachers, but this is not enough for those of us who are serious about our collections. I watch for the *good* book sales, such as buying holiday books the week or two right after the holiday when they end up on the half-price table. I still choose selectively, as holiday books are sometimes extravagant and therefore still expensive at half price. But I confess a weakness for special occasion books, and generally buy several a year in this fashion.

The chain bookstores often have good sales during the summer. One chain had a 75 percent off sale, and since the discount was on the last marked price, perhaps already half off, sometimes I paid as little as a quarter for a hardcover book which originally went for $8.00. One of my best purchases was several blank books, reduced from $3.00 to $0.25 a piece. We used them for awards in our Young Writers Conference later that year.

Don't be afraid to mention why you are buying your books. Bookstore owners are sympathetic and appreciate teachers who are fostering the love of reading (which perhaps will promote their sales). They may have more bargains for you or be able to help you out in other ways with book fairs or promotionals. I was once buying stickers on sale at a bookstore and when I mentioned that my students would love them, the owner promptly handed me several rolls of stickers free.

Discount houses often buy publisher remainders and sell them for less than a dollar after Christmas. Keep an eye out for bargains as you are doing your general shopping, making plans for stores to check after the holidays are past.

Used Book Stores

Many used book stores have a children's section which can be useful to the collector. Some have trading privileges, which is a good way to get rid of unusable books from your collection and trade them for more useful titles. You may have to trade away two to get one, but two rejects are worth one good title. If you develop a rapport with a dealer, you might be able to get advance notice of good acquisitions.

Let Everyone Know You Want
to Acquire Books

Don't be shy about letting people know you have become a "bookaholic." Once everyone knows you are actively searching for good titles at bargain prices, they will be delighted to help you with the expansion. But no one will know unless you ask. These are the three As of book acquisition: ask, ask, ask.

For example, I have a friend who organizes estate sales. She knows that I am constantly looking for good books, so she scouts out these sales for me. Once when a friend's elderly aunt died my friend presented me with a box of items designated for charity. In the box was a set of exotic rhythm instruments, probably from a Polynesian island, and a real treasure—a mint condition copy of *Eloise at Christmastime* by Kay Thompson. I had pored over the Eloise books as a child, fantasizing about being rich and living in a fancy hotel and, until that moment, I had forgotten Eloise books existed.

Parents of my students also have given me some wonderful books. Recently a parent brought me a perfect 1966 facsimile edition of the 1871 version of *At the Back of the North Wind*, by George Macdonald. She had found it when browsing through a used book store and knew I would love it.

If you enjoy auctions, watch the paper for auctions of libraries. Once a friend and I each contributed $250.00 and bought the entire library of a closed private school. We kept about 400 hardback titles each and donated thousands of books to another private school. This purchase became the core of my classroom collection.

Friends let me know when they hear about library sales, book sales, auctions, or great garage sales. I don't make it to all, but I am never disappointed when I do make the effort.

Book Clubs

I encourage my students to order from book clubs because of the free materials that can be received, and I am always amazed when teachers tell me they don't bother with them. There are many different clubs, but they all operate in a similar manner. Each month teachers receive brightly colored ordering forms, much like a newsletter, that describe the books available. For every dollar spent, for ordering in certain slower months, or just for ordering at all, teachers receive bonus points for a variety of items: books, teacher resources, classroom equipment, even VCRs. For a modest order of $30.00, I can get at least six free paperbacks. Most of my classroom sets have been built from book clubs plus what I supplement from other sources. It does take some time to order the books, but it is worth it when the box arrives. You distribute the orders and the rest is yours. See the end of this chapter for book club companies.

Reading Is Fundamental
Distributions

Reading Is Fundamental (RIF) is a program dedicated to the provision of books to all school children, recognizing that owning a book can be a powerful motivator for learning to read. Inez Dumville, a former teacher in Pekin, Illinois, devotes time every year to the Pilot Club, which has as one of its major projects the raising of money for RIF books. After various fund raisers, she finds the best source of inexpensive books (often one of the book clubs), orders the books, and sets up a distribution schedule for the town's schools. Each child gets to select a book for his or her personal library.

In some schools, the PTA manages the RIF program or gives RIF books to participants in the Young Writers Conference. If your school or district does not have this program, lobby your PTA for volunteers to organize it. The benefits to your classroom are not quite as direct, except for the free book the teacher also gets to select, but there are more books available for your students.

Book Exchanges

Betty MacMillan, a retired librarian from Park Hill School in Denver, organized the Recycle Your Books (RYB-IT) program for the alternate years when RIF didn't occur. For several weeks, students could bring in paperback or hardcover books in good condition and exchange them for tokens. After Mrs. MacMillan sorted and organized the books, students with tokens came in to make their book selections. Mrs. MacMillan always supplemented the books with leftover RIF books, so there was a good selection. And, she kept track of which classes got to go first from year to year, so one group didn't always get the best selection.

While working in a private school, I organized a variation on a book exchange. Students brought in two books and took home one. The rest went into our classroom collection. Everyone got something new to read, and we increased our class choices. Again, you need to look at the titles carefully, rejecting inappropriate books. Parent volunteers are invaluable for either of these programs.

Fund Raisers

Developing PTA support can benefit your program, not only monetarily, but with volunteers for various tasks associated with your program. Some PTAs will sponsor book fairs, during which a retailer brings in an assortment of books, giving the school a percentage of the profits. Some schools schedule their book fair during the science fair, carnival, or other special event, drawing huge crowds. Others schedule it during November or December, capitalizing on purchases for the holidays. It only seems fair that the money earned in a book fair go toward purchasing new books.

Readathons can be organized by the PTA with the help of a volunteer parent. They operate much like a walkathon, with patrons pledging a monetary amount for the number of books read. Again, the money should go to the purchase of books. This is a good way to develop classroom sets for all classes to borrow for their literature programs.

While working at a private school I set up a fee-based summer reading program while donating fewer than twenty hours of my time. Students paid tuition to read together for an hour or so per day for two weeks. The program was literature based, with individual instruction given as needed. The tuition money purchased books for our program, and one morning was devoted to going to the book wholesaler where each student chose one book for the library. This project would be more complicated at the public school level, but with some creative management (perhaps through PTA sponsorship) it should be workable.

Other Sources and Ideas

Book exhibits at conventions and conferences provide good free sources for posters and charts. Often a publishing company will offer a free paperback book. Wholesalers and bookstores usually have posters and are willing to give them to teachers.

Ask your administration if you can use what you would normally spend on reading texts and workbooks for the purchase of classroom collections of novels. If you are in a large metropolitan area, you can often order directly from a wholesaler, saving as much as one third off the retail price of the books. There are companies that specialize in compiling classroom sets of novels, but you can stretch your money by going directly to the wholesaler.

CONFERENCES AND CONVENTIONS

It requires effort to take professional leave and attend a conference or convention, even a local one. Preparing for a substitute teacher can be more work than it seems worth, and some districts make it difficult to apply for and receive the leave. Despite these difficulties, consider attending at least one per year, if only for a day or two. Conferences provide a terrific boost and are great fun.

Attending conferences is also a convenient way to get instruction on a special interest or teaching technique without registering for a graduate course. Often the one-to-three-hour workshops are more efficient than a continuing class, and by attending the workshop you can decide if you need to learn more about the subject.

I always register to hear the authors, take notes on their anecdotes about their writing, and share them later with the students. If possible, I get books autographed which I later use for gifts, the classroom, or my own collection. Often the authors give out brochures with biographical information and their booklists.

As mentioned earlier, the exhibits are a good source of free materials: posters, buttons, pencils, and even free books. Be sure to schedule time for a leisurely hour in the exhibit area.

SUMMER ASSIGNMENTS YOU WON'T MIND COMPLETING

There is nothing more luxurious than looking ahead at the first of June and seeing no classes for the next ten weeks. The summer seems to stretch ahead unendingly, and we know we will get so much done. Then it is mid-August and we never once pulled out those manuals or curriculum guides and we realize another summer slipped by. This section gives you relatively painless assignments that you can complete mostly with pleasure, returning to school in the fall feeling quite smug about your accomplishments.

Books

Every summer I look at the stack of educational journals still in their wrappers and instead round up a batch of children's books I want to read, usually from the public library or my own classroom, and retire to my hammock with an iced tea and indulge myself. Having the luxury to read during the year is rare, and this begins to satisfy my love of reading. Sometimes I have a goal in mind, such as reading ten Newbery winners. Our state has a book contest, the Colorado Children's Book Award, and some summers I try to read as many of those books as I can locate. I may later begin the school year by sharing several of them with the class.

Other summers I just browse through picture books, recommended novels, or read alouds suggested in *The Read-Aloud Handbook* by Jim Trelease. I also spend most of June getting all the dentist appointments, physicals, and eye exams completed, and I never leave the house without one of my books. No one is going to care if you are reading Judy Blume's *Freckle Juice* in public.

If you have children, you can get double duty out of your reading by sharing it with your children. My boys are in their early teens, but they still enjoy a good read-aloud book. Often I will have them read a book I have enjoyed, or I will elicit their opinion if I feel a young adult book is somewhat questionable. They also enjoy the picture books. I recently read aloud a picture book about dying and my younger son commented, "It sounds like the author was trying to say something powerful, but couldn't quite say it." His one sentence clearly articulated my vague impressions.

If you need to be recertified, get even more mileage out of your summer reading by taking a class in children's literature. Many universities offer such a class or conference featuring visits by guest authors. This is an excellent time to begin keeping a file with information about authors and to purchase an autographed book to read to your class.

Lounging by the pool or on your patio is also a good time to sample children's poetry. You can read poems with a minimum of effort between naps and still feel a sense of accomplishment. If you have a few guilty feelings about such a pleasurable past time, keep some notecards handy and organize a box of titles by subject for use later in the year.

Field Trips

Plan to visit the museums, bakery, park, zoo, or any facility that offers a tour and possible field trip. Take your children, grandchildren, or neighbor's children, or indulge yourself and go alone or with another adult. You don't need to consciously treat this as part of your school work, just enjoy it. The ideas for incorporating it into your curriculum will come naturally. Take home a brochure and keep it for future reference.

While you are traveling, be alert to materials you can use in your classroom. One summer, while visiting the Kennedy Space Center in Florida, I noticed an office marked for teachers only. I went in, filled out a card, and received a free packet of materials for teaching units on space at all grade levels. The gift shop housed other rather inexpensive treasures. I bought one set of slides with a synchronized tape about the solar system and one set on the history of space exploration. I also bought samples of astronaut ice cream.

When we got home my sons promptly commandeered the teacher packet and spent days planning a simulated space launch. Once I was able to retrieve the materials, I realized I had the potential for a great science unit. I talked with my sons about what they had done with their own project and planned to use some of their activities.

Back at school, when my class got to the study of the solar system, I augmented the unit by adding the slides, a variety of the experiments, art projects, and activities in the materials from the space center packet. The students used the minireport process found in chapter 7 to study a planet of their choice. My sons had inspired the final step which was to use the astronaut menus to plan a space shuttle breakfast. Students shared the responsibility for bringing the food, except for the Ziploc bags of applesauce that I prepared. We deviated a bit from a breakfast menu by sampling the freeze dried astronaut ice cream I had saved. My total investment for this unit was the $20.00 for the slides, which can also be enjoyed by my family and can be reused and borrowed by other teachers, and the $3.00 or so for astronaut ice cream and applesauce.

Not all tourist centers will be as accommodating to teachers as the Kennedy Space Center, but do ask if any materials are available for teachers when you travel. Even brochures or information sheets can be helpful and enliven an otherwise more routine study.

Personal and Professional Enrichment

Many outstanding conferences on special topics are held in the summer. Often they occur on college campuses and the costs are low. One summer I attended a National Endowment for the Humanities four-week workshop at the Folklore Research Center at Columbia University in New York City. There was essentially no cost to the participants, unless they wanted to pay for college credit, as they received free dorm space, a food allowance, and a small stipend that covered air fare, books, and basic living expenses. Participation in workshops such as these is competitive, but with persistence you can find opportunities to explore and learn on a budget. Many of the periodicals have announcements of these workshops, but I routinely check the listings in *Education Week*, a newspaper that publishes information on conventions including how to obtain applications for study-grant conferences such as I attended.

Consider using part of your summer to develop a new interest that will indirectly benefit your teaching: folk dancing, bird-watching, mountain biking, aerobics, relaxation and stress-reduction techniques, cooking, and photography are a few of many possibilities. Some teachers work hard at developing their units of study by reading books and guides; others travel to exotic places such as Russia or India. Do not assume such a trip is tax deductible; we all should have done this when it was easier to document the legitimacy of travel for a deduction. Nevertheless, your travels can be enhanced when you share the slides and photographs with your class, especially early in the year when your students are still intensely curious about how you live.

Even seemingly selfish activities can reach into the classroom. Terry Rodriguez, a teacher of language-impaired children, says that the best thing she ever did for herself and her teaching was to take a personal growth workshop. It enhanced her understanding of herself on a personal level, with the unexpected benefit of improving her ability to handle students, parents, and colleagues at school. Even a retreat can be so refreshing that we become better teachers as a result.

If you cannot afford the luxury of a retreat, class, or trip to Japan, and simply must teach summer school, consider teaching in an area totally unlike yours. If you are a special education teacher, teach "normal" kids. This has the added benefit of helping you regain your perspective. Often you can cut across the rigid barriers to teaching other special needs children or age groups for the summer. You might have fantasies of changing directions and this might help you decide if you wish to pursue another teaching area. Even changing from kindergarten to sixth grade (or the reverse) can be a refreshing experience.

Other Summer Projects

If you feel energetic and want to feel truly proud of yourself, go through your file cabinets or drawers. You will probably rediscover a lot of great material. After coming to my latest classroom, it took me two years to get around to going through one of the file cabinets. I discarded much of the contents, but I also found some helpful materials for myself and for other teachers to use.

Another ambitious project is to read those journals and education magazines after all. It wasn't until I had finished graduate school that I realized it was okay not to finish reading or to even skip articles in a journal. If I find something I want to use later, I use a self-stick note to label the article. I like to intersperse the reading of children's books with my journal reading because the variety is fun.

Reading journals devoted to children's books, such as *Booklist*, can cut down the time you spend reading the literature. I still maintain you should read a book yourself before using it in your classroom, but you will have students doing reports on many books you will never read (and perhaps prefer never reading). If you read the reviews, you will have some idea of what is quality literature, what is popular, and what you want to read yourself. The bibliography at the end of this chapter includes periodicals dealing with children's and young adult literature. Teachers of sixth grade (and some fifth grades) will find their students reading young adult books and should, at the very least, be familiar with the titles.

If you have created some successful lessons or units and like to write, take a risk and send in what you have done to a magazine such as *Learning*. You need not be a polished writer; editors are interested in straightforward accounts of your experiences. Editors may purchase your article for $10 or more, barely enough to celebrate with, but you will have the satisfaction and recognition of being published. Often short pieces are saved for use as a sidebar within a larger article. As you gain confidence, you might be able to sell other pieces for a more substantial payment. If you are interested in pursuing publication, review several issues of the magazine, write for their author guidelines, and adapt your work to their suggestions and requirements. Be sure to share your successes with your students. They will enjoy being even a small part of a publication.

ART AND MUSIC UNITS
TO DEVELOP WHEN YOU ARE
FEELING CREATIVE

The following ideas for art and music are for starters, not complete units. Use the titles to inspire your own ideas for use of music and art with other subject areas, and browse through records or tapes for more ideas of music children will enjoy hearing.

Ghost Studies

Danse Macabre, by Charles Camille Saint-Saens, a French composer and pianist who lived from 1835-1921, provides a spooky setting for a Halloween unit on ghosts or skeletons. Use Jack Prelutsky's poetry collections, *Nightmares* or *The Headless Horseman Rides Tonight*. Write scary poems and epitaphs (if you are not in a rather liberal district, skip the latter exercise as it has come under fire in some areas of the country). Use library books on human anatomy or a science textbook section on the skeletal system to make skeletons with toothpicks and clay on a small piece of tagboard. Use watercolors to paint graveyards with dancing skeletons. With older students, get permission to go to a local graveyard and do gravestone etchings.

Russian composer Modest Petrovich Mussorgsky (1829-1891) wrote *Night on the Bare Mountain*, also suggesting scenes of spirits of darkness.

TITLES

Prelutsky, Jack. *The Headless Horseman Rides Tonight: More Poems to Trouble Your Sleep*. Illustrated by Arnold Lobel. New York: Greenwillow Books, 1980.

————. *Nightmares: Poems to Trouble Your Sleep*. Illustrated by Arnold Lobel. New York: Greenwillow Books, 1976.

Fairy Tales and Nursery Rhymes

Cinderella, a ballet by Serge Prokofiev, a Russian composer who lived from 1891-1953, provides a universal setting for the study of fairy tales. Virtually every culture has a variant on this fairy tale, making it particularly useful for the multicultural classroom. Team this with fairy tale study in chapter 9. Study picture book illustrations of *Cinderella* and have students create their own while listening to the ballet.

Igor Stravinsky (1882-1971) used a Russian fairy tale in his composition, *L'Histoire du Soldat*, composed in 1918. If you use several musical fairy tales, compare and contrast the composers' styles, while exploring why these Russian composers were enamored of the fairy tales. See chapter 9 for further discussion on fairy tales.

The *Mother Goose Suite* by Maurice Ravel, French composer, 1875-1937, provides another setting for a literary connection. Gather collections of nursery rhymes and let students browse through them while listening to this recording. Students can select favorite rhymes to illustrate or create their own rhymes.

Sleeping Beauty, a ballet by Peter Ilyich Tchaikovsky, 1840-1893, can be used like *Cinderella*.

TITLES

Perrault, Charles. *Sleeping Beauty*. Adapted and illustrated by Warren Chappell. Music by Peter Ilyich Tschaikovsky. New York: Alfred A. Knopf, Inc., 1961.

Animals

A trip to the zoo could be enhanced by listening to Saint-Saens's *Carnival of the Animals*, a witty fantasy for two pianos and orchestra. Bring in several zoo books, draw animals never before imagined (inspired by the music), or study zoology.

TITLES

Carle, Eric. *One, Two, Three to the Zoo*. Cleveland, Ohio: Collins, 1968.

Faito, Louise. *The Happy Lion*. Illustrated by Roger Duvoisin. New York: McGraw-Hill, 1954.

Geisel, Theodor Seuss. *If I Ran the Zoo*. New York: Random House, 1950.

Munari, Bruno. *Bruno Munari's Zoo*. Cleveland, Ohio: Collins, 1963.

Folktales

Listen to Prokofiev's *Peter and the Wolf*. There are several outstanding illustrated versions of this animal folktale. Consider using one or more of the following, but don't miss the pop-up version illustrated by Barbara Cooney.

TITLES

Prokofiev, Sergei. *Peter and the Wolf*. Illustrated by Barbara Cooney. New York: Viking Kestrel, 1985.

Prokofieff, Serge. *Peter and the Wolf*. New York: Alfred A. Knopf, Inc., 1940.

_____. *Peter and the Wolf*. New York: Franklin Watts, Inc., 1961.

America According to Aaron Copeland

The music of Aaron Copeland, born in 1900, provides an opportunity to look at our heritage, folktales, geography, and musical history. Use *Appalachian Spring*, *The Tender Land*, *Billy the Kid*, and *Rodeo* to explore Copeland's musical metaphor of America.

Miscellaneous

Paul Dukas, a French composer (1865-1935), wrote a delightful work, *The Sorcerer's Apprentice*, and it is available on film. I use this primarily for entertainment, but perhaps readers can think of a more academic application.

The Planets was written by Gustav Holst (1874-1934), an English composer. Use with a unit similar to the solar system unit discussed in this chapter.

Pictures at an Exhibition, by Mussorgsky, contains musical pictures composed in memory of the works of painter Victor Alesandrovich Hartmann. Connections to art are obvious.

REFERENCES

Blume, Judy. *Freckle Juice*. New York: Dell Publishing Company, Inc., 1971.

Macdonald, George. *At the Back of the North Wind*. Illustrated by Arthur Hughes. Ann Arbor, Mich.: University Microfilms, Inc., 1966.

Thompson, Kay. *Eloise at Christmastime*. Illustrated by Hilary Knight. New York: Random House, 1958.

Trelease, Jim. *The Read-Aloud Handbook*. New York: Penguin Books, 1985.

OTHER RESOURCES

Note: Subscription rates are not included. Some periodicals are included with membership in professional organizations such as the International Reading Association. Since the content of the periodicals or journals varies and ordering several subscriptions can become costly, visit a library and browse through back issues before ordering. Be alert to half-price introductory offers with the magazines.

Periodicals Devoted to Children's Books

The ALAN Review
(Articles, plus clip and file book reviews)
Assembly on Literature for Adolescents
NCTE
Bill Subick, ALAN/NCTE
1111 Kenyon Road
Urbana, Illinois 61801

Bookbird
(Articles and book reviews)
International Periodical on Literature for
    Children and Young Adults
Publishing Firm ARNIS, Bergensvej 5
DK-6230 Røderko, Denmark
(Subscription must be paid in Danish crowns.
    Check library copy for details.)

Booklist
(Primarily reviews of books and
    other media)
American Library Association
Subscription Department Manager
50 East Huron Street
Chicago, Illinois 60611

Children's Literature in Education
(Primarily articles)
Fulfillment Department
Agathon Press, Inc.
49 Sheridan Avenue
Albany, New York 12210

The Hornbook
(Articles and book reviews)
31 St. James Avenue
Department LA
Boston, Massachusetts 02116-4167

Interracial Books for Children Bulletin
(Articles and book reviews)
Council on Interracial Books for Children
1841 Broadway
New York, New York 10023

The Lion and the Unicorn
(Primarily articles)
Journals Publishing Division
The Johns Hopkins University Press
701 West 40th Street, Suite 275
Baltimore, Maryland 21211

The New Advocate
(Articles and book reviews)
("For Those Involved with Young People and
    Their Literature")
P.O. Box 809
Needham Heights, Massachusetts 02194-0006

School Library Journal
(Articles and book reviews)
P.O. Box 1978
Marian, Ohio 43302

Top of the News
(Articles and book reviews)
American Library Association
Subscription Department Manager
50 East Huron Street
Chicago, Illinois 60611

VOYA
(Articles and reviews on books for young
    adults)
Voice of Youth Advocates
Dorothy M. Broderick
3936 West Colonial Parkway
Virginia Beach, Virginia 23452

Periodicals with Columns on
Children's Books

Language Arts
National Council of Teachers of English
1111 Kenyon Road
Urbana, Illinois 61801

Marvels and Tales
(A journal of the scholarly study of folk
    and fairy tales)
Jacques Barchilon, Editor
Campus Box 238
University of Colorado
Boulder, Colorado 80309-7226

The Reading Teacher
A Journal of the International Reading
    Association
International Reading Association
800 Barksdale Road
P.O. Box 8139
Newark, Delaware 19714-8139

School Libraries
American Library Association
Subscription Department Manager
50 East Huron Street
Chicago, Illinois 60611

Education Magazines

Classmate
(Primarily reproducibles and units of study)
Frank Schaffer, for grades 4-6
P.O. Box 10783
Des Moines, Iowa 50340-0784

Early Years: Teaching PreK-8
P.O. Box 912
Farmingdale, New York 11737-0001

Instructor
P.O. Box 6099
Duluth, Minnesota 55806

Schooldays
(See *Classmate*)
Frank Schaffer's Practical Ideas for
    Primary Teachers
P.O. Box 10783
Des Moines, Iowa 50347-0783

Learning
P.O. Box 51593
Boulder, Colorado 80321-1593

Books Devoted to
Children's Literature

Children's Books: Awards and Prizes. New York: Children's Book Council, 1981.

Dreyer, Sharon Spredemann. *The Bookfinder: When Kids Need Books*. Circle Pines, Minn.: American Guidance Service, 1985. Includes books published from 1979-1982. See earlier editions for previously published books.

Lima, Carolyn W. *A to Zoo Subject Access to Children's Picture Books*. New York: R. R. Bowker Company, 1985.

Newman, Joan E. *Girls Are People Too! A Bibliography of Nontraditional Female Roles in Children's Books*. Metuchen, N.J.: The Scarecrow Press, Inc., 1982.

Trelease, Jim. *The Read-Aloud Handbook*. New York: Penguin Books, 1985.

Other

Education Week
Subscription Service Department
P.O. Box 6987
Syracuse, New York 13217

Book Club Companies

Scholastic Book Clubs
2931 East McCarty Street
P.O. Box 7500
Jefferson City, Missouri 65102

The Trumpet Club
P.O. Box 604
Holmes, Pennsylvania 19092-0604

Troll Book Clubs
320 Route 17
Mahwah, New Jersey 07498-0003

Weekly Reader Paperback Clubs
4343 Equity Drive
P.O. Box 16628
Columbus, Ohio 43272-6112

Chapter 4

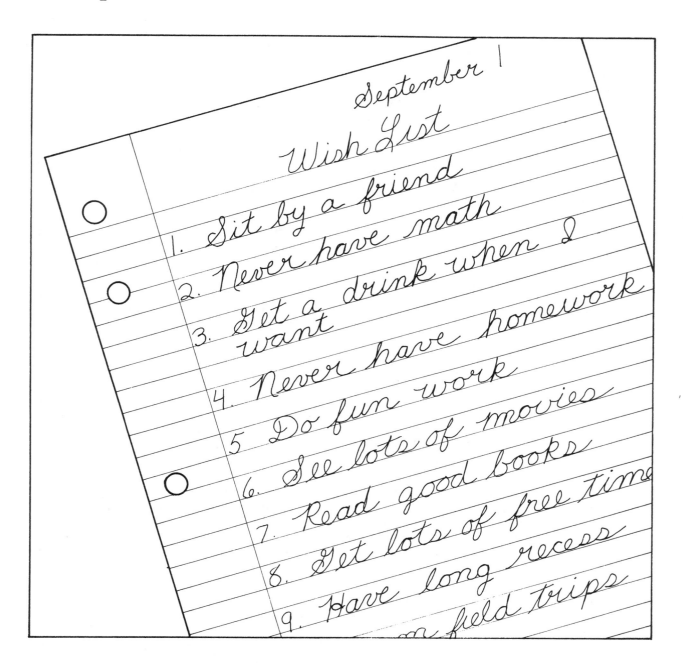

How to Implement Your Program
from 9:00 a.m. to 3:30 p.m.

Change is challenging, and often teachers abandon new programs because they are unwieldy and difficult to manage. Although management advice occurs throughout this book, this chapter deals with specific methods for simplifying your daily routine and investing your students in your program.

BEGINNING THE YEAR

On the first day I begin by having the students write "wish lists," lists of privileges they would like to have. I point out that it is worthless to write on their lists "no homework" or "no math," but a few do anyway. Generally they want to sit by their friends, go to the bathroom when they please, eat in class, or have an extra recess. Sometimes they want to have a class pet, have parties every week, or just have time to read. I read aloud most of the wishes anonymously, discussing why some are impossible, some are worth considering, and some are easy to grant.

Then I pull out my "bag of tricks" and begin to tell them about some of the privileges they will enjoy in my room. I also discuss the responsibilities that go along with them. Although I give them an overview of these privileges, I expect to repeat most of the details at a later time. There is so much to absorb during the first day that much is lost.

Many of these "tricks" you are going to read about in this chapter. Again, not every teacher will want to institute all or any of these ideas. However, you might find a few ideas to adopt or some that will inspire adaptations or alternatives which will work for you.

Getting Off to a Good Start

Beginning the year is stressful for everyone, but the teacher almost always works much harder than the students. I have never figured out how to start the year without a lot of extra hard work, but I have found that by setting the stage carefully in the beginning of the year the students eventually work as hard as or harder than I do. If you want to establish a climate in which the students keep on task and work hard, try the following tips:

1. Establish a beginning routine which is efficient and smooth. While observing my son's fourth-grade class I marveled at how quickly his teacher began the day. She had the students who needed a hot lunch stand up to be counted, told the rest to stand for the pledge of allegiance, sent a helper off to the office with the lunch count, and began the read-aloud period. Within two minutes she was into her program, and few children would want to be late for her reading of a story.

2. Never leave your class unattended. Most errands can be handled by a helper, but if you have to leave, choose a time when students are working and then be sure to return quickly.

3. Wait for complete attention before proceeding with any assignment, activity, or teaching. Waiting feels like lost time, but trying to teach over someone's chatter gives a dangerous message—that not everyone needs to listen. If a minute or two goes by and you are still waiting, move around the room, commenting quietly and positively about those who are attentive. The rest will get the idea.

4. Give direct instruction. Teach the lesson thoughtfully and thoroughly. Plan to reteach when necessary.

5. Assign meaningful work. See chapter 5 for a thorough discussion of appropriate assignments for the literate classroom.

6. Spend little time at your desk. Paper grading will have to be done when students are elsewhere or after class hours. Cruise the room, offering brief help. Do not let students monopolize you or disrupt the class with extended discussions. When you methodically monitor their work they will keep to the task. Depending on your grade level, you may be able later to provide help from your desk. I have a rule that children can raise their hands for help at their desks if I am up and about, but if I am sitting at my desk, they are to come to me for help. This is part of the question "Who's working hardest here?" The students have more energy than the teachers.

7. If you have a parent or teacher drop in, do not visit, except for brief moments. Stay in the room, facing the class, and end the exchange as quickly as possible. If you have observers, have your helper show them to a desk and give them a copy of the book you're using. I keep on my desk a file folder with various handouts which explain our atypical programs, such as our reading/writing program, relieving me of the need to ignore the class. If an observer is persistent with questions, offer to schedule a conference. One would like to think that an observer would want to see a teacher teaching and a class learning, but parents who invest the time to observe usually feel quite urgent about their need to find an acceptable school setting for their child and thus their questions are pressing.

8. Write assignments on the board after you have discussed them. If necessary, list the steps to more difficult assignments. Pat Marden, a teacher in the Cherry Creek School District near Denver, would outline a series of assignments for her first graders, using different colors of chalk for different subjects. The children could organize their work depending on their needs or moods and she could proceed with group and individual instruction knowing that her students would be working.

9. Make transitions orderly and smooth. Have the class practice "freezing" in place on a predetermined signal such as ringing a bell, playing a chord on the piano, or flicking the lights. This is a more subtle way of commanding attention than raising your voice.

   Decide how you want to dismiss students—as a whole, in rows, in groups, by the color of their clothing—and minimize the time this takes. I have never mastered the art of walking down the hall in front of a class without a great deal of socialization occurring behind me. So I walk behind the class and tell them quietly how far to proceed before the next direction. I speak very softly so that they have to listen. I also never have managed to get students to put their hands under their arms or behind their backs. It seems so rigid. However, for the children who can't keep their hands off others, I have told them to put their hands in their pockets or waistbands. This is a sufficient reminder.

10. Pay attention to each child. Children will stop you in the hall, in the lines, on the playground, and at any number of inconvenient times to convey some important message. But the inconvenience is from our perspective, not the children's. Your students will realize quickly if you don't respect them enough to give them your undivided and individual attention, and they will respond to you in like fashion. (Writing in journals, discussed in chapter 8, provides an alternative form of conversation.)

11. Use a judicious amount of positive reinforcement. Long-term reinforcement such as the Friday Afternoon Club is in this chapter. Stickers, certificates, or treats become meaningless (and too expensive) when distributed routinely. Words of encouragement and a personalized note or comment on a paper are just as effective and free.

12. No matter what grade you are teaching, remember to smile often. We forget that school is stressful and having a "nice" teacher is of great importance to children. Some teachers believe that they have to begin the year in ogre-fashion and then can ease up later. It is confusing not to know what to expect from a teacher and this confusion causes unnecessary anxiety. I have found that fairness in treatment tempered by a smile and a good sense of humor is a fairly unbeatable combination. When you hear from your principal or a parent that your students think you "make them work, but are nice," you will know that you are doing a good job.

13. Plan for an extra recess or something relaxing during the first few weeks, giving everyone a chance to ease into the routine. This is a good time for you to visit with the students, read journals, or enjoy the sunshine before the long winter begins.

14. Plan to review and rehearse your expectations often. Your students will be more comfortable and you will be confident that they know what to do.

15. Keep a sense of humor.

Beginning-of-the-Year Activities

Often teachers regroup students for instruction in math or language arts, and the groups are not established until a week or two later. This section is for beginning teachers who could use some ideas for first week activities as well as for experienced teachers who would like to expand their September repertoire.

ALPHABET UNIT

Before the students arrive, go to the library and find all the alphabet books and picture dictionaries you can. Use your public or professional library if necessary. Look especially for Mitsumasa Anno and Masaichiro Anno's *Anno's Magical ABC: An Anamorphic Alphabet*, a book which requires using a reflective cone to properly "see" the illustrations. Read many alphabet books aloud to the students, noting the differing styles.

Create a group alphabet poem using the theme of school (see chapter 10 for examples and variations). Then assign the writing of individual alphabet poems. This is a good time to introduce the use of a dictionary or thesaurus. Students will work hard at finding twenty-six words about school, especially the students who write from a negative point of view (which is helpful for you to know). They will also become adept at using these reference books.

Next have the students create alphabet art. This works well as a class project, with each student choosing a letter to illustrate in whatever media you desire. Arnold Lobel's *On Market Street* is a good model for the book, but any variation is acceptable. Either display the finished art individually or compile your own alphabet book. Students who enjoy this might make a minialphabet book on a chosen theme.

A related language arts activity for younger students would be to try to write an alphabetized grocery list: apples, bananas, corn, dog food, etc. Picture dictionaries are especially helpful for this project. Turn this into a math project by assigning prices to the items and adding them. Integrate map skills by giving students blank maps and atlases and having them find twenty-six cities, countries, or states in alphabetical order and labeling them on the blank map. For science, alphabetize twenty-six plant names, animal names, or fish names.

Choose the alphabet activities which suit your class, but don't overdo this unit. It is hard to resist having the students alphabetize your book shelves during this week. See appendix for a list of alphabet books.

SPELLING

The teaching of spelling is one of the toughest jobs a teacher faces. There is little relevance when lists are studied out of context, which is the predominant way of teaching spelling. Also, there aren't too many ways to learn spelling without plain hard work.

You can start your year with a spelling assignment which has immediate and obvious application. Students who have been best friends for years may not be able to spell their friends' first names correctly, and often have absolutely no idea how to spell their last names. Copy your class list and make your first spelling test all the first names in your class. For the second test, add their last names, plus yours, the principal's, and other teachers they may have.

If you have time, extend the list to the names of the school, city, state, nearby streets, parks, public places, the months of the calendar, and any other practical words you can list. A good alternative is to let the students create this list, based on words they feel they need to know.

MATH

Often the beginning of the year includes reams of math practice sheets for adding, subtracting, or multiplying. Consider doing some alternative math activities which develop concepts upon which you can draw throughout the year.

While apples are plentiful and inexpensive, bring in an apple for every student and a quantity of table knives. After the students wash up, have them cut the apples into halves on a piece of waxed paper. Point out that one student had one whole which is now two halves, and that two students had two wholes, which are now four halves, etc. Continue to cut up the apples. adding parts of different students' apples together to show that eight fourths once were two wholes, etc. When you have gone through as much as your grade level can understand, let the students eat the apple slices. This is probably not the assigned time for fractions, but this is the season for cheap apples, and you can refer to the experience later.

For the intermediate grades it is a good time to introduce using the calculator. I encourage students to check their work at home with a calculator, or even to practice their multiplication tables with one (they will soon tire of using them for the basic facts and get to the business of memorizing them). The skill of using a calculator will benefit them throughout the year.

Most math books on the intermediate level do not introduce averaging till the last chapter, which is too late for standardized testing. Find out all you want to know about your class by averaging the number of siblings, pets, bicycles, skateboards, whatever, per student. This can be used with the calculator lesson.

SOCIAL STUDIES
AND SCIENCE

When I returned to the public school classroom after a ten-year absence raising children and working in private schools, I was stunned that the science textbook began with a chapter on growing plants. It began with words to the effect that in the spring the earth warms and new growth appears. The incongruity of reading these lines with fall pending spurred my request to the principal that I reorganize the science curriculum to suit my sense of order.

If you are going to acquire a classroom pet, you can delay the purchase until you have studied the pet you intend to purchase, a process which can be an excellent substitute science unit. The first few weeks of school are an excellent time to do this, and you can tie in social studies through discussion of habitats, communities, or food sources.

Once at mid-year I decided to heighten interest in the science fair by bringing in two white mice for a study of nutrition. We planned to put a glass barrier between the two sides of the aquarium, separate the mice, and, in addition to a regular diet, give one mouse plain water and the other sugar water. We waited several days to initiate the experiment and meanwhile studied the mice and tamed them. We enjoyed their sociability and how they snuggled up with each other to sleep.

Finally we erected the barrier and separated the mice, leaving only a tiny space between the top of the glass and the cover. The next day the mice were once again both on one side of the barrier, snuggled up as usual. We tried again, but quickly realized unless we used a separate aquarium we could not keep them apart. After some discussion, we realized we were all too "soft" to persist with the experiment and abandoned it. We learned much more about mice as time passed. They are exceptional jumpers and would jump straight up, turning in mid air, catching the screen at the top of the cage with their paws, hanging suspended upside down. I learned not to position their cage near me while I read aloud, as they were so fascinating to watch.

Eventually we got another class pet, a guinea pig which we acquired from another teacher whose own guinea pig was pregnant when she bought it. Soon I realized the difference between the class's attachment to the pets. Getting the guinea pig was fun, but we hadn't agonized over it like we did the mice, and it never became an important part of our class.

Because of these experiences, I urge teachers to study about rabbits, mice, guinea pigs, reptiles, fish, or birds before bringing them into the classroom. It develops true ownership in the pet's membership in the class and provides you with a science and social studies focus for the first few weeks of school. A mice-unit which involves nearly all aspects of the curriculum is in the appendix.

Reading Aloud

This is the perfect time to introduce a variety of books. For primary students, read as many Caldecott winners as you can find, discussing the importance of the illustrations. You can create an entire unit just on the study of these fine books, inviting students to create and illustrate their own books.

For intermediate students, select a variety of Newbery books and read aloud only the first chapter or two, providing some idea of the direction of the book without revealing too much of the plot. The plan is to give students a teaser, hoping that when they must choose books for independent reading they will remember these books. Let the class choose one book for you to read aloud in its entirety.

GETTING THE ASSIGNMENTS IN

"What do you want me to do with my paper?" is a question I prefer not to hear from twenty-five students a dozen times a day. I never deviate from the routine I have established in the fall, which usually includes the use of folders for language arts and wire baskets for everything else. I also have a basket on my desk for notes from home and all returned office forms.

Set up a system of baskets or folders and during the first few weeks remind the students to put homework and notes in the appropriate places immediately upon their arrival. You are minimizing your work and helping your students take responsibility for their own assignments. Papers are not lost because all go in the basket. Of course, there will be those few who are sure they put their work in the basket, but my response is simply, "I didn't find it. You look." Since you are not collecting the papers, you are removed from the role of "keeper of the papers." They usually will discover the papers in their folders, desks, notebooks, or pockets.

Writing and reading folders can save you time. Set up a box or portable file box with a manilla file folder for each child. At the beginning of the period, the students retrieve their folders, and throughout the period all completed or in-progress work goes into the folder, which is returned to the box at the end of the period. Uncompleted work may go home overnight, but the folder never leaves the room. I record grades directly on the folder or sometimes insert a check sheet to help a student monitor progress on assignments (especially in the fall). When students are absent, you can slip papers into their folders which will still be in the box after class has begun. Again, the student is in charge of the assignments. You are not. Refer to chapter 8 for discussion regarding organization of the contents, grading the papers, storing assignments you wish to keep, etc.

Another challenge for the teacher is convincing students that it is necessary to do their work. Some teachers use stickers for reinforcement; some nag, threaten, or cajole; some follow the rule of natural consequences (failing grades); some simply ignore the issue. I believe that many papers end up in the teacher's wastebasket because of the nature of the assignments. They are busy work, not the work of learning. The sheer volume of paperwork makes it nearly impossible to keep up with the evaluation without hours of outside work, plus it is not particularly inspiring to grade worksheets. Even if you are among the small group of teachers who manage to keep up with the evaluation, you risk succumbing to teacher burnout.

Chapter 5 provides many alternatives to worksheets, which will eliminate much of the need to spend hours grading them. However, there will always be worksheets to grade, and it is important that there be student accountability. By the middle grades, many students have realized that some teachers aren't going to get too upset when an assignment is late or missing. They may have even figured out that many papers go directly into the circular file. The message is clear—there is not much value placed on the work of the student.

After eliminating the unnecessary work, it is time to build into the program an incentive for completing important routine and long-range assignments. An especially effective method I have used is to allow students who have completed their work the opportunity to participate in the Friday Afternoon Club (FAC). It sounds quite idle, but this is a time when important growth occurs.

In my room I keep a variety of word and card games, checkers, dominoes, math flash cards, Legos, Lincoln Logs, and a multitude of board games, such as Junior Scrabble, which reflect that I have teenage boys who have outgrown many former pastimes. If I were unable to bring in their castoffs, I would use garage sales to stock my FAC shelves.

The games and materials are for FAC time only. On Thursday I quickly go over my grade book, notifying students of missing assignments. They have until Friday morning to put them in the basket, or they can not participate in FAC. During the first months of school, I am careful to collect the assignments just after the students have arrived Friday morning, so no one is tempted to use another period to complete work—the arrangement is that the assignments are to be in the basket at 9:00 a.m., and not just before FAC.

My Friday lesson plans call for a quiet work period during which, if I can't grade the papers, I can at least check off in the grade book that I have received the assignment. When FAC time arrives at the end of the day, I formally allow the class to begin their free time. Those students who have not completed their assignments retire with me to a back table, and I give them help, oversee their work, or just keep them on track until they are done. It generally only takes one or two times of missing FAC before students regularly get their work done.

There are times when a special event, such as a Halloween or Valentine Party, replaces FAC. To avoid having a string of birthday celebrations, I bring in a treat for fall birthdays, winter birthdays, etc. With older students I give out birthday bucks: coupons redeemable for upgrading to an A on a test or for a night of no homework. At other times we watch a video which is related to our school work, such as seeing the videotape *The Secret of NIMH* after reading Robert C. O'Brien's *Mrs. Frisby and the Rats of NIMH*. These special occasions occur in lieu of FAC and that is made clear well in advance.

You might be wondering how to justify such a seemingly frivolous time to your principal or to yourself, but it is quite easy if you are adopting many of the ideas proposed in this book. Your students will not be wasting time in the classroom, they will be completing their work, and you will be available to help students who need individual encouragement. Students anticipate their participation, often planning with their friends throughout the week what they will do, and while playing, they improve their socialization skills. In final defense of a regular FAC, it is fun. Our society loves to celebrate and I believe that rewarding responsibility with fun should be an integral part of school. The bonus for you comes on those days when all students have their work completed and you can work at your desk on the next week's plans, read all the memos which have stacked up during the week, or join someone for a hand of Old Maid.

Each teacher must decide what is manageable in the classroom, but I hope that you will consider some method of internalizing accountability. It is a lifelong lesson worth learning in the very earliest grades.

LESSON PLANS AND EVALUATION

These topics are tough, especially when you are managing an alternative program. Lesson plans can be quite complicated as you try to explain the routine to a substitute teacher who is probably more used to following a prescription. Evaluation is more subjective, as you are focusing on the whole rather than the individual parts. Record keeping is a nuisance at best, but accountability for both you and the students becomes more important when there are no stacks of worksheets or tests to point to as your grading system.

Lesson Plans

Carolyn Alfredson, a Denver teacher, doesn't use a regular teacher plan book, but makes two master sheets similar to two facing plan-book pages. She writes in her schedule and blocks in vertically all the sections which remain the same every day or week. For instance, the section for journals or reading aloud would cut across every day at the same time. She follows this procedure for music, physical education, computers, lunch, and any other routine activity, and labels the rest of the blocks for the subjects. She copies a quantity of the pages, and they become her plan book. She outlines all the routine activities, and the plans for math, reading, and other subjects can be written in on a day-to-day or weekly basis. Important deviations from the routine can be entered in red ink.

I follow a similar procedure, but I have long ago given up on trying to plan out my reading program from day to day. If we are reading a group novel, I pencil in the assignments in chronological order, moving down the planning page, not worrying if they overlap into another day. As I complete the assignments I check them off with my red pen. I feel a sense of accomplishment, and any substitute can walk in and see where I left off, no matter how far I got into the week. Although math is easier for me to predict, I follow a similar procedure of lists and checks. For thematic units, the lists and checks are very effective.

Evaluation

Once you have the completed assignments, evaluating them need not become overwhelming. Many teachers use a simple check system: a check plus for work which is above average, a check for work which is acceptable, and a check minus for work which is incomplete, sloppy, or inaccurate. Some teachers use a simple plus or minus on routine work such as handwriting practice. A trained eye can tell at a glance what the general effort has been. Often I simply check to see that the work was accomplished and mark it on the writing folder or in my grade book. Many assignments require little more than this method of evaluation, and for the primary grades, where no letter grades are ever given, almost all assignments can be managed with a system of checks or plusses and minuses. Open-ended or self-selected activities, which are recommended in subsequent chapters, often require no evaluation at all. A simple "well done" or "terrific" at the top of the page is enough. You won't forget which students are going beyond the routine requirements.

I use letter grades for long-term assignments or projects at the end of a unit. With more complicated projects, such as the research minireport (see chapter 7), it is fairer to give a different grade on each aspect of the project. When my third and fourth graders completed their solar system reports, I quickly skimmed through all of them to see if there were any problems. As I reread them, I graded them on how well they had completed the research sheets, their mechanics (spelling, punctuation, etc.), and how well they had written the final reports. It took an hour to read twenty reports and grade them—a long time—but this represented two weeks of library and classwork, much of which was done independently.

Math is an easier area to grade because it is so objective. Some teachers have their students trade papers and grade them in class or have them self-grade. I have a hard time justifying class time for this, as the instructional time is so limited, and it is difficult to diagnose problems without actually seeing the work. Practice sheets such as multiplication, however, can be traded easily or self-graded. I evaluate math by giving a score reflecting how many problems were done correctly, recording that grade, and periodically averaging grades. Not a unique or simple system, but I prefer knowing what was done correctly to how many were wrong.

In all subjects I allow the students to retake tests, redo papers, or bring in work late. If students want to take tests again, they must ask me for the privilege. I always remind them that they have the option, but I leave it strictly up to them. When conference time comes and a student has a D or F in a subject, I am on firm ground when I tell the parent that the student had the option, but chose to not try to raise the grade. Late papers cannot receive an A, but they are better than Fs. I also let students use the variety of extra activities listed in chapter 5 as extra credit. I simply mark an "X" in my grade book near the appropriate date, and when report card time comes I will raise a borderline grade if there is a series of "Xs" recorded.

Because a variety of grading methods gets a bit complicated for the students, I periodically let students know where they stand if they wish to know. I plan for a quiet work period and have quick individual conferences, going over each student's current achievement. I congratulate those who are doing well, and for the others I focus on ways to improve their grades with more attention to late papers, missed assignments, retakes, or even extra credit research reports. Many students love the opportunity to pursue an interest through research and will do their best work with this option.

Just as an educator needs time to understand the many aspects of an alternative program, it also takes time for the students and parents to catch on to your evaluation system. Remember to take time periodically to explain your expectations. Students will appreciate the opportunity to improve grades through extra projects, but this should always be their choice. The grades are theirs, not yours.

HOUSEKEEPING

A literate classroom is a busy classroom. Do not try to maintain it by yourself or you will squander your own energies. A good rule is never to do housekeeping yourself if you justifiably can ask your students to do it. However, an inappropriate task is having students move heavy audiovisual equipment, especially if it is on a cart. Equipment has been ruined and children have been injured pushing carts over doorsills, moving blindly down a hallway, or simply tripping over a cord.

Involving your students in housekeeping chores should occur in moderate amounts, but if it is done routinely, it does not involve an inordinate amount of time. A clean and orderly room is more attractive and inviting than a disorderly, dusty room despite the wonderful instruction or program in progress. Limited resources in all but the most fortunate districts dictate that the maintenance of classrooms rarely extends beyond the emptying of wastebaskets and the cleaning of floors.

Keep in mind that an effective literate classroom need not look too tidy, although it needs to be organized. I once visited a school and stepped into a room that was apparently dedicated to the writing and reading process. It was beautifully arranged with books, reading corners, and writing materials. I kept wondering how the teacher managed it and then found out, to my relief, that it was the room of a reading tutor who only saw a few students at a time. If your room remains too orderly, you need to reassess its usefulness.

I do not hesitate to assign small chores routinely. At the beginning of the year I put all the children's names in a hat and each day draw out one "go-for/gopher," who is responsible for the errands, lunch count, trips to the office, feeding pets, putting up the absentee students' chairs at the end of the day, etc. In our school, which has no public announcement system, one buzz means to send someone to the office. The "go-for" automatically takes care of the chore and I don't have to interrupt my teaching to select someone. The next day the "go-for" acts as the back up for the newly drawn name. I put both names on the board so all will remember who is in charge and who will fill in.

Here is a list of housekeeping chores that you can use to involve your students in classroom maintenance.

ROOM MAINTENANCE AND HOUSEKEEPING CHORES

Alphabetize the books.

Straighten or organize the books.

Plan a new bulletin board.

Replace a bulletin board.

Pass out papers.

Feed the pets.

Water the plants.

Replace supplies.

Sort out and discard unuseable construction paper scraps.

Dust shelves.

Organize the centers.

I also have the entire class work on a major clean-up once or twice a year. I usually plan these when we are having parents visit as most students understand the rationale for preparing for company at school just as they would at home. I generally supervise rather than participate, as children often need to be taught *how* to clean or straighten, and that requires your undivided attention. It is important for students to learn that no matter who dropped the piece of paper, housekeeping is everyone's responsibility.

BATHROOMS, WATER, AND OTHER MANAGEMENT HASSLES

I dislike interruptions for drinks of water. Our classroom does not have a water fountain, but it does have a sink. Colorado is very dry, and the need for water is legitimate in the spring and fall. To reduce trips down the hall to the water fountain, I have students bring a small plastic cup and allow them to have a half-cup of water at their desks. We discuss that if a spill occurs, the child should try to save a book first. There are spills and although a piece of paper is occasionally discarded, we haven't lost a book yet. If there is no source of water in your room, invest in a pitcher and have your "go-for" keep it filled.

Trips to the lavatory can be equally disruptive. Teachers devise their own systems for monitoring this need, but I have found it convenient to give each child a bathroom card with his or her name written in large letters. The child props the card in an apple-shaped recipe holder on my desk (the chalk rail would work), takes the pass (which in this case is another card marked lav), and removes his or her card upon returning. Only one student is allowed to leave the room at a time and I can easily tell who is gone. Cards can be propped in any convenient place. Students do lose their lav cards and I assign a chore to earn a new card.

I do not allow such freedom when we have a guest speaker or when I am giving directions, but generally students do not take advantage of this system. The key is to reduce the requests made directly to you and to provide you with an easy way to be aware who is gone. A somewhat simpler method is to sign out on a chalkboard and erase that name upon the return. It would be nice if teachers could also use the lavatory when necessary instead of during rare breaks. Once the class is into a safe routine, I use the same system for myself, thus keeping the class aware of my whereabouts.

SEMISUSTAINED SILENT READING (SSSR)

This section might seem displaced, but I include it here because I use it as much as a management tool as I do a teaching technique. As you read through my adaptation, you will see how initiating this practice early in the year will benefit you every following day.

Sustained Silent Reading (SSR) has been used successfully for many years, occasionally being labeled by another acronym, USSR (Uninterrupted Sustained Silent Reading) or DEAR (Drop Everything And Read). It is characterized by an entire class or even the school, including support staff, devoting a prescribed period of time to reading books. The benefits of such a program are obvious—if an entire school regards reading important enough to dedicate a regular session to it, students will learn to value reading as well.

Yet unless the entire school is involved in a silent reading program or the district places a high value on silent reading, few teachers will use SSR for any extended time in the classroom. Even though we recognize how important reading is to school success, we feel a bit guilty using class time to indulge in a passion for books.

My usage of SSR has evolved over the years into what I call Semisustained Silent Reading (SSSR). Rather than rigidly using this period for everyone to read, I use it to have individual conferences, review what I am doing during the period or next class, read journals, or simply to sit, observe, and recoup my energies. Sometimes I use the time to read.

It is true that the teacher's involvement in SSR helps keep the students at task; thus I also read while I carefully train my students during the first month of school. Once they understand the expectations and adopt the routine of reading, I can deviate from reading without jeopardizing the program.

Usually I begin the year by telling the students that I expect them to always have a book with them. I schedule our library visit so it fits conveniently into my program. Our library has regularly scheduled times plus allows for unscheduled drop-in visits. Once the silent reading time is well established, I allow students to use this time to go to the library. I also borrow a large quantity of books from the library in addition to maintaining my own classroom collection. There is simply no excuse for being without a book.

When I teach a reading class which includes students from other rooms, I will not let students go back to their homerooms to retrieve a forgotten book. They must make do with what is in the classroom. This eliminates the phenomenon which I call the "doing the hall crawl" and keeps students in the room where they belong, presumably involved in their reading. Breaking the habits of escape artists will take some time and will not happen without some resistance. This is partly why you will need to spend the first few weeks reading with your students and making them aware of your expectations.

When your students have their books, start by reading silently, five minutes with primary students, ten minutes in the intermediate classroom. Having a timer is convenient and relieves you of the chore of determining when the ten minutes is finished. Each day, extend the time by a minute or two until you have reached a period of fifteen to thirty minutes. The amount of time will be decided by your schedule, grade level, and curricular demands. Once you have reached your desired level, continue to read with your students for a week or two to establish the routine. This is hard to do because there are always many tasks begging for attention. But, the investment of time now pays off later. And, be prepared to read silently with the class again if participation falters.

Gradually begin to do quiet activities which do not involve the students, and soon you will be able to carry on your daily chores while the students read. I discuss writing in journals in a later chapter, and this is an ideal time to read their journals. If a student needs a private conversation about what has been written, you have ample opportunity to initiate the conference.

A bonus of training your students in SSSR is that many automatically will read their books when their work is done. Sometimes the avid readers will keep their books barely concealed during other periods. I had a fifth-grade boy who wore two hearing aids and needed to depend somewhat on lip reading. He was an excellent student who often completed his work quickly and then would turn to a book. He would become so absorbed in his reading in his relatively silent world that someone would have to gently alert him that we were moving on to another activity. When you have to remind your students to put their books away, you know that your silent reading program is a resounding success.

One final comment: the purists who advocate SSR will be appalled at the above modifications. But, I believe that it is so difficult to find time during the day to schedule silent reading, that most teachers' minds are probably spinning with all the "what nexts" while they are trying or pretending to read. I maintain that using SSSR is preferable to not having any silent-reading program.

SELLING YOUR PROGRAM, YOUR SCHOOL, AND PUBLIC EDUCATION

Having spent as many years in private schools as public schools, I have decided that public schools need to learn a lesson in survival from their private counterparts. In a private school, there is a recognizable link between the tuition check from the parents of the students and the teacher's paycheck. A teacher who does not provide a marketable education does not last in a private school. Money is budgeted for advertising the school's programs, but if the school has mediocre teachers, it fails to sell, loses its clientele, and fails.

Society does not consciously recognize the link between taxpayer money and a public school-teacher's paycheck, even though we all know it exists. The clientele is primarily guaranteed and, therefore, teachers' jobs are guaranteed. Consequently, teachers have not spent much time worrying about public relations except perhaps when they want a raise and there must be an increase in taxes to acquire it. Then it is too late. In today's climate, teachers must do a better job of selling their programs. We have a tougher job than the private schools that can sell to people whose children will benefit directly. Public schoolteachers need to convince the poor, elderly, and people on fixed incomes or with no school children that education is worth their sacrifices.

It sounds like an impossible task, but I believe it can happen. Change, to be effective, must come from the bottom up. Teachers must start by selling to their constituency, and they must sell hard enough that when times are tough(er) and another generation has aged, the mill levy or bond issue will still be passed because teachers sold the public on quality education generations ago.

This section concentrates on ways to sell your program. Yes, some involve investment of money for film, punch, and cookies, but often you can get your principal or PTA to help with costs, or you can find parents to help with donated goodies.

Begin with a Back to School Night

On the first day of school I take a picture (slide) of each child. These are usually rather stiff, unnatural pictures, due to the anxiety that surrounds the first day, but they provide an important contrast later. During the next few weeks, until Back to School Night, I take more slides of the students: at work at their desks, participating in FAC, on the playground, and with their friends. With older students, I let them have a turn at the camera—this is a great icebreaker, even though the framing is not terrific.

The day or two before the Back to School Night, I make fortune cookies using a recipe from *Your Best Back-to-School Night Ever*, a helpful book by Pete Vodola and Connie Briggs. We make fortune cookies on a griddle in our room, inserting a fortune which states, "You will prosper from attending Back to School Night." (If you are in a humid climate, crisp them in an oven for a few minutes.) I send home three per student, hoping that one will reach a parent. (See recipe at end of chapter.)

Meanwhile, since our Back to School Night is for parents only, I let the students see my Back to School Night slide show ahead of time. I organize the slides with music such as Whitney Houston's "The Greatest Love" or Johnny Mathis's "Priceless." (Denver teacher Chris Blach needs no music; she uses slides to illustrate her narrative about her program.) By the time the students have taken their parents the fortune cookies and told them about the slides, good attendance is guaranteed.

On the Back to School Night, I outline my program, discuss my homework policy (see chapter 5), show the slides, and ask for questions. I then make my pitch for helpers: typists, field-trip chaperones, cookie bakers, etc. I have sign-up sheets available, and sometimes can schedule the first set of conferences as well.

I also try to have a handout available for parents. I was at my son's Back to School Night and his teachers emphasized how important it was that the students always have a book for silent reading. But, when a parent asked if they had some suggestions for good literature for this age group, the teachers replied, "No." It is understandable not to have a booklist on hand, but it is inexcusable not to offer to make even a short list available in a week or two. A list of eighty books to share is on pp. 171-73 in the appendix and may be used as a parent handout. Another successful handout is one suggesting how parents can help at home with providing a literate environment. Make your own list or use the one at the end of this chapter.

Your Best Back-to-School Night Ever is full of great ideas for this event. Most are in a form ready for reproduction for both primary and intermediate grade levels. There are invitations, clever reminder slips, personalized student projects, suggestions for sharing information, sample topics, parent letters, sign-in sheets, name tags, and a variety of parent handouts and report forms. The student worksheet, "All About Me," at the end of this chapter is taken from the book. It provides information about the student and is always of interest to parents. Be prepared to help the students with vocabulary and spelling. With younger students, send the form home for a homework project prior to Back to School Night so you will be more familiar with your families. The most frequent response when parents read the form their child completed is "I didn't know that!"

If this sounds like a lot of work for an event which should be well attended anyway, it *is*. Using pictures of children is a powerful device, and it is admittedly deliberate and perhaps a bit contrived. But it pays immeasurable dividends when the parents leave your classroom convinced that you are going to provide a wonderful learning experience for their children. You have made a major step toward selling your program.

Ending the Year

Throughout the year I continue to take slides on a more limited basis: at various celebrations such as Halloween, when a student does an especially impressive report or project, when we do something special with a thematic study, or when we have a guest speaker or performer. At the end of the year I retrieve the slides from the first day of school and, after organizing them in some arbitrary order, write a sentence or two about what I remember about each child. Once my theme was what each child taught me. The rest of the slides I organize in chronological order, with a sentence or two for each batch of slides from some special event. This is the focus of my end of the year celebration. I invite parents to join us during the last forty-five minutes of school a day or two before school is out. And, after seeing the slides in the fall, I know the majority will be there. Earlier in the day I show the slides and read my narration to the class, so if there are any reasons to giggle (and there always are) they will not embarrass themselves when our "company" comes. (Of course this is one of those special events when everyone in the class helps clean the classroom, a tremendous help when you are desperately trying to check out for the summer.)

When the parents arrive, I show the slides, and then ceremoniously bestow on each student a copy of the narration as a remembrance of our year. I also acknowledge our room mother with a summer plant. We then finish with refreshments and time to visit. (This is a time when I would advise asking parents to help with a dozen cookies, especially if your class is large.)

Other Ways to Sell a Program

Gloria Palomino, a fourth-grade teacher at Park Hill School, loves to dance and she shares that love with her class and other fourth graders. While she always begins with just a small dance or skit, because of her talent and exuberance it grows to a major production. Inevitably the whole school and parents are invited to share in the twenty- to thirty-minute show. A great amount of effort goes into these projects, but students learn lifelong lessons about stage presence, speaking, dancing, and acting. And, of course the parents love seeing their children on stage. They are convinced that if Gloria Palomino can do something like this on stage, she must be wonderful in the classroom. Those parents believe in Ms. Palomino *and* her program.

Parent Participation Month is a successful program developed by Lois Love, a third-grade teacher at Park Hill School. Mrs. Love set aside a period every morning and afternoon on Tuesdays and Thursdays for parents to schedule a visit to the class to share their vocation or avocation. Students asked all but personal questions and followed up visits with thank you notes. (One visitor showed the thank you notes to her boss, and he displayed them in the store.) Visiting parents included a ballet teacher, scuba diver, fireman, grocery clerk, educators, engraver, genealogist, and machinist. Although not required, all parents brought an item to share with the students: coupons for a free ballet lesson, coloring books, photographs, pens, and even an engraved door plate. The program was a resounding success and could have been expanded into another full month if time had allowed.

CONCLUSION

Your successful provision of a literate classroom depends on your being willing to see yourself as a manager of students. These students know the expectations for behavior and achievement. They make choices about their achievement and accept responsibility for it. They recognize their responsibility to their environment and participate in its maintenance. Finally, they know where they stand because there are no surprises. They know their teacher is there to guide, instruct, evaluate, and nurture and that they are there to participate jointly in the process of learning.

REFERENCES

Anno, Mitsumasa, and Masaichiro Anno. *Anno's Magical ABC: An Anamorphic Alphabet*. New York: Philomel Books, 1981.

Lobel, Arnold. *On Market Street*. Illustrated by Anita Lobel. New York: Greenwillow Books, 1981.

O'Brien, Robert C. *Mrs. Frisby and the Rats of NIMH*. Illustrated by Zena Bernstein. New York: Scholastic Book Services, 1971.

Trelease, Jim. *The Read-Aloud Handbook*. New York: Penguin Books, 1985.

Vodola, Peter, and Connie Briggs. *Your Best Back-to-School Night Ever*. Brea, Calif.: Peanut Publications, 1987.

CREATING A LITERATE HOME ENVIRONMENT

You can be a powerful force in your child's education by trying out some or all of the following suggestions.

1. Develop a home library containing books, magazines, and a dictionary. Find bargains at used book sales, garage sales, and discount houses.

2. Provide a good reading model. Reading with your child may mean reading the same book or cartoons or magazines to each other in turns or merely sharing the same couch while you read different materials.

3. Even if you share reading as above, and especially if you don't, try to always spend some time reading aloud to your child. Buy or borrow from the library a copy of Jim Trelease's *The Read-Aloud Handbook* or see your child's teacher for good read-aloud books. Bedtime is a fine time for this quiet activity. An even better idea from Trelease's book is to let your child clean up the kitchen while you read aloud from a favorite book.

4. Get a library card for your child and make regular visits.

5. Show the utility of reading by having your child look up numbers or addresses in the phone book, read and prepare recipes, or find the weather forecast or horoscope in the newspaper.

6. For the younger child, read aloud billboards, street signs, and signs on buildings as you drive.

7. Subscribe to a monthly magazine such as *Odyssey* or *Ranger Rick* or browse through magazines at the public library.

8. Leave notes for your children to read. If they are to come home after school before you, write out directions for special chores or privileges. Slip messages into sack lunches or pockets.

9. Teach children how to answer the phone, write messages, and politely ask a caller to repeat information (an intimidating request for a child).

10. Have children write thank you notes, letters, or messages.

11. Dictate your shopping list or memos for your child to write.

12. Encourage your child to keep a diary. A spiral notebook is adequate.

13. Take time to listen to your child. Set aside time to converse and find out what has happened in school.

14. Teach your child how to use a calculator and have him or her help with adding grocery prices, clothing costs, or estimating total bills.

ALL ABOUT ME

Full Name _____

Age _____ Date of Birth _____

City and State of Birth _____

Number of Sisters _____   Number of Brothers _____

Pets (type and name) _____

_____

Favorite Food(s) _____

Least Favorite _____

Favorite Beverage _____

Favorite Restaurant _____

Favorite T.V. Program(s) _____

_____

Favorite Movie(s) _____

_____

Favorite Pop Song _____

Favorite Musical Group_____

Favorite Radio Station _____

Easiest School Subject(s) _____

Hardest School Subject(s) _____

Favorite Library Book _____

Favorite Out-of-School Activity _____

Hobbies/Interests _____

_____

Occupational Goal (if any) _____

Additional Information/Comments_____

_____

_____

Date _____ Signature _____

FORTUNE COOKIES

Incorporate a cooking lesson in this Back to School Night reminder. Students will learn standard measuring and sequencing of steps, and enjoy the reward of a unique result.

Recipe

3 eggs

1/2-cup packed brown sugar

1/2-cup all-purpose flour

1/2-teaspoon lemon extract

30-35 fortunes

Step 1

Beat eggs with an electric mixer until frothy. Add brown sugar, flour, and lemon extract, and beat until thick. Set by stove with a pancake turner, a large platter, the folded fortunes, and a soup spoon.

Step 2

Set heavy, flat griddle over medium heat and allow it to heat thoroughly (or use an electric griddle). Place three or more spoonfuls of batter on the griddle and spread with spoon tip into three-inch rounds. Cook only until dry enough to flip with spatula; turn, cook thirty seconds, remove to platter. Lift pancake onto tips of thumb and first two fingers, poke a fortune gently into cup formed, then press edges of pancake together firmly enough to seal. It may take a few tries before you get the knack. Cookie should look like a folded pancake bent in half. If you have trouble sealing, moisten edges with uncooked egg batter. Makes 30-35 cookies.

Reproducible Fortunes

You will prosper from attending Back to School Night	You will prosper from attending Back to School Night
You will prosper from attending Back to School Night	You will prosper from attending Back to School Night
You will prosper from attending Back to School Night	You will prosper from attending Back to School Night
You will prosper from attending Back to School Night	You will prosper from attending Back to School Night

All About Me and the above recipe are reprinted with permission from *Your Best Back-to-School Night Ever*, by Pete Vodola and Connie Briggs, Peanut Publications, 1987.

Chapter 5

"I'm done, Teacher. What do I do now?"

As the school year ended, several of my students noticed I was disposing of the leftover supplemental math worksheets and asked if they could have them. While I willingly handed them over, since they were fine students who did not need any review, I asked why they wanted them. They replied that they played "school" and these would be useful. As I continued the end-of-year clean-up they carted off a wide variety of discards, saving the custodians several trips to the dumpsters. It wasn't until later that I felt some dismay; in spite of our rich and varied program, the students still saw worksheets as a routine component of "playing school."

I was somewhat reassured, however, when these same students played "school" during FAC (Friday Afternoon Club, see chapter 4) and did not use the worksheets, but assigned chapters in books for reading, writing in journals, and taught math lessons from the board. Of course students usually do not have a home full of reference books, trade books, magazines, and various other materials. If homes were so equipped, there would be less of a need for libraries or schools. It's always instructive to watch students portray you, the teacher, in the game of "school," as the portrayals are brutally honest. Using a videotape is very helpful with self-assessment, but watching your students is just as realistic. The fact that they did not use the worksheets was comforting, but the incident reminded me of the need to consistently evaluate the place of worksheets in the literate classroom.

WORKSHEETS AND THE LITERATE CLASSROOM

Where do worksheets and exercises fit in the literate classroom, if at all? Worksheets, in short, are convenient, easy to teach, and inexpensive, which is why teachers continue to use them regularly. Many students truly enjoy them because they are predictable and comfortable. There is such a sense of accomplishment when a student can look at a stack of completed exercises and declare, "I have all my work done." When Mom or Dad sorts out their tote bag every few weeks, there is this pile of work. Open-ended assignments, such as the research minireport in chapter 7, are not as comfortable at first for students when they previously haven't pursued their own interests or choices. Student success depends on the investment of the student and does not fit the parameters of typical assignments. Thus students who have been in traditional classrooms usually will choose the worksheets over less structured projects. Worksheets seem so productive, they don't require excessive thought or decision making, and, sadly for many children, they are all they have known.

Although worksheets are useful when students are mastering math or map skills or learning handwriting, which are by necessity repetitive and boring, their appropriateness is limited except for occasional usage or review. Except in those instances, however, any assignment should involve active learning, not mindless unnecessary repetition. The key distinction between a justifiable worksheet or workbook and a piece of busywork is whether the learning will occur *without* using a worksheet. If the answer is yes, find another way to teach.

Before assigning any worksheet, critique it. Workbooks or worksheets are often the fill-in-the-blank variety that require little thinking by the student, and some have the added feature of being incredibly frustrating. An example is a wordsearch puzzle. I have never been able to justify the assignment of these puzzles and have truly resented helping my son laboriously complete one. The only possible justification is to help learn the spelling, but there are other ways to use new words which are not so tedious and frustrating. Also, to assign such a complex visual task (usually on a faint copy) to a child with learning difficulties borders on being irresponsible. Finally, I suspect most teachers give the student's completed wordsearch only a glance, if they give it that much attention. Who benefits? The teacher, whose students are kept busy, and the publisher of the materials, but certainly not the students.

Another criticism of workbooks or worksheets is that they require very little handwriting because of the fill-in-the-blank format. Also, although they are inexpensive, they use precious money that could purchase trade books for your literate classroom. Finally, the students all too often complete them with little effort and *too quickly*. Most teachers would rather read a thoughtfully created poem or story than grade ten various worksheets. It takes some reorganization and a change in philosophy for those of us raised on basals and workbooks, but it is worth the change.

You will build the sense of responsibility so important to a successful learner by only assigning or encouraging meaningful work. At the end of the year, when I had my students write on the "bitter and the best" (see chapter 8), one student wrote, referring to some grammar sheets, that she didn't mind learning grammar but thought that once a student had shown understanding with nine or ten sentences it ought to be enough. She was correct, and from that day on, I look carefully not only at the content but at the amount of practice. Students know when work is pointless and if given the opportunity they will tell you so.

I could go on criticizing various types of worksheets, but the key point is the need to evaluate any assignment based on its usefulness to the students. For example, what is the value of "cloze" exercises except in diagnosis? Why color all the "red" balloons red? Why find all the three-syllable words on a page? Why list all the B words in a paragraph? When do we ever use those "skills"? If you cannot answer that question, do not use the assignment. Remember, your job is not to keep students busy, but to keep them learning.

When you critique a worksheet, ask yourself these questions:

Does this assignment:

- develop curiosity?
- teach a necessary skill?
- develop independence?
- allow for creativity?
- provide transfer to another area?
- provide achievement?

Is the assignment:

- useful, though perhaps tedious?
- individualized?
- enjoyable?
- valuable?

Does it teach?

Does it make a student think?

Does it take more work for you to evaluate it than for the student to complete it?

Would you mind doing the assignment?

JUST WHAT ARE THESE
SKILLS, ANYWAY?

First, it is important to recognize that alternative programs do not ignore the teaching of skills, expecting students to acquire them magically. It is also important to define just what skills are necessary to academic success. A lot of mindless exercises masquerade as "skills," but most teachers would agree that the successful student needs to have a degree of mastery over some basic skills.

Spelling Skills: Invented
and Traditional

An effective writing program allows for invented spelling (words written phonetically without regard to the proper spelling), reasoning that concern over spelling will impede the creative process. Correct spelling is not ignored. It is merely delayed to the revision or polishing stage, when a student uses every resource available (dictionaries, peer editors, friends) to find the correct spelling. Note that I did not include teachers on the list of resources. Of course, teachers will routinely help with the spelling, but the teacher's job is to teach and coach, and constant interruptions are counterproductive and do not foster student independence and responsibility. Students who learn to refer to other resources first become autonomous learners.

Without going through the revision stage of writing on a regular basis, there is a danger that invented spelling will be deemed an acceptable spelling form forever. Even word processors that can check spelling need an approximation of the spelling to find the word. I had a fourth-grade boy come to me from a private school in which the teachers never proceeded beyond the invented spelling stage. One day he scolded me in his journal because I was so "mean" when I insisted he begin to learn to spell. He blasted me for a full page—in invented spelling. I pretended not to be able to read it, and asked him to read it aloud to me. (I often did this with third graders who used invented spelling at the beginning of the year when I truly could *not* read some words, so this request was not seen as unusual.) This bright young man could not read aloud what he had written a mere hour earlier, which gave me the opportunity to discuss how important it is to be able to record one's thoughts so they can be read again. In a few months this same young man was writing quite readable entries, including comments such as, "I found this great word—'incognito'—it means having your identity concealed...."

Teachers of third and fourth graders face a challenge when students need to develop mastery over a basic list of words so they can communicate effectively. If revisions are done regularly, the transition to traditional spelling is a natural progression.

Making Sense of the Reading:
Phonics, Context, and Configuration Clues

Contrary to what many teachers think, the teaching of phonics does belong in a whole language or literature based program. Knowing phonics provides students with another method of making sense out of the printed word. Phonics is not taught just for the sake of being known, however. It is carefully integrated into the program when the instruction is logical and meaningful. The teaching of generalizations about words, beginning sounds, unusual blends, and so on occurs with examples from books using those words. This method relies on the teacher being willing to recognize the need for instruction and then either pulling together students with similar needs or providing instruction on an individual basis. The benefit to teaching phonics on an "as needed" basis is that through phonics instruction students see the application in the context of need and thus internalize the knowledge more effectively.

Students who love books use whatever means they can to come to terms with the text. My son became masterful at using every clue available until he overcame his reading problem. He usually could identify the "big" words, because he could get good ideas about them from the pictures and discussion, and he had an excellent speaking vocabulary. But the sight words baffled him and he thus merely read with an approximate interpretation of the text. His word recognition score would be lousy, but his comprehension would be excellent. Getting meaning from text should be the main goal. Basal readers conscientiously teach the use of context clues. This is unnecessary (and terribly boring) for most readers. They have figured out from their earliest experiences with books that the pictures and key words collaborate. For those students who need help using context clues, follow the rule of offering the help in groups or individually as it suits the reader(s).

Punctuation and Grammar

The teaching of punctuation and grammar most naturally occurs during the revision process when writers strive to ensure that their readers understand their meaning. The check sheets in chapter 8 give students help with these details. Follow the above recommendations, remembering that direct instruction in punctuation and grammar is often necessary and should be offered in a meaningful context.

Test-Taking Skills

There are certain skills students need because they appear on standardized tests, and whether or not a teacher agrees with the emphasis placed on testing, they are an inescapable influence on curriculum. Study skills can be taught and mastered quite effectively when writing research projects. Yet it would be irresponsible to ignore the fact that tests on study (or any other) skills occur outside of meaningful context. Since tests often resemble worksheets (or vice versa), I use worksheets, but as efficiently as possible. Often I will direct the class through a worksheet on grammar, vocabulary, or finding the main idea as a group, talking through the process and decision making. Other times I will teach the concept, assign the worksheet, and then check it with the class, again talking through the choices, pitfalls, and so forth. This process uses a minimum of class time, and there are no stacks of papers for grading.

A LAST WORD ABOUT WORKSHEETS

It is better to provide math problems on a worksheet than to waste student time by having them copy problems off the chalkboard. Ask yourself again: as an adult, how often is it necessary for you to copy something from a chalkboard or an overhead. The usefulness of this skill occurs only in classes or seminars where it is necessary to get information during a lecture or when information is provided spontaneously. Copying endless problems or sentences from the board in an elementary setting is a device to occupy students which wastes precious time.

The criticisms of worksheets offered here are not meant to imply that you can never allow a student the option of completing a crossword puzzle or wordsearch for relaxation or pleasure. Critique the work you *assign* and if a worksheet has any redeeming features, then it is probably justifiable.

HOMEWORK

The issue of whether or not to assign homework deserves discussion at this point because often well-meaning teachers, under pressure by the administration, educational reports, or parents, feel an obligation to provide packets of homework to their students. Often the packets or daily assignments are full of the mindless worksheets discussed above, which will taint any love of learning developing in a child.

In most households the first words usually spoken to a child arriving home from school are: "How was school?" followed by "Do you have any homework?" Asking about homework is a legitimate concern because children nowadays often participate in one or more sports during the year, play musical instruments, or take other special classes. Many families no longer have the luxury of a parent that stays home, so their children go home to a house without a parent or go to an after school activity. By the time the parents come home and eat dinner, the time left for supervising or helping with homework is very limited and places a burden on already over-burdened families, especially when the home is managed by a single working parent. Squeezing in time just for relaxation and sharing is nearly impossible.

As a parent who comes home and asks these same questions, I always am deeply relieved when the answer is "No" or "Just a little." Therefore, my students rarely have homework except for occasional book reports, and I maintain that homework is not justifiable except in a few instances.

One example is children who are missing key skills necessary for their success in a particular grade level. For example, from third grade forward, it is critical that the math facts be fully mastered. This type of homework is both appropriate and required for the child's continued success in school.

Another case is the child who has not completed the work in a class after a *reasonable* work period. I monitor the progress of the students during a particularly demanding assignment, such as long division, and if no one is getting close to the end of the assignment, I adjust my expectations. But some students vary their work rate, daydream, or procrastinate, and some days simply choose to not finish their assignments. These children will therefore need to use time at home to complete their routine assignments. If they goof off, they have assigned themselves homework.

When students are completing long-range projects, book reports that require artistic efforts, or minireports, they often will also need to spend some time out of school on their assignments. These occasions should be rare and students should be made aware of the requirements well before the deadline.

Every year at Back to School Night, I address the issue of homework, and after summarizing my philosophy the typical response is applause. However, there are always a few children who will claim they got their work done in school when they didn't. For those families I recommend a twenty- or thirty-minute study time every school night *without deviation*. If the child insists there is no homework, the period is to be spent reading together silently or aloud. Parents may have their own homework (school or job related) to do while the child is reading. Students soon adjust to completing school work during this routine study time.

When parents want homework for the sake of homework, I suggest the parent read aloud, have the student read to them, take a walk together, or have a conversation. In the case where the parents insist that the child "needs" homework, I suggest they visit the nearest school supply store, bookstore, or supermarket for work books, explaining that I simply cannot supervise more than what my curriculum already demands. I continue to encourage reading for pleasure as one of the best investments for an evening study period.

ALTERNATIVES TO WORKSHEETS AND WORK BOOKS

The lists of activities at the end of this chapter are arranged generally according to the appropriate subject. There is some overlap because of the nature of the activities. Usage of these lists will depend on your style, your class, and your grade level. If you are in the habit of using classroom centers, you might replace the worksheets with a list of activities and the appropriate materials. I must confess I have never been able to keep integrated centers adequately organized and have preferred to have separate areas for art materials, reference materials, paper supplies, etc., training and allowing students to function as independently as possible. Other teachers manage to keep centers going by teaching the students how to manage them.

For older students, you might post a list of alternatives on the board for a week, based on the curriculum. As you internalize the philosophy behind teaching in a literate classroom, you will add activities and gradually release this responsibility to the students who often can be more creative than we could hope to be. It is helpful to have a core list of activities that always will be acceptable which can be posted or kept in the students' desks or notebooks.

Examine the lists and adapt them to suit your needs. I have not divided them by primary or intermediate levels because I find it difficult to tell a student not to try a difficult activity, and if a child wishes to choose something that is too easy I don't worry about it unless it becomes a pattern. Then I encourage (and occasionally direct) the student to choose more challenging activities. Do not give all these lists to your students as you run the risk of overwhelming them. Decide which areas you wish to emphasize and select those activities that are attractive, expanding the choices as the year progresses.

Taking students from a top-down learning model that is entirely teacher directed to a more bottom-up model in which the student is actively involved in the process does not happen quickly and easily. It takes gentle introduction and review, as it is often confusing. By limiting the choices initially, you will develop a sense of confidence in your students and they will begin to take control of and responsibility for their learning.

LANGUAGE ARTS ACTIVITIES

Keep a journal or diary.

Write a letter to a friend or relative.

Make a card for a friend or relative. It could be a birthday card, get well card, or friendship card.

Write a story.

Illustrate a story.

Write a story for a wordless picture book.

Critique a book.

Make a book.

Make a book cover.

Write a paragraph about yourself for the book cover of your story—an "about the author" column.

Find a partner for shared reading of a book.

Read a newspaper or a magazine.

Rehearse a book report with a friend.

Make a card file of books you have read. Include bibliographic information about the book.

Make a notebook of writing ideas, great words, etc.

Write a newsletter or make a news report.

Write a play.

Take a familiar folk or fairy tale and make it into a play.

Practice your spelling list.

Browse through the dictionary or thesaurus looking for powerful or exciting words. Keep them in a notebook.

Practice your handwriting.

Write poetry.

Write a cumulative story with some classmates.

Make a story map.

Write about a class trip or event on chart paper.

Make a rebus story for younger readers.

Write alliterative sentences such as: Sister Susie sits on a sandy stool.

Make a list of palindromes—words that read the same forwards and backwards such as: mom, dad, radar, noon, wow.

Collect favorite riddles.

Write horoscopes.

Make a final copy of something you have written.

Turn your poem into a card or poster.

Start a "Dear Abby" column by asking classmates to submit (in writing) problems in need of solutions. Write your answers.

Write a letter to a favorite character.

Write letters from one character to another.

Write a letter to a friend about a book.

Make a crossword puzzle about a book.

Compare a story to a movie version.

Put a story in poetry form.

Write a want ad for something in a book.

Write an advertisement for a book.

Use the computer to create a banner about a book.

Start a scrapbook of major news events in the area, world, your school.

Create a brochure advertising a book or the setting of the book.

Create a travel poster to go with a book that has a special setting.

Create a grocery list for a fairy tale character. For example, what would the Wolf from Little Red Riding Hood have on his list?

Write a soap opera using fairy tale characters.

Create a wanted poster for a dastardly character.

Create a telegram to tell about a book in twenty-five words or less.

RESEARCH ACTIVITIES

Create a book list (bibliography) on a favorite subject.

Ask your teacher if you can make a book list on a topic to be taught soon.

Make a list of books you consider "must reads."

Make a list of books you consider the best.

Make a list of books you want to read.

Do a minireport.

Choose a topic and make a time line on it.

Use magazines to find pictures to illustrate your research report.

Use a newspaper to make a current events poster for the day.

Research a favorite author.

Research an author and then write a biography about that author.

If you have read a book based on a time in history, research the clothing worn by the characters. Include drawings of the clothes if possible.

Keep records of all books you have read.

Keep records of the books your classmates have read.

Find poetry to go with a certain subject, such as the solar system, trees, or an animal.

Make a crossword puzzle to go with a topic of study.

Make lists of words you want to use in Scrabble.

Play Junior Scrabble or other word games.

Find or create a recipe to go with a book or subject.

Create a trivia game about any book or subject.

Research the setting of a book—the city, geography, climate, topography, culture, and other interesting facts.

MATH, SCIENCE, AND SOCIAL STUDIES

Take a survey and make a graph of your results. For example, find out how many students have dogs and, if so, how many. Survey ideas are: number of pets, siblings, favorite color, favorite food, favorite sport, etc.

Keep records of daily temperature, indoor and out.

Keep records of daily rainfall or wind.

Make a calendar demonstrating the weather records you kept.

Chart the growth of the room's plants or animals.

Make models of the solar system.

Make a model of the space shuttle.

Make a model of an important geographical feature of your area—a hill, mountain, river, etc.

Make an illustrated glossary of geographic terms.

Measure and draw your classroom to scale.

Practice labeling the United States on a blank map.

Study state, world, or city maps with a friend.

Mark a map with all the states you have visited.

Mark a map with all the states you would like to visit.

Practice your multiplication, addition, or subtraction facts.

Map the setting of a book you have just read. Be accurate.

Create a map of the classroom, school, playground, or block.

Use a microscope to study small things you can find in the classroom: scraps of paper, dust, plant leaves, food samples. Classify and chart the differences.

Look in your science book for suggested projects and do one.

Make up rhymes to help memorize math facts.

ART, MUSIC, AND OTHER CREATIVE AREAS

Choose a familiar tune and write new lyrics for it.

Choose a familiar set of lyrics and create a new tune for it.

Find music to use for the background of a story.

Listen to music and write about the mood of the music.

Design a record cover to fit the music.

Create a rhythm instrument.

Listen to music and write poetry to fit the music.

Listen or recall Kermit's song, "It's Not Easy Being Green" and write about another color it would be difficult to be.

Make a cube story, paper cup story, or flip story.

Create an album about a book.

Make a flannel board and flannel characters.

Make an artistic transparency about a book and use the overhead projector to present a report.

Make a diorama of a setting from a book you have read.

Make a cartoon strip about a book.

Make a poster for a book you have read.

Make a seed mosaic to illustrate a book.

Give a chalk talk summary of a story.

Use clay to make models.

Plan a bulletin board to go with books you have read.

Make a "movie" of a book by using long paper or sheets of paper taped together for the illustrations and rolling them up for presentation.

Make a collage of something you have read or researched.

Design clothing for characters you have read about in a book or in social studies.

Create your own game. Write out the rules and let other students try it out.

Create a puppet show based on an assigned or original story.

Tape a story for others to hear.

Create a story in rebus form for beginning readers.

Paint a poem.

Make a poem or word into a mobile.

Create your "dream" bedroom. Sketch all the furniture, toys, shelves, and other belongings. Label everything and give measurements.

Read several picture books by the same illustrator. Find out as much as you can about the artist. Try out the artist's style or illustrate a page in your own style.

Create an ideal school. Include what it would look like, how it would function, what students would study, and so forth.

Chapter 6

Sneaking Books into the Teaching of Reading

"School readers, especially primers, should largely disappear, except as they may be competent editings of the real literature of the mother tongue, presented in literary wholes, or as they may be records of the children's own experiences and thoughts, or as they may be books needed for information in the everyday life of the school. The children should learn to read books, papers, records, letters, etc., as need arises in their life, just as adults do, and they should be trained to do such reading effectively."[1]

Although this quote reads like a contemporary criticism of basal readers, it dates from 1908 and is taken from an early major work on the teaching of reading in this country, *The Psychology and Pedagogy of Reading*, by Edmund Burke Huey.

Entire literary works or renderings of children's experiences and thoughts are rarely found in traditional basal-oriented classrooms. Children may have little experience with true books, and "doing work" is how most children perceive reading instruction. Finding out a new student's reading level is always a challenge because children never seem to learn the title of a basal, let alone the name of the publishing company. While quizzing a new second-grade student, grasping for clues to his reading level, I finally said hopefully, "Maybe you read story books in your class. What type of books did you read?" The child's puzzled response was, "We didn't read books; we did work."

His interpretation is not surprising, for reading instruction traditionally has depended more upon work books and a bounty of worksheets than upon actual reading of literature or print in any form. Basals are routinely under fire and some criticisms are legitimate. But while the experts wage the war on whether or not to use those traditional readers, we troops (classroom teachers) are left in the trenches, fighting for our very survival in the classroom. While some fantasize about leaving behind the basal readers, the mere thought of picking up the guantlet leaves many of us just plain weary.

This chapter provides the teacher with suggestions for augmenting or altering the traditional basal package. Suggestions such as routine reading aloud, literature logs, and providing a wide choice of book reports can enliven any existing program. For the teacher who would like to try some alternative methods without totally abandoning the basal, the Student Implimented Book (SIB) Guides and Vocabulary Guides are ideal for sampling literature based techniques. These are discussed later in this chapter.

A comfortable way to institute some changes is to take the reading group that is most manageable (usually the upper group) and suspend reading in the basal while reading a novel and using the SIB or Vocabulary Guides. Continue with the basal with other students. When one group finishes the novel, return to the basal and begin a novel with another group. Do try these techniques with the low groups as well. They have been successful with learning disabled, remedial, low achieving, non-English speaking, and mainstreamed mentally retarded students in the regular classroom. Students who are in these groups perhaps have not experienced success with the basal package and need a fresh approach even more than the high achieving students.

Combining these techniques with others found in later chapters can lead to the development of a program independent of the basal program, but it is not recommended that a teacher tackle a whole language or literature based program in one grand step. Any new program is challenging, and although alternative language arts programs are exciting and fun for you and the students, they require a degree of skill. A gradual process of alternating new methods with the present instructional system allows teachers to internalize the techniques and adapt them to their needs. The following models: provide for the needs of students with a variety of learning styles; develop critical thinking skills; and allow a teacher to begin the transition with activities that provide accountability and a sense of structure.

READING ALOUD

The easiest and most refreshing way of enhancing any reading program is to read aloud daily. Reading aloud inspires, soothes, instructs, and distracts. My attempts to distract my toddler with a book became so transparent that when he became cranky he'd say, "Mom, I just need a book." This works equally well in the classroom.

Scheduling a read-aloud period should be a priority, not an afterthought. Some teachers begin the day with a good book, using a picture book related to the activities in the primary classroom, or a novel in the intermediate classroom which may tie directly to the curriculum. Reading aloud just for the beauty of the words, the message, the style, or the tone is a valid justification for a choice. Other teachers use this technique at the beginning of every language arts period to set the tone. Others read to both their homeroom classes and their language arts classes. Charla Pfeffinger, a teacher at Rankin School in Pekin, Illinois, wanted to encourage her eighth-grade students to participate in the Young Authors Conference. She read a half hour daily for a week from a variety of picture books—sad, fable, ABC, funny, rhyming, counting, folk—stressing that children's books should be fun to read and to write. The students loved hearing these books, were disappointed when she quit, and followed through with creating some very good books of their own. Chapter 9, on the reading and writing connection, provides more details regarding the integration of reading aloud with instruction.

My favorite source for choosing a great read aloud is Jim Trelease's *The Read-Aloud Handbook*. After making a convincing case for reading aloud, Trelease provides an annotated treasury of his favorite read-aloud books. Although no teacher should use just one source, this is a convenient resource. At the end of the year I ask all students to write on the "bitter and the best," telling me what they liked most and least about the year (see chapter 8). Often mentioned is a read-aloud book.

A Cautionary Tale

Before reading aloud or assigning any book, read it yourself first. At a children's literature conference a presenter recommended what sounded like the perfect book for my students, who were researching their "roots" in social studies.

Soon I started reading *The Kidnapping of Aunt Elizabeth* by Barbara Ann Porte to my class. The protagonist, Ash, researches her family history, uncovering outrageous anecdotes to share with her class. She visits the library and the librarian suggests she look into folk and fairy tales, a sort of oral family history. She tells Ash, "They may surprise you."[2]

As a teacher who integrates folk and fairy tales into the program routinely, I found this section an unexpected bonus. I read on, only to stop in shock at the next paragraph as Ash recounts, "It is true I am surprised. I am surprised, for instance, to discover, in a book of creation myths, a story about first woman with teeth in her vagina. Teeth were how she controlled the world."[3]

Ash was not nearly as surprised as I was! A practiced reader's eyes are several words ahead of the spoken word, and one can usually think of a substitute for an objectionable word or two, but this time I was so stunned I closed the book stating that I could not continue. Of course the students were terribly curious and all claimed they were going to buy the book to find out why I quit. None did. But I had surely learned the dangers of not reading a book first.

LINKING REAL LIFE AUTHORS TO READ ALOUDS AND OTHER BOOKS

It would be delightful if schools regularly could host authors so that students could gain insights into their inspiration, but such an event is expensive and complicated. Fine resources for learning about authors are Sharron L. McElmeel's books, *An Author a Month (for Pennies)* and *Bookpeople: Album 1* and *Album 2*. Having biographical material or anecdotal information makes the process of writing books more real and thereby more attainable to children.

Another source that allows teachers to hear authors is a regional convention. Often an author or illustrator will be a featured luncheon speaker or will offer one-hour presentations. Take notes and keep a file of their comments. I once heard Theodore Taylor speak the day after I finished reading aloud *The Cay*. He related how a newspaper accounting of a child lost at sea during World War II had inspired *The Cay*, and how he had thought about it for ten years before the characters came together and he began to write. Through this anecdote, my students gained a new perspective on how authors work out their material. Taking back an autographed book by the author makes the story even more special.

MOTIVATING STUDENTS TO
SNEAK BOOKS INTO THE PROGRAM

Show Interest: Ask the students what they read over the weekend, what their favorite books are, what they didn't like, etc. Keep abreast of what they are reading.

Share: Share with the class titles of books you have enjoyed. Try to read as many student level books as possible. Letting them know about what you've read at book report time or whenever appropriate communicates to them how important reading is.

Read-ins: Have an occasional period during which students can read aloud sections of their favorite books to a partner. This differs from paired reading, discussed later in this chapter, which is an instructional method.

Book Posters: Pair your posters from conventions or dealers with the book it portrays. Students can create their own.

Thematic Displays: Have a display or bulletin board featuring the unit—counting books, mysteries, fairy tales, etc.

Quotations: Display direct quotations from books throughout the room. This is especially effective for thematic units.

Literary Trivial Pursuit: Have the students generate trivia questions based on their reading. Collect them and over time you will have a collection for an independent activity.

Reading Corner: Have a comfortable area appropriate for relaxed reading. A rocking chair, a small tent, beanbag chairs, pillows, or just an inviting carpeted area will attract students.

Stop Reading a Book: Charla Pfeffinger was reading aloud *Night of the Twisters* and stopped just a few chapters from the end. Soon there was a book fair, and all ten copies of *Night of the Twisters* sold out in minutes.

Read the Literature: Keep up with the newest books. Use professional reviews when there is limited time, but best of all, read the books yourself.

Book Exchange: If your school has gift exchanges for any reason, limit the gift to a book. Books can be paperback, used, etc. If your school has a book fair, schedule it before the designated book exchange; it boosts sales.

Auction: Auction students' paperbacks with play money. This could also be part of a school store or an economics lesson.

Book Swap: Have the children bring in two books and take home one. This is a good way to build a classroom collection.

Birthday Books: Make a list of desired books available to send in a birthday card to the birthday child. Ask if the parents wish to donate a book in honor of their child's special day.

Topic of the Month: Advertise a specific theme with posters, quotes on the board, etc.

Bulletin Boards: Use book themes: books for athletes, animal books, mystery books, etc.

Home Library: Encourage students to start libraries of their own. Help them get started with lists of "musts." The class could collaborate on a list.

Write Books: Have students write, illustrate, and bind their own books. Encourage "pen" names. Circulate the books as much as possible.

Tie Literature to Other Areas: Use books that have characters involved in art, music, or other special interest areas.

Develop Units Involving the Special Teachers: Share favorite books with the music, art, and even P.E. teachers, and soon they will be interested in incorporating books into their curriculums. Don't forget your principal.

Universal Themes: Use fairy tales in all forms, myths, and folklore. Discuss the universal themes.

Personal Library: Bring in your books from home to share.

Role Playing: Use books for plays.

BOOK REPORTS

"I don't mind reading the books, but I sure hate doing the book reports!" laments a fourth-grade student. Whether or not the reading of trade books is part of the instructional program, the dilemma of how to determine the student has truly read the book is commonly solved by requiring the student to write a summary book report.

Frank Smith, in his essay "Twelve Easy Ways to Make Learning to Read Difficult," writes that the eleventh way to make reading difficult is to "[t]ake the opportunity during reading instruction to improve spelling and written expression...." He states:

> Reading assists writing, but not vice versa. Apart from anything else, writing is too slow to do anything but interfere with the process of reading, just as the mechanics of the writing act can interfere chronically with children's expression of their thought. Even so, instruction in written language which aims at getting well-articulated thoughts onto paper very often finds itself more concerned with such disruptive side issues as "correct" spelling and grammar, formalized layout, page and paragraph numeration, and neatness....[4]

Jeannette Veatch, in *Reading in the Elementary School*, recommends that children follow up their reading with a "sharing time" of their books.[5] This period consists of the students sharing their books (and proving they read them) with the audience (the class and teacher) through a variety of oral or written reports, artistic creations, poetry, or related activities.

With a class of twenty-five or thirty students, it may seem a formidable task to schedule time so that all children can share their reports. To ease into a sharing program, the teacher might consider alternating traditional book reports with sharing periods. Using a timer with a predetermined maximum amount of time takes the burden of cutting off a lengthy presentation from the teacher. Students can rehearse their report in advance, knowing their limits. Ms. Veatch suggests using Friday afternoons for sharing books; the teacher can relax with the audience after a long week of work and enjoy the presentations. Most teachers have short periods just before music or art which could be used for three or four reports, scattering them throughout the week.

Although justifying class time for book sharing may seem difficult, there are many advantages to such a period. The students must rehearse their reports, and as they become more experienced, they become more comfortable in front of a group of people. They quickly learn the importance of giving a smooth report to maintain the interest of their audience. The student who is uncomfortable in front of a group can choose art-related projects, tape record the report at home, or work from a script. Students learn the importance of sequencing, organizing, and rearranging ideas. Audience skills develop. Students generate interest in other books and receive approval as others recognize previously read books. They become aware of authors' names, other books by the same author, and book series. However, for the student who is painfully shy, the choice not to share a book report should be respected.

Evaluation of book sharing can be difficult at first, as it is not easy to tell with some reports just how much effort went into the preparation. If you assign letter grades, enlist the students' help in determining the key points for evaluation by brainstorming important aspects. Points to consider are: rehearsal time, preparation time, smoothness of presentation, accuracy, audience appeal, eye contact, appropriateness of the book, etc. After one or two sharing periods, it is helpful to have the students grade their own reports. You can compare their evaluations and discuss why your assessments differ. Next have them evaluate their own as well as those of their classmates. Have the students grade the other reports confidentially and put their own grade last, so the teacher knows who is evaluating. This exercise is revealing to both the students and the teacher, as both struggle with the challenge of fair evaluation. An alternative method is simply to give credit for having presented the report.

The following list contains book-sharing ideas that are probably too difficult or too easy for any one class. Rather it is intended to be a pool of ideas for the classroom teacher which will ideally trigger new ideas. Teachers are encouraged to share their favorite books as models which demonstrate their love of reading.

125 WAYS TO SHARE BOOKS

Note: All presentations should include the book's title and the author's name.

1. *Panel Discussion:* Organize a pro and con panel with a chairperson and debate an issue. Consider including one person as the author.
2. *Dramatization:* Dramatize an incident or an important character.
3. *Radio Announcements:* Have student "broadcast" an advertisement for the book.
4. *Telegram:* Condense the essence of the book into fifteen, fifty, or one hundred words.
5. *Cliffhanger:* Read aloud, stopping at a strategic point.
6. *Costumes:* Design costumes from the period of the book.
7. *Stage:* Design a miniature stage setting for a portion of the story.
8. *Persuasive Speech:* Persuade the audience why they should (or should not) read the book.
9. *Sketch a Sequence:* Sketch action sequences. Consider use of photography.
10. *Letter:* Write a letter recommending the book to a friend.
11. *Character Dress:* Dress as a character and illustrate a section.
12. *Book Reviews:* Broadcast a review on the school public announcement system.
13. *Simplification:* Rewrite an incident for a primary grade.
14. *Pantomime:* Pantomime a character or scene and ask the class to guess the book.
15. *Map:* Make a map of the country or fantasy land from the book.
16. *Decision Making:* Take a familiar story and, at midpoint, ask what would have happened if a character had made a different decision.
17. *Past to Present:* Bring a book character from past to present. Discuss or write how the character would act today.
18. *Poetry:* Write an original poem based on one of the characters in the book or write a report in poem form.
19. *Comparison:* Compare one book with another of similar theme.
20. *Crossword Puzzle:* Use clues about the setting, characters, and plot.
21. *Current Events:* Choose a present-day situation that has been in the news. Give a character's probable reaction to the event.
22. *Diary:* Write a few pages from a diary as if you were one of the characters.
23. *Scroll:* Create a scroll to illustrate your book.
24. *Call an Author:* Plan the questions and use a conference call set-up.
25. *Movie:* Tell why a book could (or could not) become a hit movie.
26. *Dinner Date:* Invite a character to dinner. Plan an appropriate meal.
27. *Cartoon:* Do a cartoon strip using the characters or a scene.
28. *Summarization:* Get the plot down to one succinct paragraph.
29. *Book Jacket:* Prepare a book jacket that illustrates the story.
30. *Sales Talk:* Make a sales talk, pretending your audience is composed of bookstore clerks and you want them to push this book.
31. *Poetry:* After reading a book of poems, choose a poem to read to the class.

(Handout continues on page 70.)

32. *Poetry:* Create a poem in the style of the poems in a collection.

33. *Poetry:* Create a poem to illustrate an important episode of the book or to summarize the book.

34. *Best Friend:* Write to your best friend, telling why you did or did not like a book.

35. *Interesting Character:* Describe a character, making him or her come alive.

36. *Humorous Incident:* Write or tell about the most humorous incident.

37. *Exciting Happening:* Write or tell about the most exciting event.

38. *Interesting Event:* Write or tell about the most interesting event.

39. *Favorite Part:* Write or tell about your favorite part.

40. *Questions:* Have a friend, classmate, or teacher who has read the story try to stump you with questions.

41. *Facts:* Make a list of facts you learned from reading a nonfiction book.

42. *Poster:* Make a poster about the book using at least four different textures to add dimension.

43. *Role Playing:* Imagine you are one of the characters in the book. Tell what you think of the author for putting you into the book and what you think of the other characters.

44. *Folktales:* Mix the characters of several familiar folktales and write the story that results.

45. *Fairy Tales:* Read several fairy tales and list the common elements of the stories.

46. *Fairy Tales:* Read several fairy tales and create your own tale using the common elements of fairy tales.

47. *Unpopular Position:* Choose a character and defend why his or her role in a story should be different. Example: Rumplestiltskin should have gotten the queen's son to raise because he had magical powers.

48. *Book at Home:* Tell what your home would be like if it belonged to Pippi Longstocking, a "Borrower," or another well-known character.

49. *Special Words:* Think of five to ten special words to describe the book. Tell or write why you chose these words.

50. *Literary Cartoons:* Collect cartoons that use literary allusions found in books you have read.

51. *Author:* Become the author and tell why you wrote this story.

52. *Author, Author:* Research the author and give a report about him or her, why he or she writes, etc.

53. *Author's Prerogative:* Tell how you would change the story if you were the author.

54. *Bulletin Board:* Make a bulletin board about the book, showing the main characters, the setting, etc.

55. *Biography:* Write a biography of one of the characters.

56. *Interview:* Write an interview between a character in the book and the author.

57. *Interview:* Write an interview between you and the author.

58. *Interview:* Write an interview between two characters in the book.

59. *Author Appreciation:* Write a letter of appreciation to an author you admire, asking questions and sharing thoughts.

60. *Biography Imagination:* After reading a biography, pretend you visited the person when he or she was your age. Tell or write about your visit.

61. *Reporter:* Pretend that you are your favorite radio reporter and report on the book so that others will want to read it. Perhaps the school public announcement system could be used.

62. *Movie Time:* Make a hand-rolled movie of your book.

63. *Movie Producing:* You are a movie producer and have read this book to judge it as a possible new movie. Consider plot, box office appeal, and story and tell how you would script it.

64. *Book Time:* Pretend to be a book and tell what you hold within your pages. Advertise yourself effectively.

65. *Sixty-Four Words:* A very impatient person has asked about the main character in your book. Describe him or her in sixty-four words.

66. *Book Improvement:* The author has written to you and wants to know how this book could be improved. Answer the author's letter.

67. *Principal:* Your principal has asked if you would recommend this book for him or her to read. Give specific reasons.

68. *President's Address:* The U.S. president has learned that you are reading this book and wants you to tell one thing that a main character discovered about life that you think all Americans should know. Tell why you chose this message.

69. *Minor Character:* Place yourself in the role of a minor character and describe the main character as you see him or her.

70. *Television Report:* You are a television news reporter. Present an on-the-scene news report based on an incident from the book.

71. *Doll Clothes:* Dress a character doll as one of the book's characters.

72. *Paper Dolls:* Create paper dolls of the main characters.

73. *Model:* Make a model of something in the story: house, log cabin, rocket, etc.

74. *Mobile:* Make a mobile from drawings of people or objects in the book.

75. *Cartoon Characters:* Draw cartoons of the characters.

76. *Cartoon Sequences:* Sequence the main points of the book with cartoons.

77. *Coat Hanger:* Draw a significant scene on construction paper, cut in the shape of a coat hanger. Then hang the report on the hanger with paper loops.

78. *Collage:* Cut pictures from old magazines to show an idea or scene from a book and arrange in a collage.

79. *Book Talk:* Write or tell what the book would say about itself if it could talk.

80. *Your Story:* Write your own story using the same title and theme as the book.

81. *Subject of Interest:* Make a case for how a certain book could be used successfully in another subject.

82. *Next-Door Neighbor:* Choose a character and tell why you would like or not like to have him or her as your neighbor.

83. *Friendship:* Choose a character and tell why you would or would not like to have him or her as your friend.

84. *Tape Recording:* Tape part of the story for the class with appropriate musical background.

85. *Limerick:* Make up a limerick about the story.

86. *Haiku:* Write a haiku describing the story, a main point, or a character.

(Handout continues on page 72.)

87. *Postcard:* Create a postcard that describes your book.

88. *Sentences:* Make a list of the five most interesting or critical sentences in the book.

89. *Greeting Card:* Create a greeting card using the theme, characters, or setting of your book.

90. *Book Cards:* Write a brief summary on a three-by-five card and develop a file box for class-mates to use.

91. *Illustrations:* Illustrate a book written without illustrations.

92. *Poster Ad:* Create a poster that effectively advertises your book.

93. *Critical Reading:* Evaluate the quality of the book considering one of the following: charac-terization, plot, description, setting, dialogue, or theme.

94. *Comparison Reading:* Compare this book to another the author has written. Describe common elements, style, theme, etc.

95. *Book Dedications:* List the main characters in the book you have read. Dedicate another book to each character and tell why each would benefit from the reading of the dedicated book.

96. *Diorama:* Create a diorama that illustrates the setting of the book.

97. *Songwriting:* Write a song with lyrics that represent the book, its characters, or the setting.

98. *Surprise, Surprise:* Put a key object from the story inside a shoe box. Give clues about the object and see if the class can guess what is in the box and the title of the book. (Good for a mystery story.)

99. *Object Illustration:* Give an oral summary of the story, using handmade objects or objects found at home to illustrate the story.

100. *Photography:* Photograph people, settings, events, etc., that illustrate your book.

101. *Mural:* Create a mural to illustrate your book. Use charcoal, crayons, cut paper, watercolors, or other art forms.

102. *Movie Version:* Compare the movie or television version with the book.

103. *Travelogue:* Create a travelogue using pictures, postcards, magazine clips, etc., to illustrate a book that uses a variety of settings.

104. *Flannel Board:* Prepare flannel board characters or illustrate the setting.

105. *Word Sharing:* Prepare a list of unusual, difficult, or exciting words from the book.

106. *Story Map:* Make a map that illustrates the main events of the story.

107. *Time Line:* Make a time line of the events in the book.

108. *Book Reviews:* Present reviews to a younger class.

109. *Library Recommendation:* Write a recommendation to the librarian for the purchase of a good book you have read.

110. *Important Part:* Write or tell about the most important part of the book.

111. *Puppetry:* Make a puppet or puppets of the characters. Set up dialogue.

112. *Demonstration:* Show something you learned.

113. *Peep Show:* Make a peepbox of an important scene or event.

114. *Lost or Found:* Make up a lost or found ad for an object or character.

115. *Routes:* Make a map showing routes taken in the story.

116. *Chalk Talk:* Give a chalk talk summary.

117. *Experiment:* Do a scientific experiment associated with the book.

118. *Seed Mosaic:* Make a seed mosaic to illustrate a setting or event.

119. *Soap Carving:* Make a soap carving to illustrate the book.

120. *Clay Model:* Use clay to model a character, setting, etc.

121. *Book Critic:* Find a part in a realistic book that you feel could not have happened. Defend your choice.

122. *Scrapbook:* Prepare a scrapbook illustrating the book.

123. *Video:* For owners of VCRs and cameras, prepare a report for television.

124. *Charades:* Develop a game of charades based on the characters in the book.

125. *Cooking:* Prepare and serve a related food from the book.

LITERATURE LOGS

Some teachers may choose to have students keep journal-like literature logs in spiral notebooks in lieu of or in addition to book reports. These can be used for the recording of independent reading in addition to book reports or assigned reading, and they serve as an independent record of the student's literary choices. Literature logs integrate reading and writing, and develop an understanding of main ideas, summarization, sequence, and evaluation. At the end of the year, a routinely updated log becomes a satisfying source for reflection on the progress made throughout the year. But to be successful, they require active promotion by or interaction with the teacher or some students will lose interest. The following form may be reproduced for students to use as a guide for format and entry suggestions.

LITERATURE LOG

Name: _____

Date: _____

Title: _____

Author:_____

The best part was _____

_____

The worst part was_____

_____

The main problem was _____

_____

The problem was solved when _____

_____

_____

Powerful words were _____

Words I didn't understand were _____

My favorite character was _____

My least favorite character was _____

An important character was _____

I didn't understand _____

I laughed when _____

I cried when_____

I celebrated when _____

I will never forget _____

I would recommend this book to _____ because _____

_____

_____

STUDENT IMPLEMENTED BOOK GUIDES

While I am comfortable with the use of whole language techniques, I still search for ways to use literature which involve the reader in the learning process, create a measure of independence in skill development, provide accountability, and relieve the teacher of some of the more tedious mechanics of preparation. The use of Student Implemented Book (SIB) Guides was developed for instruction with multiple copies of a novel. They are appropriate for any class with students able to write complete or nearly complete thoughts (even with invented spelling) and provide one way to bridge the gap from basals to novels on a trial or occasional basis, without feeling overwhelmed by the transition.

How to Start

First it is necessary to select a novel for your reading group. For the first experience, choose a book that will entice the children into the day-to-day reading of the entire novel. Check the reading level, often indicated on the back cover. But, if a book is a bit hard yet of high interest, you can assume the students will rise to the challenge of the difficulty level—and they will. Consult librarians, Jim Trelease's *The Read-Aloud Handbook*, other teachers, and students for possibilities.

The availability of multiple copies of the title unfortunately can determine the final selection. If necessary, pair students to share a copy. If the reading period is flexible, this is easily managed. Often a student or two will have read the book previously and resist the assignment. If so, point out that rereading a book is very pleasurable, plus you will be reading with specific purposes in mind.

DAY ONE

After you have selected a novel and obtained the necessary number of copies, write numbers on the covers, and have the students sign up for a numbered copy. Explain to the group that today each student will be reading only a chapter (or two, depending on your group and book), and that during today's reading, each is responsible for recording five statements, questions, or vocabulary words and the corresponding page number. Emphasize the need to use complete thoughts or sentences, noting that their statements will guide your discussion group.

Depending upon the age of the students, you might want to give them the student handout on page 77 to get them started, but notebook paper works fine, as long as they remember to write down their page numbers—a critical piece of information for you. Take time to model this portion of the assignment, using the first page of the novel to give them examples of questions, vocabulary words, or evaluative statements.

Some students dislike interrupting the flow of their reading. Tell students they have the option of jotting down the page number and returning upon completion of reading the chapter to write the statements. Have the students turn in or file their papers in their folders when finished. While students are carrying out the assignment of silent reading and responding, you are free to work with another group.

DAY TWO

The next day, use their statements, questions, and vocabulary to guide the group's discussion. You will find that you can glance easily through the papers, organize, and lead a discussion from what they have written. This, in turn, will clarify their reading and broaden their understanding.

Have a dictionary handy to use as needed when discussing vocabulary. Occasionally ask students to read aloud a section to find an answer or to develop the use of context clues. This gives you an opportunity to check both comprehension and oral reading skills, without subjecting the group to barbershop boredom—next, next, next.

An alternative method of discussion is to let the students keep their SIB Guide for reference and let each student volunteer his or her comments as you guide the discussion sequentially through the main points of the chapter. Ask, "Did anyone have a question, vocabulary word, or comment about page 10? Page 11?" Soon the students will be eager participants, wanting to share their observations.

If no evaluative comments are forthcoming, share your evaluations, what you found funny, sad, or beautifully written. This is a perfect time to point out the use of metaphorical language, devices such as alliteration, or details of plot construction. End the discussion by making predictions about the next chapter and once again assign the writing of five statements for that day's silent reading. Continue this process until the novel's end, adjusting for length of reading assignments as necessary.

Each day will include a discussion of the previous day's reading, a period of silent reading, and completion of the next chapter's SIB Guide. It is ideal to have the discussion before reading the next chapter so that you can guide the group into making predictions, but when necessary you can assign the next chapter before meeting in the discussion group.

While this group is doing its silent reading, you can be using the same discussion process with a group that is reading a different novel or is using another instructional method. Just continue to rotate the groups as you would with basal reader instruction.

Discussion

Keep in mind that the SIB Guide is not intended for use as a total reading program. It is a supplementary system that allows you to introduce the idea of group novel reading, painlessly involving the students in their own instruction. Do not overuse it. It is perfect for a month like December, when a break from the routine is welcome, and an uproarious book such as Barbara Robinson's *The Best Christmas Pageant Ever* is appropriate.

To maximize the benefits from using these guides, use them to create future teacher-directed book guides. Jot down the best questions from each chapter and save them for another group or another year. Then, rather than assigning the SIB Guides, assign the already created questions. Use the SIB Guides with another book, thereby creating a guide for you to use another time.

With appropriate modeling and guidance the use of SIB Guides works with virtually any reading/writing level. Although my expectations alter depending on the group, I have used it successfully with groups of gifted, remedial, learning disabled, limited English speaking, and main-streamed mentally retarded students.

STUDENT IMPLEMENTED BOOK (SIB) GUIDES

_____   _____
name   date

Directions:

Read the assigned chapter or chapters.

Write down five statements about your reading for today on a piece of notebook paper. They can be questions about parts you don't understand, vocabulary words, compliments, or criticisms. Use complete thoughts.

Include the page number for each statement.

Do not use this form. Keep it in your file or notebook.

1. _____

   _____

                                                    page # _____

2. _____

   _____

                                                    page # _____

3. _____

   _____

                                                    page # _____

4. _____

   _____

                                                    page # _____

5. _____

   _____

                                                    page # _____

CREATING TEACHER DIRECTED
BOOK GUIDES

It is relatively easy to create one's own book guide or to adapt students' guides for later use (see above). Benjamin S. Bloom and David Krathwohl developed a taxonomy that is helpful for developing questions. The taxonomy has six major divisions:

1. Knowledge

2. Comprehension

3. Application

4. Analysis

5. Synthesis

6. Evaluation[6]

Many reading textbooks contain more details about this taxonomy. The key is to prepare questions that extend beyond those of a fact-recall nature. When developing book guides, review Bloom's taxonomy or the following list to determine if your questions represent a variety of thinking skills, especially as students tackle more difficult literature.

Types of Questions

Anticipation

Prediction

Details

Important facts

Character development

Motivation of characters

Vocabulary clarification

Understanding of figures of speech, expressive language

Inference

Synthesis

Opinion

Plot direction

Story structure

Reflection

Appraisal

The following teacher-directed book guide is for use with *Stone Fox* by John Gardiner. *Stone Fox* is the story of a boy whose grandfather gives up and takes to his bed because he is no longer able to support their farm. Willy enters a dogsled race, pitting his companion and pet dog, Searchlight, against a regal Indian, Stone Fox, whose motivation to win is equally valid. This powerful eighty-one-page story is appropriate for all ages. It could be read independently by strong second graders, all intermediate students, as well as older remedial readers. Note the variety of questions. For younger readers the guide might need modification.

STUDY GUIDE FOR
STONE FOX

Chapter 1: Grandfather, p. 3.

1. On the first page you read that Grandfather won't get up from bed. Why do you think he just gave up?

2. Why did Willy think this was not just another trick of Grandfather's?

3. Doc Smith said Grandfather didn't want to live anymore. How did such a sickness happen?

4. If you were ten years old like Willy and this happened to you, what would you do? Explain why.

Chapter 2: Little Willy, p. 12.

1. Grandfather is still sick. What did Doc Smith say would happen to Grandfather?

2. What was Willy and Grandfather's communication system?

3. What did Willy learn when he went to the strongbox for money?

4. Willy wouldn't accept any help from friends. Why do you think he wouldn't let others help him?

Chapter 3: Searchlight, p. 22.

1. Why would a person need to be ready for Wyoming winters?

2. Willy wanted to grow potatoes when he grew up, but Grandfather wanted him to go to college. Why do you think this was so important to Grandfather?

3. What is a "city slicker"?

4. Why would they race home just to win against themselves?

Chapter 4: The Reason, p. 30.

1. What type of man was Clifford Snyder? Give details.

2. Why did Searchlight growl at Snyder?

3. What information had Snyder brought about their farm?

4. What do you think Willy will do next?

Chapter 5: The Way, p. 37.

1. What does it mean to "meet a situation head on"?

2. Why was Willy determined to take care of Grandfather?

3. Why do you think the bank president told Willy to sell the farm?

4. Lester tells Willy about Stone Fox, but Willy doesn't pay attention. Why do you think the author lets the reader know about the Indian at this point?

(Handout continues on page 80.)

Chapter 6: Stone Fox, p. 46.

1.   Why did little Willy feel "ten feet tall" after he entered the race?

2.   Describe Stone Fox. Use details from your reading.

3.   Why did Stone Fox refuse to speak?

4.   Both Stone Fox and Willy had important reasons to win the race. Whose reason do you think is more important. Why?

Chapter 7: The Meeting, p. 55.

1.   What does Doc Smith mean when she tells Willy that she would be rooting for him?

2.   Why would that embarrass Willy?

3.   Would you have investigated the barking from the old barnhouse like Willy? Why or why not?

4.   Why do you think Searchlight couldn't sleep all night either?

Chapter 8: The Day, p. 62.

1.   Why wouldn't Willy want Grandfather to see his swollen-shut eye?

2.   Willy thought everyone came to the race to see Stone Fox. What could be another reason so many people came to the race?

3.   Willy knew he and Searchlight would win. How could he be so confident against such experienced racers and dogs?

4.   Describe how Willy felt physically just as the race began.

Chapter 9: The Race, p. 69.

1.   Why do you think Stone Fox got off to such a slow start?

2.   What was Willy's shortcut?

3.   Why couldn't others use the shortcut?

4.   What made Grandfather get up at last?

Chapter 10: The Finish Line, p. 77.

1.   As they entered the town, Searchlight was ahead and Stone Fox was catching up when Searchlight died. How did you feel when this happened? Why?

2.   What were the reactions of the townspeople just as he died?

3.   Why do you think Stone Fox stopped the racers so Willy could carry Searchlight across the finish line?

4.   What do you think happened next?

5.   Why do you think the author didn't tell the readers what happened next?

PREDICTING VOCABULARY DEFINITIONS IN A NOVEL

Another way to approach the teaching of a group novel is to examine the book's vocabulary, especially if the novel is a challenge to the group. Vocabulary development continues to receive attention because of its importance in standardized testing. Using this method of prediction and clarification expands a student's vocabulary, while emphasizing the need to use context to clarify the meaning of words.

After selecting a reading group's novel, reread it, listing four or five words (or more depending on the age of the students) from each chapter. With primary students or with a lower achieving group, use the list to discuss with the students what they think the words will mean in the chapter. On the board list all the definitions the students suggest, and, if possible, leave them there. Assign the chapter and give the students a reproduced list of the words, including the page numbers, instructing them to write down the contextual meaning of the word.

With intermediate students, an alternative method is to have them first write the predicted meaning, read the chapter, and then write the contextual meaning. However, unless you carefully separate the activities of prediction from the reading and clarification, some students will skip the prediction and use one meaning for both. This discussion method works best if you structure the lesson in the following manner.

Day One:

Introduce the story.

Do the vocabulary prediction.

Assign the reading and the accompanying contextual vocabulary clarification activity.

Day Two:

Discuss the previous day's story in general:
   comprehension questions, character development, sequence of events, and other appropriate comments.

Discuss the contextual meanings versus the former day's predictions.

Introduce and predict the meaning of the next set of vocabulary words.

Assign the next chapter and the accompanying contextual clarification activity.

Continue through the book in the same manner.

Sample Vocabulary Guides

The first vocabulary guide is from Jane Yolen's *Commander Toad in Space*. Though the book is for the very early reader, it is not written with a controlled vocabulary.

The second vocabulary guide is from Armstrong Sperry's *Call It Courage*, a story about a young boy who leaves his island home to conquer his fears of the sea with only his dog for companionship. Stranded on a distant island with no resources, he is challenged by a shark, a wild boar, and a man-eating tribe. This Newbery Medal book is good for the upper intermediate reader as it lends itself well to intense discussions about different customs, values, challenges, and environments. The list for this book is long and may be reduced as needed. There are also many other vocabulary words that are associated with the island or sea which can be discussed in the context of the story.

COMMANDER TOAD IN SPACE

p. 7, porthole

p. 8, fleet

p. 8, mission

p. 8, galaxies

p. 8, alien

p. 10, crew

p. 12, shimmering

p. 14, computer

p. 17, lily pad

p. 19, milkweed fluff

p. 22, plump

p. 26, folderol

p. 29, trembling

p. 31, shivering

p. 33, attention

p. 36, horrible

p. 45, emergencies

p. 51, ballet

p. 53, hot-air balloon

p. 58, explorers

p. 64, leapfrog

CALL IT COURAGE

Chapter 1: Flight, p. 1.

    p. 2, chants
    p. 3, millrace
    p. 3, frigate
    p. 4, thwarts
    p. 5, pinnacle
    p. 6, scorn
    p. 7, jibes
    p. 8, albatross
    p. 9, serenely
    p. 12, tense
    p. 15, jeered
    p. 16, hovered

Chapter 2: The Sea, p. 17.

    p. 17, dismal
    p. 18, desolation
    p. 19, ominous
    p. 19, tentacles
    p. 20, parched
    p. 20, ballast
    p. 21, squall
    p. 22, supernatural
    p. 23, buoyancy
    p. 26, luminous
    p. 30, tier
    p. 31, tumult
    p. 33, cascade

Chapter 3: The Island, p. 35.

    p. 35, gusto
    p. 38, extinct
    p. 39, cauterize
    p. 41, eerie
    p. 42, testimony
    p. 44, breach
    p. 44, resolution
    p. 45, impaled
    p. 47, clambered
    p. 48, toboggan
    p. 49, irresolute
    p. 55, haunches
    p. 58, resolved
    p. 58, inevitable
    p. 60, famished

Chapter 4: Drums, p. 63.

    p. 65, score
    p. 67, rout
    p. 68, multitude
    p. 70, imperative
    p. 71, deference
    p. 72, formidable
    p. 76, adze
    p. 78, defenseless
    p. 80, succulent
    p. 84, detached
    p. 85, truce
    p. 89, abandon
    p. 91, piteously
    p. 93, prodigious
    p. 95, sustained

Chapter 5: Homeward, p. 97.

    p. 98, reverberated
    p. 100, guttural
    p. 102, pursuit
    p. 103, zephyr
    p. 104, vengeance
    p. 105, stoutest
    p. 108, implacable
    p. 108, conflagration
    p. 109, monotony
    p. 111, despair
    p. 113, triumphant
    p. 115, transformed

NOTES

[1]Edmund Burke Huey, *The Psychology and Pedagogy of Reading* (New York: Macmillan Publishing Company, Inc., 1908), 381.

[2]Barbara Ann Porte, *The Kidnapping of Aunt Elizabeth* (New York: Greenwillow Books, 1985), 36.

[3]Ibid., 36.

[4]Frank Smith, "Twelve Easy Ways to Make Learning to Read Difficult," in *Essays into Literacy* (Exeter, N.H.: Heinemann Educational Books, 1983), 21-22.

[5]Jeannette Veatch, *Reading in the Elementary School.* 2nd ed. (New York: John Wiley and Sons, 1978), 576.

[6]B. S. Bloom and D. R. Krathwohl, *Taxonomy of Educational Objectives* (New York: Longmans, Green and Company, 1956).

REFERENCES

Gardiner, John. *Stone Fox.* Illustrated by Marcia Sewall. New York: Harper and Row, Publishers, 1980.

McElmeel, Sharron L. *An Author a Month (for Pennies).* Illustrated by Deborah L. McElmeel. Englewood, Colo.: Libraries Unlimited, Inc., 1988.

Robinson, Barbara. *The Best Christmas Pageant Ever.* New York: Avon, 1973.

Ruckman, Ivy. *Night of the Twisters.* New York: Harper and Row, Publishers, 1984.

Sperry, Armstrong. *Call It Courage.* New York: Collier Books, Macmillan Publishing Company, Inc., 1940.

Taylor, Theodore. *The Cay.* New York: Avon, 1977.

Trelease, Jim. *The Read Aloud Handbook.* New York: Penguin Books, 1985.

Yolen, Jane. *Commander Toad in Space.* Illustrated by Bruce Degen. New York: Coward, McCann, & Geoghegan, Inc., 1980.

Chapter 7

Research and the
Reading and Writing Program

When planning any unit, a teacher's first stop should be the library. School libraries often have a vast variety of materials, and by investigating the available materials before planning your unit, you can save time by letting the materials help shape your plans. Don't automatically exclude older materials, unless having current information is necessary to the project. Ask for films, filmstrips, videos, books, magazines, articles—anything related to your unit.

RESEARCH MINIREPORTS

This chapter discusses a method of research that links the curriculum directly to the library. It is designed for upper primary and intermediate students, but may also be useful for older students who have never done research work, or lower primary students who are capable or in need of an extra challenge. Minireports are useful introductions to the library and they can be used to temporarily replace or supplement textbooks for many subjects.

These reports substitute a bibliography with a student research worksheet. This provides practice in recording bibliographic information without going into the more complex forms of bibliographic entries. However, for the teacher who wishes to teach bibliographic form, the research worksheets function like the more traditional notecard, and subsequent teaching of the bibliography is a natural extension.

The tip sheet provides step-by-step guidance for the students. It may seem difficult for upper primary; however, it is not intended for use with any grade level without teacher introduction and extensive discussion. The purpose of the sheet is to provide you and the students with guidance and a permanent record of your expectations. You will avoid endless repetition of key points by directing the students to reread their tip sheets before asking for additional help. You will also build student accountability and help parents who choose to help their children through the process. If you spend time thoroughly discussing the tip sheet with your students, you will have provided an excellent start to their research.

In general, follow this outline of steps for teaching minireports, adapting the list to what is available to you or to what is comfortable for you.

Minireport Outline

TEACHER PLANNING

1. Choose a topic. It could be on any subject or be a seasonal topic on a special event or holiday.

2. Investigate the resources in the library. Make sure there will not be competition for the materials.

3. Order additional resources from the professional or public libraries.

4. Select a film, filmstrip, or other audiovisual material for your introduction, if you desire.

5. Determine the requirements of the project. Remember this is a minireport and therefore should be short. Decide if students will be able to collaborate. How many resources are necessary? (For students new to research, limit it to one encyclopedia and one nonfiction book.) Students get uneasy about new learning experiences and having your plans worked out clearly in advance will be helpful when they ask you questions about the particulars.

6. Schedule work sessions in the library.

7. Prepare a letter to send home with the students describing the project, asking for any resources parents might have, and requesting that they let you know of any experts who might visit your class. Include the requirements, the deadline, and other pertinent information.

Teaching the Minireport to Your Students

1. Introduce the topic to the class.

2. Brainstorm components of the topic. Use semantic webbing or a similar strategy to show the relatedness of the topics. Ask students what they know and what they want to know about the subject.

3. Make assignments or allow for topic selection.

4. Provide the outline worksheet and discuss the types of questions that would be appropriate for the report, avoiding questions that can be answered in one word. There are ten blanks for questions on the reproducible outline on page 89. Assign only what is reasonable for your group. Have students fill in the due date for the report.

5. Give students time to generate questions. They might collaborate with others, exchanging lists for other ideas during this time or prepare their own webs of ideas.

6. Go over their questions before moving on to the next step. Some questions will be too broad and need revision. Others will be too obvious, brief, or unnecessary. Learning how to write good questions is an essential aspect of any research project. They will also need to be reminded that they may not find answers to all their questions and will thus need to revise or create new questions.

7. Provide the handouts for the research worksheet and the student tip sheet and carefully review the steps. Have the students record the due date on the tip sheet.

8. Take the class to the library and provide an overview of references, the nonfiction section, and other resources.

9. Guide the students through the scheduled work periods in the library. Once they have begun their research and are familiar with the resources, they will learn to retrieve resources and continue working with minimum help from you.

10. Provide support as needed throughout their research.

11. When students are nearing the completion of their research phase, hand out and discuss in detail the guide sheet, "How to Write Your Report." Make certain that the students understand that they are to rewrite the information into an organized report. You will want to amplify certain points based on the needs of your group.

12. When the deadline has arrived, collect and evaluate the papers and worksheets. Evaluation is often difficult. I assign three grades: the first for the report itself, the second for the research based on the attached sheets, and the third for mechanics such as punctuation and spelling. I merely skim the research sheets, looking for completion of the required publication information, page numbers, and other details. Vary the evaluation based on your needs.

13. Plan a sharing time. Have students read aloud their reports or ask permission for you to share portions of their work. The collective knowledge is the purpose of the report, therefore the sharing is an important step.

14. Gather copies of the papers into a central folder or bind or staple them, making them available for reference. (Make these copies before adding comments of an evaluative nature.)

MINIREPORT OUTLINE

_____   _____
    name   date

Topic _____ Due Date _____

Questions About My Topic

1. _____
   _____

2. _____
   _____

3. _____
   _____

4. _____
   _____

5. _____
   _____

6. _____
   _____

7. _____
   _____

8. _____
   _____

9. _____
   _____

10. _____
    _____

Ask your teacher to check your questions before you begin your research.

RESEARCH MINIREPORT WORKSHEET

_____   _____
name   date

Topic _____

Title of resource _____

Book? _____ Magazine? _____ Other? _____

Encyclopedia? _____ If yes, what volume number is it? _____

Author or editor _____

Publisher _____

Place of Publication_____ Date_____

Information _____

_____

_____

_____

_____

_____

_____

_____

_____

_____

_____

_____

_____

Page number(s) of information _____

STUDENT MINIREPORT TIP SHEET

How to fill out the research minireport worksheet:

1. Complete the blanks for topic, name, and date *every time* you complete a worksheet and you won't lose your valuable research.

2. Put the name of the book, magazine, or encyclopedia in the blank for "title of resource."

3. Mark which type of resource it is. If it is something other than an encyclopedia, book, or magazine, write what it is in the blank after "other."

4. Books will usually have an author. Magazines or encyclopedias will have editors. If a book has both an editor and an author, include both.

5. The publisher is the company that printed the book. Its name is usually on the page with the title and the author's name. It will often look something like A. B. Smith & Co.

6. The place of publication is usually a city's name and is on the same page as the publishing company. If there are several cities listed, just put down the first city in the list.

7. The date is harder to find. It may be on the same page with the publisher and city, or it may be on a following page in small print with other information. Scan the page for numbers. The word "copyright" is usually near it.

8. Once you have found some facts that you want to remember, write them in this section. It is important that you use your own words. Often you don't need all that the author says anyway. If you do copy from the book, put it in quotation marks so you will know they are the author's words.

9. Put down the page or pages on which you found the information. This will save you time if you need to go back to it later and will be necessary if you want to include a quote.

HOW TO WRITE YOUR MINIREPORT

Once you have completed several research worksheets, you have done the hardest part of the report. You are now ready to begin to organize and prepare for the writing of your report. Follow these directions.

1. Read through your worksheets, checking for publication information, page numbers, spelling, etc. Go back to your sources if you left out anything.

2. Check to see if you answered all your questions. If you didn't, go back to your sources and try again.

3. Spread out your papers and decide on the order of your report. You can put numbers on the pages or paragraphs in the order in which you want them to appear. If you need to reorganize paragraphs, use a colored pencil to number the paragraphs in the order you want.

4. Read through the numbered pages or paragraphs and decide if you have enough information and if it makes sense.

5. If you need more information, go back to the library and use more research worksheets to fill in what you need.

6. Write your report using the research sheets as your source. Remember to put quotation marks around anything you have copied. *Do not* write the information from one source, followed by information from another source. Your information should be grouped by the questions or topic of paragraph, not by the sources you used.

7. Reread your paper, checking for spelling, punctuation, and indentation of paragraphs. Make sure your writing makes sense.

8. Have a friend read and check your paper.

9. Make any needed changes.

10. Gather together all your research worksheets.

11. Be sure your name is on every page.

12. Turn in your report with your outline and research worksheets stapled or clipped together.

THE CRICKET IN TIMES SQUARE
RESEARCH PROJECT

This next portion describes a research unit (minireport) implemented with third and fourth graders who were reading George Selden's *The Cricket in Times Square*. It can be as short or long as you wish, but for the first report two written pages plus the research worksheets are generally adequate. It also serves as a model for other literature and research projects suggested at the end of the chapter.

The Cricket in Times Square is a story about a cricket suddenly transported to New York City. His new home is a newsstand in the center of Times Square. The cricket and his animal friends have several adventures, but the greatest occurs when he becomes famous for his singing.

Unless you live in the New York City area, most students are not going to be familiar with the places mentioned in this book, or realize the significance of events such as performing at Carnegie Hall. Thus the research project provides the background information that increases student interest and knowledge about the importance of setting and description.

Planning

Read or reread *The Cricket in Times Square*, keeping in mind possible topics for research and concepts that you believe are necessary for understanding the book. Investigate the number of resources about New York City in your library. Plan to use films or filmstrips as you introduce the project. These will provide an overview and give students a visual framework. Alert the public librarian to your plans and line up any assistance available for your students. If you have been to New York City, share any slides, photographs, or mementoes you have with the class.

Teaching the Unit

Introduce the book, explaining that the setting of this book is integral to the plot and that therefore the class is going to investigate New York City before beginning the book. Find out how many students have been to New York City and have them tell what they remember about their visit. Share any materials you have brought in and show any films or filmstrips you have found.

Brainstorm topics that might be useful. At this point you will need to mention some of the key events or places in the story to ensure that your research list includes the necessary topics. If your students are not experienced with this type of brainstorming activity, ask them to think about what they would want a visitor to their area to know about and draw parallels to New York City. You might also have a visitor's guide such as Fodor's and use the index as a springboard to the discussion. Even if you are prompting responses, it is important that you involve the students in this activity, as it develops ownership in the project. A list of recommended topics might include the following:

Times Square

Chinatown

Carnegie Hall

Central Park

Subways, transportation in the city

Geography (boroughs)

Geography of Manhattan

History

Famous places: Statue of Liberty, Empire State Building, etc.

Other topics that are helpful but are not as directly related to the story are:

Places to stay

Places to visit

Cost of living

Climate

Variety of cultural enclaves within Manhattan

Things for children to do

When you have your list generated, describe the nature of the minireport. Explain the requirements: that it is a two page report plus the research worksheets. Have in mind whether you want students to work in pairs or individually. You will know from your reading of the book that certain topics need to be covered if the book is to be meaningful. You might begin with the recommended topics and then move on to the secondary list. In the case of individual research, some topics will be duplicated; however, duplicated topics do not necessarily mean duplicated information.

Give the students the outline form and assign the number of questions you want them to answer. Have the students use semantic webbing or brainstorming techniques to generate their questions. Checking questions with another student or collaborating is useful at this point.

Pass out several minireport research worksheets (copied from page 90 or modified to suit your students' needs). Explain that the students are to do their research on these pages, keep them to use during the final writing of their report, and turn them in with their report. (A folder with pockets to hold their work is helpful during the process.) Provide a central place for students to obtain additional research worksheets.

Hand out a copy of the student tip sheet to each student. Go over it very carefully, elaborating on how to find the publication information. Have students use the books in their desks to practice finding names of publishers, copyright dates, and cities. List on the board some of the publishers so the students become familiar with the process.

Schedule library time for the initial research. Guide the students while they locate resources and plan their papers. The use of encyclopedias, travel guides, magazines, nonfiction books, almanacs, and atlases should be encouraged.

Once you have reached this point, you might want to put off reading of the novel allowing for uninterrupted research for several days until the topic is ready for sharing. If you do decide to proceed with the book, allow a period or two to get into the research, and then introduce the reading assignment. Give a deadline for the research papers that will occur when you are within the first four or five chapters of the book. This will allow the students to see the relevance of their research, while still providing adequate background information.

Using peer editing (see chapter 8) is a good method of collaborative learning. The students learn about the other students' topics, while developing their own skills. When the papers are complete, provide a sharing time when you or the individual students read the reports aloud. Discuss how they relate to what is already known about the novel.

The study of vocabulary is suggested for this novel. For a more complete description of how to use the following vocabulary list, refer to chapter 6. Briefly, use the list to predict the meaning of the words, assign the reading, and have the students write the contextual definitions of the selected words. On the following day discuss the chapter and the vocabulary. Discuss the events of the chapter and how it ties into the research as you progress through the book.

VOCABULARY

Chapter 1:

    p. 1, abandoned
    p. 2, subsided
    p. 4, gust
    p. 6, lurch

Chapter 2:

    p. 9, shuttle
    p. 9, thicket
    p. 10, soot
    p. 10, antennae
    p. 12, rummaged

Chapter 3:

    p. 20, wistfully
    p. 20, eavesdropping
    p. 22, tuffets
    p. 26, crouching

Chapter 4:

    p. 27, frantic
    p. 28, acquaintance
    p. 31, long-hairs
    p. 31, venturing

Chapter 5:

    p. 36, toppled
    p. 39, din
    p. 40, downbeat
    p. 41, prophesy

Chapter 6:

    p. 43, abrupt
    p. 44, craned
    p. 46, pagoda
    p. 48, ancient

Chapter 7:

    p. 53, browse
    p. 56, luxury
    p. 60, spongy
    p. 60, burrowed

Chapter 8:

    p. 62, furiously
    p. 64, forlornly
    p. 64, evidence
    p. 69, gamboling
    p. 70, peril

Chapter 9:

    p. 75, squinting
    p. 78, solemn
    p. 81, deduction
    p. 82, contented

Chapter 10:

    p. 84, luminous
    p. 86, haunches
    p. 87, amateur
    p. 91, vaudeville

Chapter 11:

    p. 98, soothe
    p. 99, reproaches
    p. 99, jinx
    p. 100, scorched
    p. 104, dumbfounded

Chapter 12:

    p. 107, precious
    p. 111, blurted
    p. 114, passage
    p. 115, sublime
    p. 116, illustrious

Chapter 13:

    p. 118, celebrity
    p. 120, flex
    p. 123, throngs
    p. 123, delicacy
    p. 128, entomologist

Chapter 14:

    p. 132, fame
    p. 134, summit
    p. 136, encore
    p. 140, standstill

CONCLUSION

Teaching the first research project is admittedly a frustrating and difficult job. Midway through I often wonder why I have subjected myself to such a challenge. Then the students seem to settle into the research and are reaching for their research folders when other work is completed. They start spending long stretches of quiet time working. Rather than completing endless stacks of worksheets requiring tedious evaluation, the students are involved actively in the process of research. The advantage becomes suddenly apparent—the students are becoming independent learners, freeing the teacher for other tasks.

The big bonus comes when you tackle the second research project, as it takes a minimum of instruction from you. I have used the above technique in science, social studies, and language arts; with broad topics such as topics related to the solar system, and narrow such as *The Cricket in Times Square*. I have never done more than three research projects in the period of a year, as I appreciate variety as much as the students do. By the third project, students are experienced writers of reports who have acquired lifelong research skills.

REFERENCES

Selden, George. *The Cricket in Times Square*. Illustrated by Garth Williams. New York: Farrar, 1960.

OTHER RESOURCES FOR RESEARCH PROJECTS

Arkin, Alan. *The Lemming Condition*. New York: Bantam Books, 1977. 58 pages. Grades three and up.
    Bubber is an atypical lemming, questioning why the lemmings are preparing for mass suicide. His dilemma raises sensitive points about blind following of others. Use in the study of lemmings or rodents. When reading aloud, be prepared to make substitutions for the occasional "damn."

Avi. *Captain Grey*. New York: Scholastic Book Services, 1982. 142 pages. Grades four and up.
    Combine the study of the Revolutionary War with this adventure story of a young boy captured by pirates.

Banks, Lynn Reid. *The Indian in the Cupboard*. New York: Doubleday, 1981. 182 pages. Grades three and up.
    An English boy acquires a magic key and cupboard that bring to life small plastic figures. The study of England is an obvious application, but also consider having some students research the time of the Indian and the cowboy to develop an understanding of the conflicts of the different periods.

Beatty, Patricia. *The Coach That Never Came*. New York: William Morrow and Company, Inc., 1985. 164 pages. Grades four and up.

Paul resigns himself to a summer with his grandmother in Colorado. While examining a trunkful of old newspaper clippings he is drawn into a mystery involving a missing stagecoach and $40,000. Based on a true incident, this suspenseful tale sets the stage for researching local history or the west.

Bishop, Claire. *Twenty and Ten*. New York: Penguin Books, 1978. 76 pages. Grades three and up.

A class of fifth graders hides ten Jewish refugees during World War II. Study the Holocaust, France, or World War II while reading this book about courage.

Blos, Joan W. *A Gathering of Days*. New York: Charles Scribner's Sons, 1979. 144 pages. Grades four and up.

Life in the early 1800s in New Hampshire is seen through the diary of a young girl. Use this Newbery Medal winner in a study of early America.

Byars, Betsy. *Trouble River*. New York: Scholastic, Inc., 1969. 105 pages. Grades three and up.

To escape Indians, Grandma and Dewey set off down the river on a raft. The study of pioneer times is enlivened by this rousing adventure book.

Cleary, Beverly. *Dear Mr. Henshaw*. Illustrated by Paul O. Zelinsky. New York: William Morrow and Company, Inc., 1983. 134 pages. Grades three and up.

A young boy reluctantly writes to an author for a class assignment and his letters provide an intriguing novel, requiring students to infer Mr. Henshaw's responses. Although authors can hardly provide this type of interaction, this book is a good backdrop for research about authors using available printed sources, films, or filmstrips. Of course a fan letter to an author may be a part of the study, and it often results in at least a postcard, but expectations should be reasonable.

Coerr, Eleanor. *Sadako and the Thousand Paper Cranes*. Illustrated by Ronald Himler. New York: Dell Publishing Company, Inc., 1977. 64 pages. Grades three and up.

This is based on the true story of Sadako who is dying of leukemia because of the bombing of Hiroshima. She learns of a legend that promises the granting of a wish if a thousand paper cranes are folded, and she vainly tries to forestall death. The study of World War II, Japan, cancer, and nuclear war are possible research areas.

Collier, James Lincoln, and Christopher Collier. *My Brother Sam Is Dead*. New York: Scholastic Book Services, 1974. Grades four and up.

A study of the futility of war would be dramatized by this story of Sam's family, brutally split by the differing views during the Revolutionary War.

_____. *War Comes to Willy Freeman*. New York: Dell Publishing Company, Inc., 1983. 178 pages. Grades four and up.

After Willy's father is killed by Redcoats and her mother is taken prisoner, she disguises herself as a boy and sets out in search of her mother. The slavery issue and the Revolutionary War are study topics for the Colliers' first volume of the Arabus Family Saga.

Dana, Barbara. *Zucchini*. Illustrated by Eileen Christelow. New York: Harper and Row, Publishers, 1982. 148 pages. Grades three and up.

Zucchini, a renegade ferret, finds a friend in Billy, a shy boy who is still adjusting to his parent's divorce. Their individual and joint adventures, separation, and eventual reunion make for heartwarming reading. Use in the study of ferrets or rodents, perhaps in preparation for a classroom pet.

de Angeli, Marguerite. *The Door in the Wall*. New York: Scholastic Book Services, 1949. 121 pages. Grades four and up.

Robin is taken to a monastery until he can join his family at the Castle Lindsay. Their reunion is threatened by the hostile neighboring Welsh, and it is up to Robin to save the castle. Use in the study of England during the Middle Ages.

Dunn, Mary Lois. *The Man in the Box: A Story from Vietnam*. New York: McGraw-Hill, 1968. 120 pages. Grades four and up.
   A Vietnamese village boy wants to free an American airman held captive in a box. Use when studying American history, Vietnam, or war.

Forbes, Esther. *Johnny Tremain*. Illustrated by Lynn Ward. New York: Dell Publishing Company, Inc., 1943. 256 pages. Grades five and up.
   In contrast to the rural setting of *My Brother Sam Is Dead*, this title provides an urban backdrop for this Revolutionary War novel.

Fritz, Jean. *And Then What Happened, Paul Revere?* Illustrated by Margot Tomes. New York: Coward, McCann & Geoghegan, Inc., 1973. 47 pages. Grades three and up.
   Though this title and the others that follow are essentially nonfiction, they read like fiction. Their applications are indicated by the titles.

_____. *Make Way for Sam Houston*. Illustrated by Elise Primavera. New York: G. P. Putnam's Sons, 1986. 105 pages. Grades three and up.

_____. *Shh! We're Writing the Constitution*. Illustrated by Tomie de Paola. New York: Scholastic Book Services, 1987. 64 pages. Grades three and up.

_____. *What's the Big Idea, Ben Franklin?* Illustrated by Margot Tomes. New York: Scholastic Book Services, 1976. 48 pages. Grades three and up.

_____. *Where Do You Think You're Going, Christopher Columbus?* Illustrated by Margot Tomes. New York: G. P. Putnam's Sons, 1980. 80 pages. Grades three and up.

_____. *Where Was Patrick Henry on the 29th of May?* Illustrated by Margot Tomes. New York: Coward, McCann & Geoghegan, Inc., 1975. 46 pages. Grades two and up.

Gardiner, John R. *Stone Fox*. New York: Crowell, 1980. 96 pages. Grades two and up.
   An Indian who is reclaiming lost land and a boy who is trying to save his grandfather's farm are adversaries in a dog sled race. Use this absorbing story while studying the loss of Indian lands or other related areas of Indian history.

George, Jean Craighead. *Julie of the Wolves*. Illustrated by John Schoenherr. New York: Harper and Row, Publishers, 1972. 170 pages. Grades four and up.
   Julie is forced into a young marriage and flees into the Alaskan terrain after her husband becomes amorous. She learns to survive with help from the wolves. Alaska, survival, and wolves are potential research topics.

Gilson, Jamie. *Hello, My Name Is Scrambled Eggs*. New York: Simon and Schuster, Inc., 1985. 159 pages. Grades four and up.
   Harvey welcomes Tuan Nguyen who has just arrived from Vietnam and they experience a variety of outrageous adventures, while indoctrinating Tuan to American culture. Immigration and Vietnam refugees are related areas for study.

Henry, Marguerite. *King of the Wind*. Illustrated by Wesley Dennis. New York: Scholastic Book Services, 1984. 192 pages. Grades four and up.
   This is the ultimate horse story, spanning Africa, Europe, and America, with a plucky hero who faces an almost redundant set of adventures. Tie in the study of Morocco and map skills with research on horses.

Houston, James. *Frozen Fire: A Tale of Courage*. New York: Atheneum, 1977. 149 pages. Grades five and up.
Study life in the Canadian Arctic with Matthew Morgan and Kayak who brave the rugged wilderness to search for Matthew's lost father.

Hunt, Irene. *Across Five Aprils*. New York: Berkley Books, 1986. 223 pages. Grades five and up.
Jethro's life is disrupted when he must take over the work of the farm while the men fight in the Civil War. The historical details of this rich novel make it ideal for study of the Civil War.

Levitin, Sonia. *Journey to America*. New York: Macmillan Publishing Company, Inc., 1970. 150 pages. Grades four and up.
Lisa Platt's father escaped to America in 1938, and she waits with her mother and sisters in Switzerland till they can join him. Use in the study of Jewish immigration.

Lord, Bette Bao. *The Year of the Boar and Jackie Robinson*. Illustrated by Marc Simont. New York: Harper and Row, Publishers, 1984. 169 pages. Grades three and up.
Shirley Temple Wong's first year in the United States entertains readers with stories about language misunderstandings, school-time events, and the country's fascination with baseball. Research reports could include Chinese immigration, New York City, or baseball.

MacLachlan, Patricia. *Sarah, Plain and Tall*. New York: Harper and Row, Publishers, 1985. 58 pages. Grades two and up.
Sarah leaves the sea she dearly loves to join a motherless family on the prairie. This Newbery Medal book is excellent for the study of pioneer life.

McSwigan, Marie. *Snow Treasure*. Illustrated by Mary Reardon. New York: E. P. Dutton and Company, Inc., 1942. 179 pages. Grades four and up.
Based on a true incident, this is the tale of how Norwegian children sneaked gold bars past the Nazi invaders. Use while studying World War II or Norway.

Magorian, Michelle. *Good Night, Mr. Tom*. New York: Harper and Row, Publishers, 1981. 318 pages. Grades four and up.
Willie is sent to rural England to escape World War II and is placed in the home of crusty widower Mr. Tom. Willie's transformation, his return to London to a mentally ill and abusive mother, and his rescue by Tom provide strong adventure against the realities of war. This is for mature readers or listeners. Use in a study of World War II, England, London, or the general lifestyle of the period and setting.

Morey, Walt. *Gentle Ben*. New York: Avon, 1976. 192 pages. Grades three and up.
The theme of having an adopted bear in the house provides the opportunity to study endangered species and environmental science.

Moskin, Marietta. *Waiting for Mama*. New York: Coward, 1975. 92 pages. Grades two and up.
This simple but poignant story relates the anguish of a Russian immigrant family forced to leave Mama behind due to a baby's illness. Use with the study of New York, Russia, or immigration.

O'Brien, Robert C. *Mrs. Frisby and the Rats of NIMH*. New York: Atheneum, 1971. 232 pages. Grades four and up.
Rats, who have become amazingly intelligent during laboratory testing, escape and set up their own society. Although this reads like fantasy, recent laboratory experiments have led to improved cognitive memory in rats. The study of rats, experimental medicine, or societies are possibilities. (Another related activity is to rent the video *The Secret of NIMH* and compare the alterations to the original version.)

O'Dell, Scott. *Sarah Bishop*. New York: Scholastic Book Services, 1982. 184 pages. Grades five and up.
Sarah flees the Revolutionary War, taking refuge in the Connecticut wilderness. Study the effects of war and survival through this novel, based on a true incident.

_____. *Sing Down the Moon*. Boston: Houghton Mifflin Company, 1970. 124 pages. Grades three and up.
The injustices of the move of the Navahos from Arizona to Fort Sumner, New Mexico, is detailed in this suspenseful novel. Use in the study of the American Indian.

Pyle, Howard. *Otto of the Silver Hand*. New York: Dover Publications, Inc., 1967. 173 pages. Grades five and up.
The story of this young boy's struggle is set in Medieval Germany, an ideal background for the study of this period in history.

Roberts, Willo Davis. *The Girl with the Silver Eyes*. New York: Scholastic Book Services, 1980. 198 pages. Grades five and up.
Katie's silver eyes and paranormal abilities become even more bewildering when a mysterious man becomes uncomfortably interested in her. Use this suspenseful tale when studying paranormal phenomenon with mature readers.

Ruckman, Ivy. *Night of the Twisters*. New York: Harper and Row, Publishers, 1984. 153 pages. Grades four and up.
Dan Hatch, his baby brother, and his friend must face alone the devastation of a series of tornadoes in this gripping personal narrative based on a true Nebraska disaster. Use in a study of weather, tornadoes, disasters, or heroism.

Selden, George. *The Cricket in Times Square*. Illustrated by Garth Williams. New York: Farrar, 1960, 1970. 156 pages. Grades three and up.
See this chapter for in-depth discussion.

Speare, Elizabeth George. *The Sign of the Beaver*. Boston: Houghton Mifflin Company, 1983. 135 pages. Grades three and up.
A young boy survives two seasons in the northeast woods while his father returns to their former home for his wife and other children. Unexpected help from Indians leads to a dilemma when the new friends are forced out of their lands. Use in the study of Indians or early colonial times.

Steiner, Barbara. *Oliver Dibbs to the Rescue!* Illustrated by Eileen Christelow. New York: Four Winds Press, Macmillan Publishing Company, 1985. 122 pages. Grades four and up.
Ollie is intensely interested in the rights of animals and takes on the challenge of saving a town of prairie dogs from destruction during the construction of a mall. The study of any endangered species is enhanced by meeting Ollie.

Taylor, Theodore. *The Cay*. New York: Avon, 1977. 144 pages. Grades four and up.
A blind white boy and an old black man are shipwrecked on a Caribbean island during World War II. Prejudice, the Caribbean, and World War II, are possible topics for study.

Turner, Ann. *Dakota Dugout*. New York: Macmillan Publishing Company, Inc., 1985. Unpaged. Grades 1 and up.
Life in a sod house is described including the killing winter, the summer drought, and the unending isolation. Finally their existence improves, but the beginning is remembered fondly. Use in the study of the early settlers.

Uchida, Yoshiko. *Journey Home*. New York: Atheneum, 1978. 131 pages. Grades four and up.
Yuki and her family return from Topaz, a concentration camp for American Japanese during World War II, only to find distrust and prejudice. Use when studying Japanese/American history.

Chapter 8

Management of
the Writing Program

THE TEACHER AS WRITER

"... I am interested in what made [writers] start writing, and what kept them at it. Many writers mentioned school. But none of the writers who mentioned school said anything about programs or tests, about exercises or drills. Not one of them cited inspiring grammar lessons or unforgettable spelling lists. They all mentioned a person; they mentioned a teacher. And the teachers whom the writers mentioned were not necessarily tender and permissive. Some of these teachers were difficult and demanding curmudgeons. But they were all teachers who respected students and who respected the subject that they taught. They thought that writing was worthwhile."[1]

Many teachers find any form of writing a formidable task. Other than the requisite term papers or projects during our training, we are rarely expected to demonstrate writing skills. Indeed, thinking of teachers as poets, journalists, essayists, or novelists is an uncommon concept. Therefore, it is difficult for a teacher to expect students to write when they are hesitant about the writing process themselves. Perhaps that is why many of us give little more than passing attention to the writing process.

Therefore the first step in teaching writing to your students is becoming comfortable with the role of the writer yourself. By writing you will develop an understanding of the challenges a writer faces and gain valuable insights into the process. You will be able to articulate to your students how you arrived at your story, essay, or poem. Also, you will find it immensely satisfying to have stretched your skills.

You as teacher/writer will be reminded throughout this chapter to have your own writing samples ready and to lead group writing assignments with the class. The processes presented were developed to make the transition from literature to creative writing as painless as possible. Although a creative writing class is useful, you do not need to take such a class to begin your transition to teacher as writer. Nor do you need to prepare every sample before class, although having a poem or two ready is certainly helpful. Take the time to struggle through the process *with* your students during some of the assignments. Struggle with them on the board, at your desk, at their desks. And yes, you *will* have time if you believe your writing is as valuable as theirs.

If you are still unconvinced, consider this. Teaching is a lonely profession, and except for that occasional observation or chance comment, the compliments and recognition are all too rare. This is a chance for some recognition. If you are supportive of your students' efforts, they will adopt the same attitude toward you. When you share what you write with your class, you reap applause, compliments, and admiration. Indulge.

DEVELOPING TRUST

After modeling a poetry writing session on "My Secret Place" with a fifth-grade classroom in a nearby district, I was once again reminded of how critical it is to have an internalized value of student writing. As I was leaving, one teacher excitedly told me that her nonreader/nonwriter had asked to miss his session with his resource teacher to stay for the poetry writing. She predicted that since he could hardly read or write, it would all stay in his head, so I suggested I return and ask him to dictate his poem. However, an hour later she brought me a laboriously printed four-line poem. It was composed of the few primer words this student knew and expressed his feelings about his "Secret Place." We celebrated his achievement and planned to build upon this personal triumph.

The next day I modeled the same lesson in another classroom. The students also were intrigued with the topic, and before writing, one student came to me bubbling about the treehouse that she and a friend had decorated and stayed in through a rainstorm. I urged her to put this in her poem, as it was a very special place. After sharing the poems with the class, with predictably mixed levels of accomplishment, the teacher followed me to the hall, expressing his amazement, "You are really going to accept this stuff as poetry?" I explained that it was a first effort, and that we would begin during the next session to shape and polish the poems. But at this point, yes, these were fine efforts. He was not convinced, stating that he obviously needed to talk to me more about this. He added he would be ashamed to publish these under his name.

"Under his name" is the key phrase. We as teachers are not producing products. We are producing writers. The process is more important than the product. Though this teacher is a warm, vibrant, energetic, intelligent person, beloved by all his students, he is decidedly product oriented. His room sparkles with the students' polished art projects. Behind all this glitz, he has missed the main point—that students are *developing*, not accomplished writers.

Happily, once the poems were polished and typed, the teacher recognized that the process was successful and satisfying, and, in fact, produced an acceptable product. He reports that many of the students have continued to write poetry independently, often sharing it informally.

MANAGEMENT OF THE WRITING PROGRAM

Planning for the smooth management of the reading and writing program is challenging. This chapter assumes that a language arts period allows for a one-and-one-half to two-hour period for an integrated instructional program. If writing and reading are offered separately, your first step is to lobby for a new schedule. It takes time to write, read, share, meditate, reflect, and rewrite. Students need an uninterrupted block that provides time for adequate processing. Meanwhile, if your language arts time is split, some modifications will be necessary because of time restraints. But the management techniques will be useful with some adaptations. (And keep lobbying for a new schedule.)

Getting Ready to Write

Students introduced to a new class or process need time to learn the teacher's expectations and the new routine. Time spent modeling the appropriate behaviors will be well invested. At all grade levels, take time to answer several "what ifs?" A student check sheet that guides the student through appropriate choices during a daily writing period is provided on page 105. Adapt it by blocking out the inappropriate choices on a copy; or make your own sheet and laminate and post it; or make multiple copies. Then rehearse the options with the class, making certain everyone understands your expectations.

Organize your room so that materials and books are available and review with the students how to gain access to materials. The teacher's goal should be to develop independent students who invest in the learning process and thus are responsible for their activities. Having a literate classroom with an ample supply of books, reference materials, or alternative activities requires good organization and student responsibility. Be clear regarding what is allowable when all work is completed. If centers with alternative activities are not available, students should always have the option of reading a library book. Having leisure time to browse through magazines and picture books is often a real treat, requiring minimal teacher preparation and supervision.

Maintaining an independent classroom means students must have access to materials as they need them. This can result in students becoming casual about the use of materials, replacing them on the shelves and so forth. Copy or adapt for students the suggestion sheet entitled "What to Do When Your Work Is Done" (provided on page 106) and enlist their help in maintaining a functional room. The key to making self-management work is being ever alert to the students who regularly help keep the room in working order. Be sure to notice those who are truly faithful in maintaining the environment and reinforce their actions. Some teachers reward these students with coupons for special privileges, stickers or other small tokens, or certificates of recognition. Usually verbal recognition is adequate. Use whatever system is comfortable and works for your class.

Writing Folders

The use of folders to hold writing samples and/or reading assignments is especially convenient. They can be stored in a portable file or ordinary box, and the students can retrieve them at the beginning of the period. Students can be instructed to put all work in their folder, whether completed or in progress. A technique that simplifies evaluation is to have the students put work in need of the teacher's attention on top, works in progress next, and graded work last in the folder. This management does not happen unless time is spent during several periods, training the students how to organize their work. It is well worth the effort. The teacher can go through the folder every day or two and keep abreast of the student's progress. Grades or comments can be entered on the inside of the folders.

Once every week or two, folders can be purged of rough drafts, completed reading forms, and other extraneous material. Selections worthy of keeping for possible publication, in draft or revised form, can be stapled to the back of the folder. Incomplete assignments might be taken out of the room as homework, but it is critical that the folders never leave the classroom. They are a permanent record of the students' progress.

"WHAT IF?" CHECK SHEET

What to do when:

You run out of paper or pencils:

   Use the materials in the supply center.

   Use the materials in the writing center.

   Borrow from a friend.

You can't spell a word:

   Use a dictionary from the reference shelf.

   Ask another student for help.

   Write it like it sounds and correct it later.

You need help from the teacher and he or she is busy with another student:

   Sign up for a conference.

   See a student editor.

   Keep busy with other assignments.

You get stuck while writing:

   Browse through the literature for ideas.

   Jot down new ideas.

   Ask a friend or student editor to read your work and make suggestions.

You have completed your work:

   Put it in the folder.

   Put it in the basket.

You have turned your work in:

   Read a book or magazine.

   Write in a journal.

   Write poetry.

   Go to the activities table.

WHAT TO DO WHEN YOUR WORK IS DONE

Personal Management

Check to make sure your assignments are complete.

Review your writing folder and reread past work.

Work on a list of writing ideas.

Write poetry using forms you have learned with new subject ideas.

Read a library book.

Read a picture book.

Read a magazine.

Offer to help another student.

Polish a former work that is still in draft form.

Sign up for a conference.

Write in your journal.

Work on a book report.

Write a letter or to a pen pal.

Read other students' works.

Room Management

Alphabetize the classroom library.

Organize the reference shelf.

Put dictionaries and other books away.

Check at the tables for other unshelved books. Put them away.

Refill the supplies from the main storage area.

Tidy the supply area.

Look around the room for any area in need of tidying.

GUIDING WRITING THROUGH CONFERENCES

It is unfortunate that often by intermediate grades, many students have been programmed not to disturb the teacher to get help. Students who are shy or who do not want to risk censure either drift through the period or find some nonacademic pastime until class is over. The following techniques for holding conferences should help solve this problem.

Assigned Conferences

Some teachers find that assigning a conference time to guarantee that no student is missed is most effective. Others have a sign-up sheet and monitor conference times informally. The advantages are that you have good records and can monitor participation. A major disadvantage is that if students come to your desk or to a table, many will prolong the conference because they enjoy this private time with the teacher.

Cruise Conferences

Another method is to "cruise conference." Methodically work from desk to desk, going through each folder, reviewing the work in progress, stapling samples to the folder, recording grades, etc. It is amazing what can be accomplished with a minute or two at each desk. Student accountability is developed because it is difficult for students to escape being responsible for an assignment if they know the folders will be checked regularly. If the students are kept busy with their writing or reading assignments, a teacher who cruises can do virtually all paper grading within the class period. The teacher remains in control of the time spent at the students' desk, without searching for a tactful way to ask students to return to their desks.

Combination Approach

Another system is to have a period of assigned conferences, followed by student initiated conferences, followed by the cruise conferences. Each period might last ten to fifteen minutes. Any conferencing technique that works for a teacher is right for that teacher. It is important, however, to review what happens during the conference.

Managing the Conference

During the conference, you will read (or have read before class) the student's writing, spelling or grammar assignments, literature forms, etc. This is your opportunity to focus on the writing process, especially when a work is in progress. Ask open-ended questions that lead the student to self-assessment, but be sure to allow time for the writer to give thoughtful responses.

Often a developing writer makes sizable leaps in the narrative, leaving the reader perplexed. Ask what the student meant to tell the reader at that point. Often the writer knows exactly what was intended and articulates it clearly. Other times the writer simply didn't bother to develop the story line. Once it has been stated, then the writer can incorporate the missing sections into the narrative.

Skills are best taught in the context of the student's writing because they are more immediately understood and internalized. Keep grade-level novels at hand to illustrate skills such as indenting paragraphs, putting conversation in quotes, etc. Often the beginning writer strings together sentences with connectors such as "and then" or "so." Having materials available for modeling saves you time. Remain alert to the kinds of skills several students (or even the whole class) need help with and teach them as needed.

Use this time for positive reinforcement of progress, even if it seems minimal (see "What to Say During Sharing" on page 111). By reviewing work stapled to the inside back of the folder, you will see that progress truly does occur. Make written comments on the work. If a work is in progress, put a star on the paper where you quit working together. The next conference time you can skim to that point and then continue your more thorough reading.

The content of the conference period is not as important as the time spent individually with the writers. Your questions should lead to a reflection of the work in progress, and they will be a natural outgrowth of what is being written or read. You will quickly become adept at leading students to explore new ideas and refinements. This is a good time to share your own challenges as a writer and to explain how you tackle problems. Keep a copy of "Writing Conference Responses and Questions" available for reference as you initiate conferencing techniques. You will soon be adept at efficiently guiding your students. Your role is to inspire progress through modeling, sharing, and advising.

WRITING CONFERENCE RESPONSES AND QUESTIONS

Tell me about your piece.

What inspired this idea?

How is your work going?

Are you stuck?

What were you thinking about as you wrote this?

Where do you want to take this?

Let's think of some new directions. Can you think of some options?

What do you want the reader to think?

Who do you want to read this?

Have you reread aloud what you wrote?

Have you read this to another student?

Has another student read this?

Are you pleased with what you have written?

Do you want to make any changes?

What can you do with this now?

You seemed to be uncomfortable with this part. What could be done with it?

How can I help you?

What do you plan to do next?

Do you want to polish this?

Do you want to publish this?

REVISIONS

Everyone would like to be able to write a polished piece in one attempt. But it is the rare writer who does not revise in the process. For developing writers, there needs to be a balance between editing pieces and getting on with the next creation. A good policy to follow is to polish pieces intended for definite publication, to staple to the folder those pieces that seem worthy of possible editing and publishing, and to set aside the rest in draft form. The drafts should never be seen as failures, but might be considered works "in progress." They are worth retaining for several months if only to mark the student's growth.

Each teacher needs to develop an editing style that will vary according to grade level. Although you will help with revisions as a routine component of the conference, you will not usually supervise all the steps. Also, your goal should be to develop more and more student independence. For the very youngest student who is primarily using experimental spelling, the task of revision may be overwhelming. Enlist the aid of parents, older students, or paraprofessionals to write out the revision for the student to copy or file as is. If the work is to be typed, the revisions can be noted for the typist. For completed revisions that will not be typed but still have errors, put a check mark in the margin in pencil. The student can make the change, you can monitor the revision, and then either you or the student can erase the check mark.

Generally, it is best to have a variety of revision expectations, depending on the work, your time, the student's level, and the involvement with the piece in progress.

Modeling revisions is an important aspect of this stage. Again, it is effective if the students see you work through a revision. Take a work of your own that is in progress or create one and put it on the board or on an overhead projector. Think out loud and discuss problems you are facing, changes you need to make, and possible alternatives. Enlist the students' help in deciding what to revise. Let them see and hear that there are many ways to polish a piece and that sometimes a conclusion is not reached. Show students that work in progress may have cross-outs, notes, sentences on the side of the paper, arrows that reorganize the paragraphs, omissions, inserts, and so forth. If it is understood from the beginning that completion of a piece doesn't mean just copying it over neatly, and that polishing involves several important stages, students will be more receptive to revisions.

Occasionally students will volunteer their work for a revision lesson. This means either the student is quite secure or prefers the teacher handle the revision task. When this happens, preface the revision by making it clear that though you will give ideas you are not going to let the student copy suggested revisions. This is generally acceptable to the student and while help is given, the student is still accountable.

Self and Peer Editing

Many teachers successfully develop self- or peer-editing programs. The students are trained to be supportive readers of works in progress, offering constructive criticism, punctuation and grammar advice, and generally serving as sounding boards for the authors. Again, the teacher as a model plays a crucial role. Using supportive conference techniques provides a system that can be adapted to the student editor. The students can be encouraged to critique their own work carefully and then enlist the aid of another student. Students who learn to subvocalize their writing while rereading it uncover many errors, particularly omissions and incomplete words. A checklist for peer editing or self editing is on the next page.

WRITING CHECKLIST

Style:

Does the writing say what it is meant to say?

Will a reader understand the writing?

Is each thought complete?

Do most sentences begin *without* words such as "so," "and," or "then?"

Is there variety? (Not all short or all long sentences?)

Are powerful words used?

Should some parts be rearranged?

Does more need to be written?

Does some need to be changed?

Should parts be taken out?

Form:

Are there periods or other end marks at the ends of complete thoughts?

Is the writing organized into paragraphs?

Are the paragraphs indented?

If there is conversation, does each speaker's statement have a new paragraph and appropriate quotation marks?

Do you need to check the spelling?

Considerations for the peer editor:

Tell a student what the main point is. Do you both agree?

Does your piece flow? Can it be understood?

Give two positive statements about the work.

Does the author need to explain more?

What is the author going to do next?

SHARING

Sharing works in progress or completed works is an important part of the writing process. Students realize quickly how critical it is to write with accuracy. Omissions, misspellings, and incomplete words are sharply reduced when work is shared.

Again, the stage is set by the sharing of the teacher's work. This step also influences the manner in which the student works are received. Some students will not read their work aloud, but will allow the teacher to read it. Some students will not want their work shared orally, but I have never found a student who won't share a work in print. Do respect a student's wish not to have works shared in any form. If a student has a particularly fine piece, sometimes he or she will read it or allow it to be read after others have shared theirs. Remember those pieces during a sharing period and come back to them toward the end and try again (with a bit of gentle coaxing). Often the student is then more comfortable.

Sometimes a poem or story is so rough that finding a positive aspect is a challenge. Review the following list of comments periodically, so you will always have something positive to say. If you are sharing with the group, a positive comment is always the first appropriate comment. Some classes can move on to offering criticism and asking questions. Keep a pencil handy and make written notes during class comments or just put checks as you read when you see items in need of attention. If you are having a personal conference, once you have praised some portion of the writing, you can then work on the revisions needed.

A visitor once observed my writing class and asked how I got them to be so eager to offer their works for sharing. I talked about the importance of modeling, building trust, and allowing risks, but I felt I was missing something. During the next session I asked the class if they could tell me how they became so comfortable with being praised and critiqued. Hands went up immediately. I called on one student, and he said, "You bribed us!" I was stunned and asked for more details. "Don't you remember at the beginning of the year? No one wanted to share their stories, so you gave out stickers for anyone who would let you read their story to the class." It then came back to me. I did indeed bribe students. It was only needed during one or two sessions. This reminded me of how important it is to use whatever method works—even bribery.

What to Say during Sharing

FOR THE EARLY OR DEVELOPING WRITER

(Or What to Say When It Seems Like There's Nothing Nice to Say)

I like the sounds of your words.

The word "_____" is a favorite of mine. I'm glad you used it.

I'm glad you shared this.

I get the picture of what you wrote about.

I appreciate that you put this into words.

This must be important to you.

I can tell this is a special place (thought, experience, etc.).

You worked hard on this! Congratulations!

I appreciate your effort.

I enjoy seeing your work.

I can tell that you are thinking about your work.

GETTING MORE FROM A WRITER

This is a great start—can you write more?

You got me interested in this and it made me want to read more. Can you expand on your ideas?

I didn't want this to end so soon. Can you develop the middle (beginning, end)?

This has caught my fancy. Can you give me more to read?

You have some terrific ideas. Tell me more.

FOR THE STRONG WRITER

Your writing is exciting to read.

Your words are powerful.

Your characters are carefully described.

You have a good voice.

You express yourself so well.

You have good variety of thoughts.

Your work is a joy to read.

I look forward to reading more.

You put so much into your writing.

PUBLISHING WORK

Another aspect of sharing work is the publication stage. Often resources of time and money are limited and it is not possible to copy every worthwhile piece. Poetry is often an exception to this because several poems can share a page, especially if both sides of the page are used. Poetry collections for special days are quite effective. Get parents involved early in the year to act as volunteer typists for those pieces you do want typed. Have a sign-up sheet at Back to School Night or at fall conferences. A word of caution: when you do send a packet home to be typed be sure: you include directions; that each student's first and last name appear on the paper; and allow *plenty* of lead time. Make no assumptions about the background or knowledge of the typist or you will have a volunteer whose hours of work are unacceptable. Include examples if necessary. When the work is published later, add a note of appreciation at the beginning or end such as, "This work is presented thanks to the gracious support of Mr. or Mrs. _____ who did the typing."

If you have a computer center, computers in the library, or the luxury of a computer in your room, acquire software for word processing and use the computer for part or all your publishing efforts. The computer is especially beneficial when formatting poetry. Students can create their poems and see graphically how adjusting the format can influence the flow and meaning of a poem. Revisions become less painful if they are done on a computer. If you have a computer teacher, collaborate on getting the students' works into print. Many students have computers at home and enjoy the accomplishment of having completed their own final version. The ideal situation would be to have computers available in the classroom for a variety of writing activities, especially for modeling revisions and formatting. (Occasionally minigrants are available which would cover the cost of a computer and printer.)

No matter how you publish the work, make the students responsible for proofreading their own work. You will inevitably miss something if you try to do it yourself. I had typed up Mother's Day poems for each student to use in the making of a card. The day after Mother's Day one student informed me, "My mother said to tell you that you spelled 'occasion' wrong." I reminded him that proofreading was his responsibility, but it reminded me once again of the need to develop student ownership. This *was* my typing error, but it was his proofing error. Any computer work is easily modified and even typed versions from volunteers can be fixed with White Out.

If you are able to publish several collections or one large collection, consider having a reading at the end of the year. Invite parents and guests to attend. Have the students select and prepare two or three short pieces to read aloud to the group. At the end, present the collections and allow time for visiting and refreshments if this is possible. (Enlist volunteer or student help with the refreshments.)

Other Publishing Ideas

Short oral readings throughout the year.

Post all over the school: bulletin boards, lockers, halls, desks.

Have a classroom mailbox.

Have a literary magazine.

Publish a newsletter.

Illustrate and create a small book.

Set a story to music.

Have a shelf in the room for student works.

Have a shelf in the library for student works.

Have students copy a poem with markers, crayons, paints, etc.

WAYS TO EXCITE STUDENTS ABOUT WRITING

It is important that students remain excited about their writing projects. You can be an example by maintaining your own interest level. Finding autobiographies by authors familiar to the students and reading vignettes is especially effective. In *Me Me Me Me Me*, M. E. Kerr writes of her years as a child, explaining how various experiences led to characters or themes in her novels. "I think that whenever you find a smart-mouth tomboy kid in any of my books, you have found me from long ago...."[2]

Trina Schart Hyman writes of her youth and early years as illustrator and mother in *Self-Portrait: Trina Schart Hyman*, "I was a really strange little kid. I was born terrified of anything and everything that moved or spoke."[3] She actually lived the role of Little Red Riding Hood for years, complete with red cape, a basket of goodies, and a dog for the wolf, and father for the woodsman; thus it was not surprising that she illustrated this famous tale. She writes eloquently of her mother and learning to read: "It was she who gave me the courage to draw and a love of books. She read to me from the time I was a baby, and once, when I was three or four and she was reading my favorite story, the words on the page, her spoken words, and the scenes in my head fell together in a blinding flash. I could read!"[4]

Check the library for other autobiographies. At conventions pick up brochures on authors and save them for later sharing. Conventions or conferences are excellent places to hear authors speak about their works, and bringing an autographed book back to share with students is exciting.

Magazines such as *Instructor*, *The New Advocate*, and *Learning* are other good sources, and the book clubs for student paperbacks occasionally feature authors. See the end of chapter 3 for additional resources.

Charla Pfeffinger set up mailboxes for all her kindergarten students and encouraged them to create cards for classmates who were absent or had a birthday, or for other special occasions. The child who had been home ill would return to a mailbox full of cards and know that the class truly cared. This writing project expanded during the year with birthday cards being written to each other's parents and staff members.

Another activity that generates interest is the submission of copies of good stories, poems, or essays to contests. Many school districts host an authors' conference in the spring. A few students are selected from each school to display their written book and/or illustrations. Some districts give certificates, have authors as guest speakers, have a RIF distribution, or bring in a storyteller for the event. When participation is limited, grade-level awards within the building spread out the recognition. A good award for the budding writer or illustrator is a small blank book, available from bookstores at a small price.

Larger metropolitan areas often have vendors who sponsor poetry or short story contests. There is generally only a few awards of value, but often certificates of recognition are given to all participants. Consider inspiring a local bookstore to start such a contest if none exists in your area. There are several children's literary magazines which also provide an excellent outlet for the polished pieces. See the end of this chapter for sources.

Some teachers are uncomfortable with the competitiveness of writing contests. Participation should be voluntary, except perhaps in those cases where certificates are given to all students. Ideally students would write because the program is so strong that the need to write is internalized in each student. If this is the case in your class, contests are probably just the frosting on the cake. If you are looking for a way to stir up interest but are not fully comfortable with the competitiveness of a contest, mention a contest to the class and let their reactions help you with the decision. It does take a fair amount of work, but if you have kept samples and polished works in their folders, and if you have volunteer typists, you can generally pull together some submissions with ease. See references for contest or publication possibilities.

More Ways to Excite Interest in Writing

If you learn about local authors at conventions, try to arrange a visit to the school.

Have a writing contest on a theme such as Halloween (scary story or poem), Veteran's Day, or Valentine's Day.

Use book fair proceeds to pay for a visit from a famous author.

Use the book fair setting for a writing competition. Ask the sponsor to provide books as prizes.

Invite the principal to read and comment on fine works.

Have students orally share their works with the principal.

Read aloud parts of authors' autobiographies.

Read the author notes on the cover of a book.

Write to an author as a class—authors are hard pressed to answer thirty individual letters.

Use a copy of *An Author a Month (for Pennies)* to introduce a year's worth of authors to your students.[5]

Have a Write-In (modeled after a Read-In).

Use poems and stories as gifts.

Have poem or story swaps.

Have a shelf in your room and in the library for student works.

Illustrate, bind, and decorate stories and collections of poetry.

Write under pen names just for fun.

Have students develop their own "about the author" section.

Dramatize a student work. (Fairy or tall tales work well.)

Ask students "What are you writing about lately?"

Have students collaborate on a piece.

Use tape recordings for oral stories. It could be transcribed later by the student or a typist (this is especially good for the early writer).

JOURNALS

How would you react if you received this advertisement?

* *

SPECIAL OFFER!

This revolutionary program will teach your students:
Writing Skills
Spelling Skills
Grammar
Appropriate Behavior
Social Skills

In addition, you will receive:
Heartwarming Anecdotes
Compliments
Confidences
Laughs
Kudos
Jokes
and
An Occasional Tear

Your cost (believe it or not!):
LESS THAN ONE MINUTE PER CHILD PER DAY!

* *

Sounds incredible doesn't it? Would you buy such a program? Less than one minute per child per day seems like a small price to pay for such a big return. Yet teachers often say that they can't find the time to read journals and thus a valuable writing experience is ignored.

There are several ways to use journals, but this section will concentrate on interactive journals. Most classrooms have ten or fifteen minutes sometime during the day, between regrouping or before or after specials, which is an excellent time to use journals. I watch the sales in August and buy spiral notebooks when they are on sale for 20 cents each and have them on hand the first day. Some teachers list the notebooks on their student's supply list for the fall, but I prefer spending my own $5.00 just so they are all the same size.

Think of journals as a way to have twenty-five to thirty private conversations with your students every day. You can scan and respond to a journal entry much more quickly than you could have individual conversations, and your students will keep you updated on nearly every important aspect of their lives. It also allows you to keep in touch with your homeroom students if they are regrouping with other teachers and classes throughout the day.

Introducing the Journal

The first day of writing in journals, explain that this is a journal for writing to you, the teacher. Students can write anything they want in the journal: about school, about homework, about the teacher, about home, about what they like to do, etc. Explain that you will not be checking spelling or grammar and this is just a time of sharing thoughts and ideas.

Again, take time to model the types of things you want the students to write, brainstorming ideas on the board. Explain that you will write back to them, however briefly. After the writing, direct the students to put their journals on a designated shelf or somewhere convenient to your desk. Give them large paper clips so they can clip the pages together as they use their notebook. You can then open directly to the appropriate page.

Emphasize that the journal is private and that you will respect their confidences. However, it is wise with intermediate and older students to note early in the journal writing, if not on the first day, that you are obliged by law to seek help if the student writes about suicide or physical or sexual abuse. This does happen. I had a fifth-grade boy who began writing about how awful the world was, how it wasn't worth living, and so forth. After several exchanges and reoccurrences, not wanting to breach the trust within the journal writing yet knowing I had to alert the parents, I reluctantly called them in. The father agreed that the last thing he wanted to do was risk breaking my line of communication, and fortunately the family was able to solve the underlying problems.

Student enthusiasm for journal writing is generally high at first. Primary students will need more convincing that creative or inventive spelling is acceptable, and you may have to have young students read their journals aloud to you until you learn their individual styles. Primary students often supplement their writing by using a rebus here or there, helping you with the interpretation.

Intermediate students may need more coaxing or want to know how many sentences to write, etc. Consider stating that they must have a minimum number of sentences corresponding to their grade level, for example, fourth graders must write four sentences, fifth graders must write five, etc. (Several students will invariably think this means writing five lines.) Soon, they will forget this injunction and write what feels right for the day.

Reading the Journals

The key to making these journals effective is your response to them. Students love reading the teacher comments, no matter how brief. If you are absent, they will ask why you didn't write back, totally forgetting you were gone. Through positive responses, compliments of good behavior, pertinent questions, and thoughtful answers, you can influence their behavior much more effectively and efficiently than you would have imagined possible. Your answers need not be long—a word or two is often sufficient. Upon occasion, you may want to spend more time on an individual response. Set that one aside until a later time, so the others can be finished quickly.

If you have the students write early in the day and have a planning period shortly thereafter, you can get a handle on each child's state of mind before the day is over. It truly takes less than a minute a day for most journals.

What Do Children Write About?

Students who have not previously written in journals will take a while to find their style. They will write about home, school, their friends, their favorite television shows, what they did over the weekend, what they like about school, what they hate about school, etc. A newly arrived Vietnamese student's questions ranged from the political system to standardized testing to Halloween. He wrote that he was sad because he didn't have a costume, and since I read it early in the day, I was able to call the room mother and make sure he was able to participate.

One shy fifth grader wrote about a murder she had witnessed, telling me this was why she was having trouble concentrating that day. No wonder!

One young man was struggling socially and academically, and on an appropriate day I commented on how nicely he had behaved during the first hour. He was starved for appreciation and that casual comment set off a series of entries, increasingly longer, discussing how "nice" he was. Of course, I methodically reinforced each entry. He stretched from a sentence to a paragraph to pages about his niceness. (At times as I laboriously read through pages of his invented spelling about being nice, I wished I had never mentioned it.) But he became nicer in the process and changed from a volatile, unpredictable student to a functional class member.

Students who are comfortable with you will keep you in line through the journals. They will scold when you have forgotten something or have been unjust. They will criticize you, sometimes unfairly. They can wound you with their words. But generally a quick apology or explanation or a response of "I understand" clears the air without a confrontation.

More often you will be the recipient of compliments and bravos, especially if you set the tone for positive thoughts through your responses. The journal is not the place for you to scold or criticize. It is your opportunity to model behaviors you find desirable.

How Can Skills Improve If You Don't Correct Errors?

Students write about their interests. For weeks in the fall I would read about "socker," "socur," "socer," and "soucre" games, and I would write a phrase about my son's soccer games. Eventually the students would internalize the correct spelling. Using a reflective style while modeling the correct spelling is subtle, yet effective.

What to Do When Interest Lags

After a few months, and especially when the writing has lost its initial interest or has become particularly sloppy, tell the students to take a period or two to reread their entire journal. This is the rare occasion when I tell them the theme of their next entry: telling me their thoughts upon reading their journal entries. Typical comments are about how much they had forgotten had happened, how much they enjoyed reading their (and your) entries, and many will write how hard it was to read what they wrote. There is generally a sharp improvement at this point. Sometimes an older child who has used the journal to vent anger or frustration with peers or the teacher will express some regrets. I had one girl write some rather explicit observations about the anatomy of young boys, and her rereading made her feel quite ashamed. This is a good time to let that student know that such feelings are normal.

Another tactic to increase interest in the journal is expanding its use. Bring in magazines and have the students use a page for a collage that tells you visually about them or a special interest. Suggest they use crayons or markers and write in the color that they feel suits them that day. Ask them to write something you are *not* to read and fold the page over with the message "Do Not Read" on the outside. And, of course, *don't read* that page. Try a few changes now and then, and generally their interest will pick up again. Everytime I have wanted to quit for a week or two, someone has shared something important with me, and I was glad I didn't quit.

Bitter and Best

At the end of the year, consider having the students read their journals again and then write on the best and the worst of the year. This is for the confident teacher, as it invites criticism along with the praise. I explain to the students that by having them write about the bitter and the best helps me become a better teacher. I usually brainstorm some of the highlights (and low points) of the year and also add that I want their personal reflections, not just what was fun for the entire class.

I do this activity during journal time, but instead of having them write in their journals, I have them write on looseleaf sheets so I can collect and save them. I keep them from year to year, and they do help me evaluate my program and teaching, providing fascinating glimpses of how I am perceived by the students. Just like the students, you will learn and grow also.

If You Are Still Not
Convinced, Read This:

Journals are justifiable for many academic reasons: they build independent writing skills, develop proofreading skills, improve spelling, provide an avenue for improvement of behavior or self-esteem, develop acceptable and safe methods for airing complaints or arguing for a cause, plus they provide solid evidence of progress.

Whenever I am asked what system of discipline I use, I am at a loss. I can't articulate what I do. Then I remember my journals, my best secret disciplinary technique. I can reinforce, chide, argue, praise, and joke through those pages. I had one new fourth-grade boy come into my room late in the year, very angry about being there. I gave him a journal and he wrote (in beautiful script) about how he liked me and the school (despite behavioral evidence to the contrary). I methodically praised his behavior, and his journal became an obvious effort to internalize improved behavior. His questions were about me and my children. Did I ever have a fight? Did my son? Was I a good student? Did I ever get sent to the principal? Was my son overweight? Did he like jokes? And so on. Meanwhile he became a delightful contributing class member. I haven't figured out why his handwriting deteriorated simultaneously, but decided that was an acceptable trade-off.

Finally, journals provide a personalized bond to each student with the bonus of being entertaining and rewarding.

Other Types of Journals

Dan Kirby and Tom Liner describe four types of journals in their book *Inside Out: Developmental Strategies for Teaching Writing.*[6] The "Writer's Notebook" contains ideas for future writing, the "Class Journal" is a combination of personal entries and responses to class activities or literature, the "Project Journal" is a record of progress while doing a research paper or long creative writing, plus a record of group or individual projects, and the "Diary" is similar to the interactive journals described above. Refer to Kirby and Liner for an excellent overview on using journals with older students.

NOTES

[1]Frank Smith, *Insult to Intelligence* (New York: Arbor House, 1986), 170.

[2]M. E. Kerr, *Me Me Me Me Me* (New York: Harper and Row, Publishers, 1983), 75.

[3]Trina Schart Hyman, *Self-Portrait: Trina Schart Hyman* (Reading, Mass.: Addison Wesley Publishing Company, Inc., 1981), unpaged.

[4]Ibid.

[5]Sharron L. McElmeel, *An Author a Month (for Pennies)*, illus. Deborah L. McElmeel (Englewood, Colo.: Libraries Unlimited, Inc., 1988).

[6]Dan Kirby and Tom Liner, *Inside Out: Developmental Strategies for Teaching Writing* (Upper Montclair, N.J.: Boynton/Cook, Publishers, Inc., 1981).

OTHER RESOURCES

Books

Bergstrom, Joan M., and Craig Bergstrom. *All the Best Contests for Kids.* Berkeley, Calif.: Ten Speed Press, 1988.
Hundreds of contests are described, ranging from writing and book contests to a Frog Festival.

Frank, Marjorie. *If You're Trying to Teach Kids How to Write, You've Gotta Have This Book!* Illustrated by Judy Howard. Nashville, Tenn.: Incentive Publications, 1979.
This book is full of ideas for inspiring young writers. Process, evaluation, and management are touched on, but the primary focus of the book is providing hundreds of inventive ways to involve students in creative writing.

Graves, Donald H. *Writing: Teachers & Children at Work.* Portsmouth, N.H.: Heinemann Educational Books, 1983.
Graves provides an in-depth look at teachers involved in writing conferences, and offers advice on teaching skills, developing confident writers, and documentation of progress.

Contest and Publication Opportunities

Write to the following magazines or contests for details regarding submissions. Include a self-addressed, stamped envelope for return of information. There are other publication possibilities, but these are included because of positive experiences and responses to my inquiries.

Cricket Magazine
P.O. Box 300
Peru, Illinois 61354

Highlights for Children
803 Church Street
Honesdale, Pennsylvania 18431

National Written and Illustrated by ...
    Awards Contest for Students
Landmark Editions, Inc.
1420 Kansas Avenue
Kansas City, Missouri 64127

Publish-A-Book Contest
Raintree Publishers, Inc.
310 West Wisconsin Avenue
Milwaukee, Wisconsin 53203

Shoe Tree Competition for
    Young Writers
National Association for Young Writers
P.O. Box 452
Belvidere, New Jersey 07823

Stone Soup
P.O. Box 83
Santa Cruz, California 95063

Young Writer's Contest
P.O. Box 6092
McLean, Virginia 22106

Useful Magazines for Writers

The Writer
120 Boylston Street
Boston, Massachusetts 02116

Writer's Digest
Subscription Department
P.O. Box 1952
Marion, Ohio 43306-1952

Chapter 9

Making the Reading
and Writing Connection

LITERATURE AS A BRIDGE
TO WRITING

Using certain forms of literature to inspire student writing is an important aspect of a strong writing program. Story forms such as fairy tales, folktales, tall tales, and fables provide developing writers with a familiar and easily internalized structure, giving them a predictable and comfortable framework for writing. This chapter thoroughly explores the use of traditional fairy and folktales for creative writing, and provides suggestions for the teaching of alternative folktales, tall tales, modern urban legends, and fables. These techniques can be adapted to suit other genres as well.

FOLK LITERATURE

It is difficult to distinguish between traditional fairy tales and folktales. Although some basic generalizations can be drawn, there is much overlapping between the tales. For the purposes of this writing experience, traditional folktales and fairy tales will be considered interchangeable.

To spark interest, give the folk literature survey on the next page. If you have primary students, use it for general discussion rather than as a survey. With intermediate students, make copies for independent work and then discuss their answers. Although the responses might seem quite poor initially, as you discuss the tales students will begin to remember them, even though they may not have read or heard them for some years.

To begin your writing unit, gather several collections plus individually illustrated tales from the library. Browse the library 398 section and find tales that appeal to you. Folktales and fairy tales are oral traditions; start by reading aloud familiar short tales such as "Cinderella" or "Sleeping Beauty," which will set the stage for other tales. Use your read-aloud time and instructional reading time for the tales. Progress to sharing several of the beautifully illustrated tales that are also familiar. For the multicultural classroom, spend some time reading from a collection that includes tales from around the world, particularly from cultures represented in your room. Joanna Cole's *Best Loved Folk Tales of the World* is a collection of 200 tales including tales from the remotest parts of the world. Jane Yolen's *Favorite Folktales from Around the World* is another excellent resource for various cultures, with the added bonus of being organized thematically ("The Fool: Numbskulls, and Noodleheads," "Shape Shifters," "Fooling the Devil," etc.).

Vary the reading assignments with other activities to keep the students actively involved. Use your film library to show and compare films to the book versions. If you have a VCR available, rent a cassette of a fairy tale or folktale. The use of a variety of media keeps your students involved in the unit while you build upon their backgrounds of fairy tales. As you expose your class to as many forms of the tales as is reasonable, begin to draw them into an understanding of the elements of the traditional tale. Lead them to realize the following key points, listed on page 124.

FOLKTALE AND FAIRY TALE SURVEY

Write the name of the tale you think of when you read these statements.

1. A wolf gets to grandmother's house before a young girl.

2. A fairy godmother helps a girl go to the ball.

3. A wealthy man's bride opens a locked closet.

4. A girl saves her brothers from a life as water birds.

5. Everyone in the castle sleeps till the princess is rescued.

6. A girl spins straw into gold.

7. A witch comes to a fiery end.

8. The youngest son is helped by a clever cat.

9. The youngest daughter drops a golden ball into the well.

10. A girl runs away to the home of several short miners.

11. A poor man gets a black pudding stuck on his nose.

12. Knights ride up a slippery hill to get the golden apple.

13. A tiny boy has adventures while he travels the world.

14. A boy's wishes are granted by a genie.

15. A prince climbs a girl's hair to get in the tower.

16. A poor man gives his daughter to the white bear.

17. A beast becomes a handsome prince.

18. Gerda rescues Kai from an icy future.

19. A girl's visit upsets a home of furry creatures.

20. Some musically talented animals scare off some robbers.

The above survey was inspired by Sister Margaret Mary Nugent's "How Is Your F.Q. (Folklore Quotient)?"[1]

Answers to Survey

1. Little Red Riding Hood
2. Cinderella
3. Bluebeard
4. The Wild Swans
5. Sleeping Beauty
6. Rumplestiltskin
7. Hansel and Gretel
8. Puss and Boots
9. The Frog Prince
10. Snow White and the Seven Dwarfs
11. The Foolish Wishes
12. The Princess on the Glass Hill
13. Tom Thumb
14. Aladdin's Lamp
15. Rapunzel
16. East of the Sun and West of the Moon
17. Beauty and the Beast
18. The Snow Queen
19. Goldilocks and the Three Bears
20. The Bremen Town Musicians

Elements of a Fairy Tale
or Folktale

1. *Story Length:* The tales are generally short and simple.

2. *Time:* Tales often begin with "Once upon a time." The time of the tale may not be given, and time may even stand still, as in "Brier Rose."

3. *Characters:* Generally there is only a minimum of information provided about characters. Stereotypes are common, such as the beautiful princess, the handsome prince, and an evil antagonist. At times the characters are not even given names. They are described simply as the daughter, son, prince, princess, mother, father, or evil witch. Characters are generally either good or evil, strong or weak, beautiful or ugly.

4. *Setting:* The setting often receives little description. It may include a castle or a forest. Few details are provided.

5. *Style:* The simple style of the fairy tales and folktales is what makes it appealing to the early writer. Only words necessary to the flow of the tale are included.

6. *Action:* Adventure is important to a fairy tale or folktale. The action gives the tale its interest, is intertwined with and carries the theme, and it builds quickly to a climax.

7. *Theme:* This is the main idea of a tale and is often hardest to articulate at first. In traditional tales it is usually one of journey, rescue, quest, and/or conquest. Often tasks must be performed while on a journey or quest. When reading tales aloud, take time to summarize the theme of the tale so the students develop an understanding of the message of the tale.

8. *Magic:* The presence of characters who have magical powers often distinguishes fairy tales from folktales. Although this generalization is not consistent, the role of magic is often important to the conflict or resolution of the plot.

9. *Ending:* Nearly all traditional fairy tales and folktales have happy endings with a solution to the problem. They often include marriage of the male and female heroes.

Expand your classroom collection by using all available libraries so each student can choose a collection or individually illustrated tales to read. Instruct the students to choose folktales for their independent reading for several days. Use the form on the next page or construct a similar form to help students become adept in identifying the elements of a tale. Continue to read tales aloud when possible, using your form of choice to model how students are to analyze the tales. Pay particular attention to the difference between the true resolution of the tale in contrast to the ending, which often is "happiness ever after" and/or marriage.

As the students complete the accompanying form, either collect them or have the students put them in their reading/writing folders for evaluation. You will be able to examine them quickly and determine if each student is mastering the analysis method. Offer support and redirection as necessary, discussing what comprises a good analysis.

ELEMENTS OF FAIRY TALES AND
FOLKTALES WORKSHEET

Name _____ Date _____

Directions: As you finish the reading of your selected tale, complete the following blanks. If your
tale did not have a certain element, write "none" in the blank.

Title _____

1. Setting _____

    _____

2. Female Hero_____

3. Male Hero_____

4. Other Main Characters _____

    _____

    _____

5. Animals_____

6. Theme   (What was the problem?) _____

    _____

    _____

    _____

    _____

    _____

7. Resolution (How was the problem solved?)_____

    _____

    _____

    _____

    _____

    _____

FAIRY TALE POETRY

Since little writing happens during this immersion period, it is a good time to use the fairy tale theme to introduce or continue your poetry writing. Again, students meet with greater success if their first poetry experiences are somewhat guided. The acrostic and diamante forms are excellent for first attempts at poetry and for use with fairy tales. They are discussed in chapter 10 but are also included here for convenience.

Acrostic Poems

An acrostic poem uses a key subject word vertically and each line begins with the vertical letters. For example:

Quite grandly is how she steps in

Unison with the king on the ballroom floor

Especially if she has just

Eaten--then she dances very

Nicely.

Emily White
grade four

King Caloban

Inspiring his queen

Nodding yes to his queen

Gazing at her with happiness

Atiba Nunnally
grade four

Before teaching this form, create one or two acrostic poems yourself and be ready to share them. Begin with the class by brainstorming key words found in fairy tales: castle, kingdom, king, queen, dragon, peasant, fairy, witch, prince, princess, squire, and so forth. Choose a word and work with the class, creating a poem or two together on the board or overhead projector. Share what you have written with the class. It is important that the students see and hear these forms. If the students still seem reluctant to write, do another group poem. Leave the poems and key words on the board and let the students begin. You will have provided just enough input when students are surreptitiously reaching for their pencils and papers.

Diamante Poems

Another successful, though more challenging poetic form is the diamante poem. Teaching this form provides an internal grammar lesson and is a natural for thesaurus instruction. Before beginning, if you do not have a classroom set of thesauri, round up enough copies from the library or other classrooms for at least half your students.

Again, spend some time preparing your own examples before class. Follow the same general brainstorming procedure. Then introduce the following specific form:

Line one: a noun (indicating the topic).

Line two: two adjectives.

Line three: three verbs or "ing" action words.

Line four: a four-word phrase.

Line five: three verbs or "ing" action words.

Line six: two adjectives.

Line seven: a noun, that is a synonym for the noun in line one.

Examples:

Prince

Handsome, kind

Daring, sharing, caring

Always   there   when   needed

Helping, giving, protecting

Strong, brave

Man

Atiba Nunnally
grade four

King

Royal, rich

Waiting, wanting, wishing

Always   needing   more   money

Taxing, demanding, taking

Selfish, greedy

Figurehead

Bryce Milton
grade four

Ideally the poem forms a diamond shape, but as in the above poems, it is sometimes necessary to stretch the spacing between the words in line four to get the desired effect.

Again, practice with the class, creating diamante poems on the board, while reminding students of the features of verbs, nouns, adjectives, and synonyms. Use a few of the nouns your class has contributed to search for synonyms in a group thesaurus lesson. Looking up "king" might result in majesty, sovereign, figurehead, monarch, and others. Soon the students will become adept at turning to the thesaurus for new ideas.

The next day share what the students have created (with their individual consents) and review the poetic form. Then introduce a new twist. The alternative diamante form changes focus in the fourth line and ends with an antonym. It may split the focus between the four words in the middle line, or it may simply introduce the new theme with the phrase. This is more challenging, yet can be managed with some practice. Start by generating antonyms: castle/cottage, royalty/peasantry.

Examples:

Princess

Pretty, sweet

Wishing, dreaming, searching

Rescued, kissed--married, ignored

Cleaning, cooking, mothering

Tired, wrinkled

Queen

Suzanne Barchers
(author)

Prince

Nice, handsome

Looking, finding, marrying

Always   getting   new   clothes

Shopping, buying, spending

Tired, broke

Pauper

Bryce Milton
grade four

FAIRY TALE LETTERS

Janet and Allan Ahlberg have created a charming collection of letters from fairy tale characters entitled, *The Jolly Postman or Other People's Letters.* The postman begins by delivering an apology from Goldilocks to Baby Bear, and continues his rounds, delivering clever missives to a variety of fairy tale characters. Check out this book and read it to your class. Then brainstorm fairy tale characters and possible communiques through discussion and on the board. Assign a letter writing period and be ready to share the results.

Examples:

Dear Cinderella,

We're sorry we treated you so bad, so to make it up to you, we would like you to come to a big party on June 22, 1988. Bring your husband. There will be a lunch and dinner and a dance contest. It is at 1430 Palace Road and it's the third palace on the left.

P.S.Please dress nicely

Love,

Your Sisters

Written by: Chris Meyer
October 15, 1987

Dear Goldilocks,

I am meeting you in court and if you want to know why -- two weeks ago you came into our house. You broke my chair and ate our food. How do we know if you have a cold or bad breath and it got on the silverware that you ate on? Oh yeah, I remember something else too. You were sleeping on my bed and you got in my father's bed and my mother's bed. The worse thing is, you have a home too!

Your Enemy,

The Baby Bear

Written by: Bryce Milton
October, 1987

FOLK LITERATURE AND PROBLEM SOLVING ACTIVITIES

George Shannon has gathered a collection of folktales entitled *Stories to Solve: Folktales from Around the World* and has structured them so that they become lessons in critical thinking. Each brief tale is presented on one page, with the solution or ending following on the next page. The listeners can try to solve the problem or riddle and then hear the solution/ending. Have your students experiment with known tales, structuring them like Shannon's collection, or create their own riddle tales.

WRITING THE FAIRY TALE

During the above reading and analysis of folk and fairy tales, plus the poetry writing, the students have been building and expanding on prior knowledge of this universal form; they have been preparing to write. Review their favorite tales and point out once again the key elements of a traditional tale. Leave these points on the board or have the students use the form for analysis while outlining their own tale. Use peer editing, conferring, group editing, or whatever your chosen revision process is to work through the rough draft. Share completed tales and, if possible, publish a collection of the poetry and/or tales. Once again use volunteer typists, although some students will be delighted to type up their own finished tales. Depending on your schedule, the above process can take three to four weeks to complete. Use your judgment as you move through the process and adjust activities accordingly.

Example:

The Princess

by Emily Waters
grade four

Once upon a time there was a princess named Kristle. She was very pretty and every single prince in the kingdom wished to marry her.

Her hair was golden brown, and her eyes were turquoise blue. She always wore a different white dress. She collected many jewels like crystals, diamonds, sapphires, and rubies. But her favorite was a magic ball made of diamonds. She never misplaced it.

Even with the magic ball, she had one fear. The evil witch was mean and jealous of Kristle. She did everything she could to kill Kristle. But she had never succeeded.

One day the king decided that he would have a contest to see who could kill the witch. The prize would be to marry the princess. The king told the page to announce it at once.

As soon as the whole kingdom knew the good news, princes from all over the kingdom were talking about it except for one. His name was Michael and the princess loved him just as much as he loved her.

Michael went to the castle to see Kristle. He was determined to marry her. When he got there, he was greeted at the door by the page. Kristle was holding her magic ball.

"I have an idea," she said. Then she rubbed her ball and said, "Oh golden ball, the one and all. I need a magic sword."

Suddenly she was holding a magnificent golden sword. She gave it to Michael and he left. About a week later he came back with the witch's head. He never told her how he killed the witch. Three days later they got married and lived happily ever after.

Animal Tales

Standard fairy or folktales with animals as the main characters are common to most countries and appear in large collections. If your students have read and enjoyed the animal tales, suggest writing a tale with animals as the main characters. The following tale was submitted to the Young Writer's Contest and won inclusion in the *1987 Rainbow Collection: Stories and Poetry by Young People.*

Example:

Sir Hopalot the Frog

by Doug Kingsbury
grade five

Once upon a time a little frog hopped away from home. He acted like he wasn't afraid, but he was. He wanted to save a lady in trouble. All he could save was a nickel and penny from his allowance. Yes, it looked hopeless for him until he met his fairy-god-frog. He got three wishes to help him get going in the real world. He asked for some food, and some clothes, and a sword.

He saw a broken down shack and it looked deserted so he helped himself in. It was the best he could get, so this became his home now. The shack had cobwebs and a damp floor. He was hungry so he took out some meat and opened the window. Soon about ten flies flew in and the frog had supper and threw the meat out. Sir Hopalot (the frog) made a bed out of leaves and went to sleep on them.

When he woke up, he heard the croaking of a female frog in trouble. He got his sword and hopped as fast as he could to the noise.

When he got there he saw his school teacher in a huge spider web. He hesitated to save her because he hated school. Then he croaked, "I'll save you if (ribbit) you never give me any work (ribbit) again!"

"It's a (ribbit) deal!" So Sir Hopalot hopped up and cut the web so she fell to the ground, safe from the spider. He finally saved a female in trouble. He wasn't going to get married or anything, but it's a start![2]

Writing the Alternative Fairy Tale

Fairy tales present an excellent opportunity to explore the stereotypes represented in our society. By now the students should be well aware that most tales feature passive, beautiful females who are rescued by heroic, brave men. Several collections are available featuring women in active, heroic roles (see this chapter's resources). Reading these and contemporary alternative tales provides another opportunity to examine and write fairy tales. Use the above process, substituting these collections for the traditional tales. Since often these collections are not as readily available in large quantities, read several aloud, exploring their differences as a group.

To add a light touch, read aloud Roald Dahl's *Revolting Rhymes*, a truly outrageous collection of alternative fairy tales in verse form. Proceed with the writing assignment, specifying what are the signs of an alternative tale: women are not passive; successful characters are not necessarily beautiful or handsome; the ending is not always predictably happy.

Example:

The Lost Child

by Marta Whearley
grade five

"Come back! Come back with that child!" called Jack Fleming. The child was his, and some crook had run off with her.

After six days of searching for his long lost daughter, he decided to give a reward to anyone who could find his child. Each person had a week to find her. Many men searched, but never came back.

On the other side of town there was a women's club. They had heard of the reward and since Jack had not decided what the reward was, they thought up a plan.

"Ladies, ladies," said Barbra Omaz, the lead of the club. "We all know about Mr. Fleming's daughter and our plan. We have chosen Mrs. Leak to find her."

The next morning Mrs. Leak went to Jack's house to find out which way to go. "Mr. Fleming, I am going to look for your daughter. Which way did the horrible man take her?"

Jack burst out laughing. "If every brave man could not find her, there's no way a woman could find her!"

"Which way?" Mrs. Leak stammered.

Jack pointed to the woods and ran off laughing.

Mrs. Leak walked for many miles, searching every step, before she came to a little cottage. She knocked on the door and a small girl answered. It was the child! Jack Fleming's child!

Mrs. Leak merrily walked her back to Jack's house where she found him and all his friends playing poker. When he saw his child he said, "Oh thank you, thank you. Will thirty dollars be enough?"

"No, no, I have what I want," said Mrs. Leak, and she marched off with the child. The plan had worked!

MODERN URBAN LEGENDS

For the experienced writer, studying collections of modern urban legends, such as those found in *The Vanishing Hitchhiker* by Jan Harold Brunvand (Norton, 1981), can be an intriguing extension of this unit. These tales are the folktales of the twenty-first century, and students are fascinated by them. However, be sure to preread any collections of urban legends before offering them to students. Some are a bit bawdy.

READING AND WRITING
TALL TALES

A good bridge to the reading and writing of tall tales is to discuss why our heritage of traditional fairy tales and folktales was largely drawn from Europe. Using a world map, review the early migration of Europeans to America, exploring why they came and speculating about the life of the poor under the rule of royalty. While European tales were concerned primarily with royalty and the dreams of the poor, tall tales deal with people involved in the settling of America, whose feats became larger than life. Lead the class through questioning to realize how important it was for us to develop our own body of tales, and why America dispensed with the theme of royalty and adopted the working man's life as a model.

Read aloud some tall tales and discuss the elements of tall tales in contrast to the fairy tales and folktales just read.

Elements of Tall Tales

Story Length: The story may be short or may be collected into a series of stories or chapters with a common theme.

Time: The specific time is not important, but it is generally implied that the tall tales occurred during the settling of America.

Characters: The main character is usually male. Upon occasion there is a female love interest.

Setting: Usually the setting is related to the work of the male hero — the woods, the country, the railroad line.

Style: The style is characterized by hyperbole. Characters and events are exaggerated beyond belief, with no apologies provided.

Action: There is plenty of action in a tall tale, again wildly exaggerated. This is the trait that distinguishes the tall tale and should be emphasized during their study. The characters are in control of the action.

Magic: The use of magic is either overt or implied by the deeds of the heroes. Animals may play an important role in the plot.

Theme: There is nearly always a problem in need of a solution. The hero tackles it and uses whatever powers available to him or her to resolve the tale.

Ending: The ending is not as predictable as in the fairy tale or folktale, as the hero may face another challenge in the next chapter or tale. But generally the ending brings closure to that particular episode.

Again, immerse the students in the tall tales, using collections, individually illustrated tales, films, videos, and read-aloud time to build their understanding of the genre. Use the accompanying form or devise your own to help the students analyze the structure of the tale. Discuss the elements whenever possible, and pursue the same writing process. You will find that the tall tale is much easier to write after the students have had experience with the fairy tales and folktales.

Examples of tall tales written by students:

Polly Byers

by Kate Finger
grade four

Polly Byers was a giant. She had a mother, a father, and a sister. She also had a boyfriend. His name was Jon Prindle.
One day, Jon asked Polly to marry him. Polly said she wanted time to think about it.
Polly went into the forest to think about it. While she thought, she paced. She paced for fourteen months. By that time there were five big holes in the ground.

(Examples continue on page 135.)

TALL TALES WORKSHEET

Name _____ Date _____

Title: _____

Author:_____

Location of tale: _____

Male Hero: _____

Female Hero: _____

Other characters:_____

Animals: _____

Give three examples of hyperbole (exaggeration). Use complete sentences. You may quote directly from the tale.

1. _____

_____

2. _____

_____

3. _____

_____

Describe the funniest or most outrageous part:

_____

_____

_____

Rate this tale on a 1 (ok) to 5 (great) scale and tell why:

_____

_____

_____

Example by Kate Finger (*continued*)

Now as you know, a lot can happen in fourteen months, and a lot had happened. Her mother and father had died, and Jon had married someone else.

When Polly found out, she began to cry. All her tears landed in the five holes she had made. She cried for fifteen years. And that is how we got the Great Lakes.

Jim Patrick

by Colin Strickland
grade four

One day there was a big storm in Colorado. Jim Patrick woke with a start. The lightning was so big it looked like it was cracking the sky in half.

More and more the water flooded the land. The animals had to climb trees to get away from the water, it was so high. Jim liked animals, so he called in some men. He had an idea that if he made some mountains he could channel the water and at the same time provide higher land for the animals.

It only took one week and the mountains were made. They had two good things. They gave higher ground and they would channel the water toward the Colorado River. There was so much water it dug the Grand Canyon.

When the water was all gone, it had washed away the dirt and sand. There were only rocks left. These rocky clumps were called the Rocky Mountains.

In doing this work, Jim Patrick got caught in the current and was never seen again. Some folks say he was just washed away. Some other folks say he got out, went down to Texas and rode Widow Maker without Pecos Bill's permission and was bucked away.

FABLES

Writing fables is especially challenging because of the need to write a succinct, concrete story to tell a symbolic message. Although some tales do not have an explicit moral, all express a lesson, and this is the best way to explain a fable to students. Again, start your unit by gathering collections of fables, reading them aloud, and using filmstrips, films, and videos of fables. Begin with the traditional fables by Aesop. Then share *Fables* by Arnold Lobel and some of the appropriate fables from James Thurber's *Fables for Our Time and Famous Poems Illustrated*. The students will quickly see how Thurber and Lobel used the genre to develop humorous literary fables. As you share them, bring out the following key points.

Elements of Fables

Characters: The characters are usually in sharp contrast to each other: good versus bad or wise versus foolish.

Plot: The characters often solve a problem.

Length: Fables are a short, one-act lesson.

Style: Though the characters are animals, fables poke fun at human foibles.

Resolution: Fables may have a specific moral at the end of the fable.

If your students have had success with the preceding folk literature assignments, using a form to analyze the fables might be unnecessary and they could proceed with reading several fables, followed by writing their own. If you wish to use a form, consider the following one or create your own. The students' completed fables are especially fun to publish with illustrations, as each fable is short and often fits easily on a single page.

FABLES WORKSHEET

Name _____ Date _____

Title: _____

Author: _____

Characters: _____

_____

_____

Problem or Plot: _____

_____

_____

_____

_____

Resolution: _____

_____

_____

_____

_____

Moral or Lesson: _____

_____

_____

_____

Example of a fable written by a student:

The Fox and the Frog

by Ryan Pleune
grade four

One day a frog heard a fox saying that he could do anything anybody else could do. The frog went over to the fox and said, "I bet you can't do this."

The frog spotted a fly, shot his tongue out, snatched the fly and ate it.

Then the fox looked around, spotted a fly, and tried to shoot his tongue out, but it was so short it wouldn't stretch an inch.

All the animals watching started to laugh.

"Laugh if you wish," said the fox, "but I shall succeed tomorrow."

The fox went home, put his tongue in a clamp, and started stretching it. When his tongue was about one foot long, he stopped.

The fox rolled up his tongue as much as he could and went outside to try it. He spotted a fly and shot his tongue at it. When the fox tried to bring it back in, it wouldn't come. The fox had to live that way for the rest of his life.

Moral: Don't try to be who you are not.

OTHER TEACHING IDEAS

Oral Histories

Folktales are basically recorded oral histories. Have students develop their own oral histories by interviewing their relatives and compiling the information in reports or story form.

Folktale Comparisons

There are hundreds of variants of *Cinderella* in existence. Your librarian can help you find several versions in the library. Make a chart with the elements listed down the left side of the page and the sources (authors, countries) across the top. Fill in the details of each tale's elements, comparing the differences and similarities. This can be repeated (with any often found tale) as a research project by intermediate students who have developed a good background in folk literature. Compare book versions to film versions for more application.

Drama

Use folktales or fairy tales as the source for a short play. Let the students decide what portions of the story are important to the script. It is easy to work with a familiar tale because the students have internalized the story. This could be a good follow-up to the above comparison activity. Students could select the elements they like from a variety of countries and construct their own variants of *Cinderella* or another similar tale. Paul Nolan's *Folk Tale Plays Round the World* is a collection of one-act royalty plays that are useful.

NOTES

[1]Sister Margaret Mary Nugent, "How Is Your F.Q. (Folklore Quotient)?" in "News Letter for Professors of Children's Literature," edited by Elliott D. Landau. *Elementary English* 45 (1968), 667-668.

[2]*1987 Rainbow Collection: Stories and Poetry by Young People* (McLean, Va.: Young Writer's Contest Foundation, 1987).

OTHER RESOURCES

Recommended Traditional Folktale and/or Fairy Tale Collections

Note: The following have been included because they represent a variety of countries. Check your library's 398 section for collections from specific countries.

Cole, Joanna, ed. *Best Loved Folk Tales of the World*. Garden City, N.Y.: Anchor Press/Doubleday, 1983.
    Two hundred tales are included from Europe, the Middle East, Asia, Africa, the Americas, the Caribbean, and the West Indies.

Lang, Andrew, ed. *The Blue Fairy Book*. New York: Dover Publications, Inc., 1965.
    This is a republication of the 1889 edition of thirty-seven tales. It is the first volume in a series of many colored collections: Violet, Pink, Gray, etc.

Yolen, Jane, ed. *Favorite Folktales from Around the World*. New York: Pantheon Books, 1986.
    This collection has a wide variety of countries represented and is conveniently organized by theme.

Recommended Alternative Folktale and/or Fairy Tale Collections

Barchers, Suzanne I. *Wise Women: Folk and Fairy Tales from around the World*. Englewood, Colo.: Libraries Unlimited, 1990 (in press).
    Tales celebrating strong women who prevail and triumph using their intelligence, courage, or resourcefulness.

Minard, Rosemary, ed. *Womenfolk and Fairy Tales*. Illustrated by Suzanna Klein. Boston: Houghton Mifflin Company, 1975.
    These eighteen, predominantly European folk and fairy tales, also include stories from Persia, Japan, China, and Africa.

Phelps, Ethel Johnston, ed. *The Maid of the North: Feminist Folk Tales from Around the World*. Illustrated by Lloyd Bloom. New York: Holt, Rinehart & Winston, 1981.
    Twenty-one tales from Europe, West Pakistan, Africa, Japan, Russia, Canada, North America, and Persia are decorated with black and white line drawings. An informative introduction prepares the reader for the tales.

_____. *Tatterhood and Other Tales*. Illustrated by Pamela Baldwin Ford. New York: The Feminist Press, 1978.
    Tales from Africa, Egypt, America, Japan, India, China, and Latin America are interspersed with European tales.

Riordan, James, ed. *The Woman in the Moon and Other Tales of Forgotten Heroines*. Illustrated by Angela Barrett. New York: Dial Books for Young Readers, 1984.
   Riordan includes eighteen tales from America, the Arctic, Estonia, Mongolia, Russia, Africa, Japan, Vietnam, Europe, and the Aztec Indians, plus a bibliography.

Recommended Individually Illustrated Tales with Female Heroes

Anderson, Hans Christian. *The Snow Queen*. Retold by Amy Ehrlich. Illustrated by Susan Jeffers. New York: The Dial Press, 1982.

_____. *The Wild Swans*. Retold by Amy Ehrlich. Illustrated by Susan Jeffers. New York: The Dial Press, 1982.

Apy, Deborah, reteller. *Beauty and the Beast*. Illustrated by Michael Hague. New York: Holt, Rinehart & Winston, 1983.

Bell, Anthea. *The Wise Queen*. Illustrated by Chihiro Iwasaki. Natick, Mass.: Picture Book Studio, USA, 1986.

Grimm Brothers. *Hansel and Gretel*. Illustrated by Susan Jeffers. New York: Dial Books for Young Readers, 1980.

Mayer, Marianna. *Beauty and the Beast*. Illustrated by Mercer Mayer. New York: Four Winds Press, 1978.

Mayer, Mercer, reteller and illustrator. *East of the Sun and West of the Moon*. New York: Four Winds Press, 1980.

Yolen, Jane. *Sleeping Ugly*. Illustrated by Diane Stanley. New York: Coward, McCann, & Geoghegan, Inc., 1981.

Other Fairy Tale Books of Interest

Ahlberg, Janet, and Allan Ahlberg. *The Jolly Postman or Other People's Letters*. Boston: Little, Brown and Company, 1986.

Dahl, Roald. *Revolting Rhymes*. Illustrated by Quentin Blake. New York: A Bantam Skylark Book, 1986.

Hall, Nancy Christensen, ed. *Fairy Tale Alphabet Book*. Illustrated by John O'Brien. New York: Macmillan Publishing Company, Inc., 1983.

Shannon, George. *Stories to Solve: Folktales from Around the World*. Illustrated by Peter Sis. New York: Greenwillow Books, 1985.

Fairy Tale and/or Folktale Resources

Bosma, Bette. *Fairy Tales, Fables, Legends, and Myths: Using Folk Literature in Your Classroom*. New York: Teachers College Press, 1987.

Nolan, Paul T. *Folk Tale Plays Round the World*. Boston: Plays, Inc., 1982.
  The sixteen royalty-free plays are adapted from relatively unfamiliar tales.

Zipes, Jack, ed. *Don't Bet on the Prince: Contemporary Feminist Fairy Tales in North America and England*. New York: Metheun, 1986.
  Zipes has collected sixteen feminist tales plus four articles on the subject of fairy tales and feminism. Not all tales are suitable for children and should be carefully preread.

Tall Tales

Fleischman, Sid. *Jim Bridger's Alarm Clock and Other Tall Tales*. Illustrated by Eric von Schmidt. New York: E. P. Dutton and Company, Inc., 1978.

Stoutenburg, Adrien. *American Tall Tales*. Illustrated by Richard M. Powers. New York: Puffin Books, 1966.

Urban Legends

Brunvand, Jan Harold. *The Choking Doberman and Other "New" Urban Legends*. New York: W. W. Norton and Company, 1984.

_____. *The Mexican Pet: More "New" Urban Legends and Some Old Favorites*. New York: W. W. Norton and Company, 1986.

_____. *The Vanishing Hitchhiker: American Urban Legends and Their Meanings*. New York: W. W. Norton and Company, 1981.

Fables

Carle, Eric, reteller. *Twelve Tales from Aesop*. New York: Philomel Books, 1980.

Kennerly, Karen, ed. *Hesitant Wolf and Scrupulous Fox: Fables Selected from World Literature*. New York: Schocken Books, 1983.

Kent, Jack. *Jack Kent's Fables of Aesop*. New York: Parents' Magazine Press, 1972.

Levine, David. *The Fables of Aesop*. Boston: The Harvard Common Press, 1975.

Lobel, Arnold. *Fables*. New York: Harper and Row, Publishers, 1980.

Thurber, James. *Fables for Our Time and Famous Poems Illustrated*. New York: Harper and Row, Publishers, 1983.

Chapter 10

Finding Hidden Poets

Reading and writing poetry can be an exciting component of a literate classroom. Yet teachers often are uncomfortable with teaching poetry, perhaps believing that it takes a special talent to write it. To the contrary, many forms of poetry are quite easy to write, because the structure provides the poet with a format that helps guide the actual writing. Being told just to write a poem, even with a subject provided, would cause "writer's block" in most of us, but guided through the experience with a confident mentor would probably result in a successful product. This chapter discusses a method of teaching poetry which you can master and use with assurance, learning the poetic forms and expanding your writing skills as you use it. Remember, you do not need to be a poet to teach poetry, but you might become a poet while teaching poetry.

GENERAL TECHNIQUES FOR
TEACHING POETRY

To start, choose a topic that relates to a subject your class is studying. If your class is studying the solar system or fairy tales, your students already have a background of images and thoughts upon which they can draw. Next, consider what poetic form to use. (You will be given several examples in this chapter.) Certain forms lend themselves better to different topics, so the form might be influenced by the topic in use. For the beginning poets, choose a predictable and easy form. It is generally easier to teach nonrhyming poetry first, as students will focus on the poem in total, rather than on finding rhyming words.

Before teaching any poetry, gather together several examples of the type of poem you are going to teach. Familiarity with several collections helps, and recommendations for volumes that contain a variety of poetic forms are at the end of this chapter. Also valuable are additional resources such as *Calliope*, an activity book of poetic forms and figures of speech, and the *Handbook of Poetic Forms*, which provides an overview of the forms plus examples.

Once you have chosen a topic and a form, try to create one or two examples yourself. However, if this step makes you uneasy or stops you from teaching poetry, skip it and go on to the next step. You will gain your confidence by working through the process with the students. Remember, don't expect more of your students than you are willing to tackle yourself. If you are threatened by writing poetry, they will sense this and you are destined for failure. Instead, adopt the attitude of learning with the class. Let them know that you are going to meet the challenge together, and you will be quite surprised at the poet hiding inside you.

Introduce the topic and form to the class. Try to have an example or two on the board or in handout form. Read or share in print as many examples as you can. Be sure to include student examples, if possible, so your students realize that writing poetry is within their reach. Certain forms, such as diamante and acrostic (see chapter 9), rely upon the visual message as well as the oral, and reading these and designating the line changes with your hand (in the fashion of an orchestral conductor) will give students an idea of the style of the poem.

Use the board or overhead projector to generate many words related to the subject. With older students, you might also have the students use scratch paper to jot down a list of ideas or words. This is an important step because it will stimulate the writing and provide some support to those students who are not comfortable with the process. As the students suggest words or thoughts, respond positively with comments such as "That's a great word ... I like that thought.... That makes me think of another powerful word, _____." If you have chosen a topic that is currently under study, use those resources (even textbooks) to generate words. Have a thesaurus handy and use it often to expand on a suggested word. The teaching of poetry is a good way to acquaint students with the advantages of a thesaurus and should be seen as an integral part of the word play of creating poetry. It is *not* cheating to use resources such as a thesaurus for ideas and the process is more comfortable when a student can legitimately and methodically search for inspiration. Don't shortcut this stage and don't erase the collection of words you create. Students need the support and will use what you've written for additional ideas.

The next step is the creation of group examples. Use some of the words on the board to start the poem. It is wise to control the first line of the poem yourself so that you know it is workable. Otherwise you run the risk of having either to struggle with a student's inappropriate suggestion or rejecting a student's idea. Once you have developed a level of trust with your class, you will be able to take more risks.

After writing the first line on the board, ask for ideas for the next line. Get several ideas, putting them all to one side of the board. Choose one that seems workable—not necessarily the best—and write it under the first line. Continue in this fashion, adding lines until the poem is complete. Leave it on the board and create more examples with the class. Don't forget to use the thesaurus and dictionary routinely as you work with the class.

Have an example or two from a collection or resource in reserve in the event the session begins to flounder. You can use an example on the board and rewrite it into a totally different poem, while relying on the sense of the poem for the new version. Discuss and show that it is acceptable to struggle, rewrite, and use existing poetry for inspiration. Few of us have totally new ideas, we usually take the known and improve upon it or lend it our own interpretation.

When a poem has a definite structure, such as the diamante, knowing how to format or arrange the poem on the page is integrated into its creation. Other types of poetry which depend on format for part of the interpretation are often quite complex and should probably be delayed until students are more experienced. To alleviate fears of being unable to format the poems, reassure students that they will be given guidance shaping the final version of their poems.

Knowing when to let the students begin writing their poems takes only a bit of observation. Inevitably you will have some students who work laboriously over one poem, taking more time than you can allow, while others will be done in five minutes. In anticipation of those who will hurry through the process, tell the students that if they get done with their poems quickly, they are expected to create another one (or two or three), adding that you will be looking forward to reading *all* their poems. This generally elicits more thoughtful efforts.

Allowing an uninterrupted work session at this point is most ideal, although I have seen students set aside their writing and return successfully to it later. Be sure there are thesauri and dictionaries available centrally or throughout the room to enable the students to work independently.

Circulate through the room while students work, reading poems in progress, and offering help as needed. Make note of especially good poems for sharing later in the period or the next day. You can ensure a good sharing period by quietly complimenting an individual's poem and asking if you can share it with the class later. If the student hesitates, ask if you could share it anonymously. Once you have established an atmosphere of trust, you will have an ample number of volunteers.

It is generally more successful for the teacher to read the students' works to the class, rather than asking the students to read their own poems. You may need help with reading creatively spelled words (remember to read phonetically), but if you are in control of this portion of the session, you will maintain the necessary dignity.

If you have time, share some of the students' poems during the same period. Reassure them that you don't expect polished work, but that their poems will help others who are still struggling for ideas. Once you have shared several poems, ask if anyone else would like to have a poem read. Often a reluctant poet will feel more comfortable by that time. Planning to share more poems on the next day as well allows students to work up their courage and provides more reinforcement for the next step of the process.

Revision

The day after students have had a writing session, put an unpolished poem of your own on the board. Discuss where you are having problems and ask for help from the class. Beginning writers often use crutches such as "and then ..." or "so...." Show how the meaning usually remains the same without these mundane connectors. Work through your poem, cutting, revising, deleting, or adding, discussing each change you make. At times, leave some changes unresolved. This gives the message that poems may be "in progress" for some time.

Ask for volunteers for public revision and first read through the poem aloud. Before proceeding to *any* revision make several *positive* comments about the poem and ask for other compliments (see "What to Say during Sharing" in chapter 8). Then quickly write the poem on the board in approximately the same format as the student's poem.

Begin the revision with some comments of your own. It is important that you not dictate changes. Begin your sentences with words such as:

You might consider changing ...

One suggestion might be ...

Did you think about ...

A small change here might ...

This made me think of _____ —is that what you meant?

You might want to add ...

It won't take much to clarify ...

Then ask the class to suggest modifications the poet *might* consider. If you have modeled the above process tactfully, your students will follow your lead. Interspersing positive statements with the student suggestions will also help maintain a balance. Always close with the positive comment, "I'm looking forward to the final version."

After your students have become familiar with revision techniques and have learned supportive behavior, use paired revision, much like paired peer editing. Students can work on their poetry in pairs or small groups, coming to the whole group when problems can't be solved.

Formats

Learning to format poems is a challenging process. Having several collections or copies of poems available for study is particularly helpful. Ask your librarian for suggestions or browse through the poetry section for useful anthologies.

Plan a session on the format, and structure the lesson in the same fashion as the revision session. Use a poem of your own and struggle through the formatting process with the class. Then ask for a volunteer's poem, read the poem aloud, compliment it, put it on the board and begin the revision process with the same types of nondictatorial comments as above. Then write the new version alongside the draft, so there is a visual record of the format. If the students struggle with writing, I often allow them to copy the revision from the board. With more confident writers, I go through the formatting and then erase the poem, forcing them to make their own format choices.

After doing several on the board, most students will get the idea. You will have to do a session of formatting nearly every time you introduce a new type of poem, but the students will catch on more quickly as they become more experienced. Some poems allow for refinement of the format during the earlier revision stage, eliminating the need for a separate session. There will be some who simply won't understand the process. With those, individual conferences take only a few minutes and provide the support that permits them to keep trying and risking. Use a bright pen and put slashes where line endings are appropriate. For the student who is wrestling with this step, you might want to rewrite the poem quickly, asking if this is acceptable, and letting the student copy it. Modify the process to fit the needs of both the group and the individual, but always keep in mind that the mechanics of the format should never stall the creative process.

TEACHING INDIVIDUAL FORMS OF POETRY

The following forms of poetry are chosen because they have been routinely successful with elementary students. They will be described without further discussion regarding the process outlined above, except when modifications in presentation are indicated. Note will be made of the level of difficulty when appropriate.

Acrostic Poems

An acrostic poem, explained in further detail in chapter 9, is an excellent form for various holidays or special needs.

Examples:

<u>V</u>ictory and

<u>E</u>xecution are different

<u>T</u>riumphs of the always

<u>E</u>xcrutiating war.

<u>R</u>emember the

<u>A</u>rmy,

<u>N</u>avy and other

<u>S</u>oldiers who fell in the war.

>   Colin Strickland
>   grade four

<u>S</u>piders

<u>P</u>erfecting their

<u>I</u>nvisible webs.

<u>D</u>evouring insects foolish

<u>E</u>nough to dumbly

<u>R</u>un into the spider's trap.

>   Colin Strickland
>   grade four

Alphabet Poems

Alphabet poems are the ultimate acrostic, except that the letters do not relate to the subject. Rather, the subject is shown in the title, and the beginning letter of each word is dictated by the alphabet. This is a good way to begin the school year, especially using the subject of school. You will quickly learn who has a positive or negative attitude about school; I once had a fourth-grader who spent a couple of hours poring over the dictionary and thesaurus looking for every negative word he could find to include in his alphabet poem.

The alphabet poem in particular is an excellent device for introducing the use of the thesaurus and dictionary. It is necessary to cheat a bit when you get to the letter x. Put some examples on the board such as "xcellent" and "xciting" to show how sometimes it is okay to use "poetic license."

For the younger students, finding twenty-six words in alphabetical order is quite a challenge. For older students, you can introduce the idea of using phrases that tie together lines with each line beginning with the letter of the alphabet. "School" is a mixture of words and phrases:

Example:

School

An apple for the teacher	Noisy
Books for reading and math	Overworked
Correcting papers	Principal
Desks and drawers	Quiz
Exclamation marks	Recess
Friends	Summer vacation
Graphs	Teachers
Hoping school's over soon	Understanding
Ignoring the teacher	Verb
Joking around	Wise
Knowledge	eXhausting
Learning	Young
Math book	Zany

Benjie Hiller
grade two

Another variation is to write the poem in phrases, but each word begins with the letters of the alphabet within the phrases.

Example:

A Bright Child Doing

Educational Fractions.

Getting Homework.

Innovative Jumping, Kicking,

Laughing, and Mingling

Nicely in Outdoor Play.

Quietly Reading.

Sitting Tight Until

Vigorously We eXit.

Yeah, Zoom!

Paige Nilson
grade five

In this third variation, each line has several words starting with the same letters. The example, "Animals," follows this style with the added stipulation of having to use a noun, verb, and adverb. This is an excellent way to integrate a bit of grammar and thesaurus usage, but it should only be undertaken with experienced writers due to its level of difficulty.

Example:

Alphabet Animals

Aardvarks ate anxiously

Bears bite badly

Cats climb carefully

Dogs dig desperately

Elephants eat earlier

Ferrets fight fiercely

Goats gobble grossly

Hippos hitchhike hurriedly

Ibex improvise impulsively

Jellyfish jiggle joyfully

Koalas kiss kindly

Leopards leap lethally

Monkeys meddle menacingly

Newfoundlands nod nervously

Octopi oggle oddly

Peacocks parade proudly

Quails quake quietly

Raccoons race rapidly

Snakes slither silently

Turtles toil tiresomely

Unicorns unite unanimously

Vipers violate violently

Whales whistle wildly

X

Yaks yoddle yearly

Zebras zap zealously

Philip McGrath
grade four

Diamante Poetry

As discussed in chapter 9, diamante poems have a specific form that is a bit more challenging, but is generally very successful. A bonus is that your students become acquainted with grammar terminology. For the specific format see page 127.

Examples:

Soldier

Brave, bold

Fighting, daring, shooting

Always   trying   to   win

Falling, trying, winning

Tired, proud

Warrior

Paige Nilson
grade four

Moods

Sad, happy

Crying, eating, singing

Moods   change   every   moment

Walking, sleeping, watching

Mad,   glad

Feelings

Tim Miller
grade five

A variation of the diamante is to have a shift in the fourth line, indicating a new focus and ending with an antonym (see chapter 9).

Examples:

Friends

Great, nice

Understanding, caring, sharing

helping you-------------------mean, evil

Hurting, hating, killing

Terrible, horrible

Enemies

Tami Doi
grade five

List Poem

The Teachers and Writers Handbook of Poetic Forms discusses the list poem. "It is particularly suitable for people just beginning to write poetry, because its form is flexible and its content has authenticity by virtue of its often being derived from the writer's personal experience."[1]

The list poem details an event, describes a series of events, or lists the qualities of someone, something, or someplace. Rhymed or unrhymed, it is an excellent way to reinforce organization of thoughts, as it is important that the lines are in the proper sequence.

Examples:

My First Day of Kindergarten

"Go into the office, the big door on your first right."

Clickitat, clickitat ding, zooom, dering, dering.

"Oh let's see, Mrs. Stein, first floor. I'm sure you'll find it."

     step

       step

         step

           step

            step

              Mrs. Stein

Butterflies beat, flap, beat

What a large room — and a small me.

There are five children, and an old teacher, tables, books,

       chairs, toys, signs, and a

          Piano

To the corner I go, blang, blang, blang.

Dragging me away

Screaming, kicking, whining tears, bulgy eyes

     tears

       tears

       tears

         Hush!

Stillness, very quiet.

Scary, very scary.

I am fine now. We read, write, play, sing, and work.

The day is over.

Good-bye Mrs. Stein.

Sleepy

ZZZZZZZZZZZZZZ

                 Emily Waters
                 grade four

Scoring My First Goal

Riding to the game, sweaty and nervous,
I'm there, practicing, wondering about the game.
Game time, the butterflies have taken over,
The whistle blows and we're off,
Running
Kicking
Tripping
The most fun I've ever had.
Charging to the goal
Dribbling the ball.
Knowing they will take it away like always,
But they miss the ball,
A clear shot on goal,
I kick the ball—it's in the air gliding
Into the goal.

Running
Jumping
Slapping hands
Yelling
And then to await the kick off,
The first goal I ever scored!

> Kevin Smith
> grade four

Couplet

A couplet is a good introduction to the use of rhyming words, as it can be limited to one couplet or expanded to include several couplets. A poem of one couplet requires an economy and power which is challenging. Demonstrating to the class how couplets can be written in pairs in an aa, bb, cc fashion is a good foundation for other forms that require sequential understanding.

Example:

A Walk in a Rainstorm

I walk around and smush the worms.
Oh, how they squiggle! How they squirm!
I try and try but don't know why
The worms come out when it ain't dry.

> Benjie Hiller
> grade two

Epistle

Teaching the epistle provides a lesson in letter writing while allowing students an opportunity to use free verse. It does not have to rhyme; it merely must be in letter form and sound poetic. This is a good form for Valentine's Day, Mother's Day, Father's Day, or any time when a letter would be special.

Example:

Dear Mom,

You are like a sun out of a valley of flowers.

You give me light when I am lost.

When I fall you touch my soft skin with rays of tenderness.

When I grow tired I lay down and you darken the sky,

letting me rest.

For you are my mother, my generous, loving mother.

Emily White
grade five

Limerick

Limericks may seem easy, but the requirements of rhythm make them challenging. Lines one, two, and five have three beats and they rhyme. Lines three and four have two beats and they rhyme. The sound of a good limerick is unmistakable and they are always expected to be humorous. Older students will have to listen carefully to hear the three beats versus the two beats. Using nonsense syllables and chanting while tapping the accent helps internalize the pattern:

Ta <u>da</u> ta, ta <u>da</u> ta, ta <u>da.</u>

Ta <u>da</u> ta, ta <u>da</u> ta, ta <u>da.</u>

Ta <u>da</u> ta, ta <u>da.</u>

Ta <u>da</u> ta, ta <u>da.</u>

Ta <u>da</u> ta, ta <u>da</u> ta, ta <u>da.</u>

Example:

There was an old teacher one day

Who realized she wanted to play.

She sent the kids home

And stayed all alone,

But never received any pay.

Concrete Poetry

Concrete poems are visual forms of word play. For the experienced poet, they provide a whimsical alternative to lines and prescribed format. The words are arranged on the page to enhance the message of the poem visually. Since it is difficult to describe these poems in words, you need to have copies of concrete poems available or put several on the board. Students will enjoy using their markers, different styles of printing, and other special effects. Those with computers will especially enjoy the challenge of creating a poem using the capabilities of a computer.

Example:

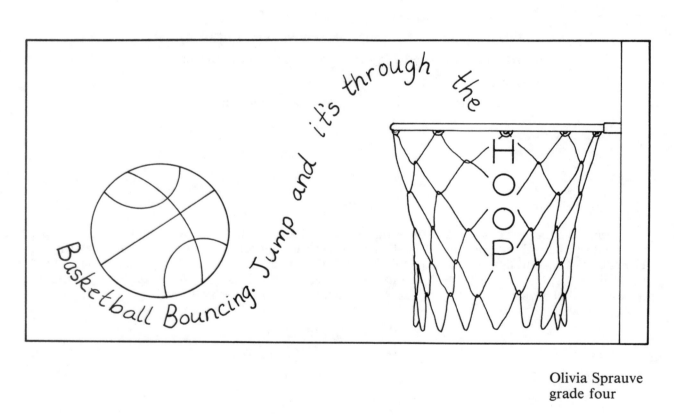

Olivia Sprauve
grade four

Chants

Often students know several chants from jumping rope or playing hand games. Chants are most easily taught by reading several, asking students for chants they already know, generating themes to use for the chant line, creating one or two, and letting them create. The form is most easily explained if you point out that the poem is a rhyming one with the chant line coming between each rhyming line. Use these examples on popular themes to show the form:

Examples:

She is my friend.
She has brown eyes.
She is my friend.
She eats yellow fries.
She is my friend.
Does she like any guys?
She is my friend.
Why must she say good-bye?

Hadley Smith
grade three

School is making me sick.
But summer's almost here.
School is nothing but ick.
But summer's almost here.
School is making me ticked.
But summer's almost here.
School deserves a big kick.
BUT SUMMER'S ALMOST HERE!

Benjie Hiller
grade two

School's almost out.
Winter is a bummer.
School's almost out.
I love summer.
School's almost out.
You do get dumber.
School's almost out.
Your brain gets number.
School's almost out.
In fall I'm a newcomer.
BUT SCHOOL'S ALMOST OUT!

Gina Dardano
grade four

Let's go sailing on a sailing ship.
When the wind blows.
Let's go sailing on a sailing ship.
What the captain says goes.
Let's go sailing on a sailing ship.
While the sun glows.
Let's go sailing on a sailing ship.
And the water flows.

Chris Guillot
grade four

THEMATIC POETRY

I Remember Poems

A form of poetry introduced to me by poet, writer, and teacher Jack Collom, is the "I Remember" poem. It has no particular form, although it is similar in style to the list poem. It provides a good introduction to free verse, as the students become more fascinated with their remembrances than with rhyming or rhythm. This type of poem often requires a fair amount of revision, as the first drafts are usually in prose form. Use all types of revision processes: giving individual conferences, using the overhead projector or board to revise a volunteer's poem (or your poem), and paired revision. Try introducing this with Cynthia Rylant's book, *When I Was Young in the Mountains*.

Examples:

The Christmas I Remember

I remember a Christmas when the dog knocked down the tree.

I remember trying to stay up late to see Santa.

    I was too tired.

I remember decorating the tree and putting up the star.

I remember visiting Santa, but his beard fell off.

I remember making cookies and eating half the dough.

    I still liked what was left of them.

                        Emily Waters
                        grade four

The First Day of School

The first day of school

I was shivering and whivering.

I was certainly scared.

I did not know my teacher very well.

The class room was funny and weird,

    weird and funny.

I did not know my room number,

    but of course it is room 122.

My teacher looked nice, very nice.

But she just isn't my mom.

                        Julia Steiner
                        grade one

Hiding Places Poetry

Poet Craig Czury believes that secret hiding places are the primary entrance to all children, and, from his experience with teaching poetry, it is apparent that children (and grown-up children) love to share their secrets. I have used Czury's theme with *Your Own Best Secret Place* by Byrd Baylor and Peter Parnall. The theme intrigues even the most reluctant learner; I have watched a nearly nonreading fifth-grade boy struggle for an hour to tell about his secret place using his limited primer vocabulary. Those four simple lines were a major achievement. (If a student claims to have no hiding place, adapt it to "special place.")

If you have the *Random House Book of Poetry*, edited by Jack Prelutsky, use "Keziah," "I'm Alone in the Evening," "Up in the Pine," and "Waking" for examples. With older students, add Baylor and Parnall's book.

Examples:

My Secret Place

A small hammock by my cabin
It comforts you so very tight
Lean to your right
      and hear the river as it rushes fast
Lean to your left
      you hear the river in the background
      of the crisp silence that flows through your ears.
Then you fall asleep into a world of dreams.

> Kevin Smith
> grade four

A small cave big enough for two
      behind a clear waterfall glistening in the sun.
The trees shadow the small river below.
Great mounds of sand tower above my head.
The sun beating down on the hot sand and
      the constant trickle of the waterfall
      rings in my ears.

> Chris Meyer
> grade four

My secret place is in my room.
I read and hide there.
It's under my bed, hidden very well.
One of these days I'll read there again,
And it will be how it has been for ever and ever.
My other secret place is hidden even better.
It's in the dining room corner, behind a little bench.
No one knows about that, except for me.
It's my favorite one, and it always will be.

> Steven Kingsbury
> grade three

Big Trouble Poetry

Getting in trouble is another concept originated by Czury that can be used as a classroom writing exercise. Using examples of getting in trouble from your own childhood as a warm up will intrigue your students and disarm any reluctant poets. Initiating this theme by writing a group poem allows all students to participate. This is especially effective when introducing poetry or at the beginning of the year. The following finished poems were created by Czury from fragments of the students' writing as a group collaborative.

Examples:

Big Trouble

Means I can't go out of my house
after school.

Not allowed to watch TV.

No radio.

I have to stay in my room
for a week.

I can't leave my yard
for the weekend.

Have to pooper-scoop the yard.

And lose my allowance.

And can't ride my bike
for the whole summer.

No dinner or worthwhile snacks.

Can't have any friends over.

And I'm not allowed to talk
on the phone for at least 1 week!

Big Trouble means school.

Having to stay in the office
for recess 2 weeks.

And not being able to go
to the last 2 soccer games.

Getting a detention
and having to write:
I'll never get in trouble again
for 3 hours.

You Know You're in Big Trouble When ...

Your sister comes up to your room
and says: Mom wants to see you!

You're alone with your mom
and a vase flies across the room
and the dog whines.

You kick the soccer ball
and hit the outside light.

You come home from the creek
4 hours late soaking wet.

Your dad yells at you for having
a kick fight under the table.

You put eye shadow on your baby brother.

You kick the bathroom door
and make a hole in it.

Your dad falls into a trap
you forgot about at your fort.

You roll toothpaste onto layers
of toilet paper to make a sandwich.

Big Trouble when ...

You break the lamp in a rented house.

You sneak your dad's fishing pole
and it breaks.

You wake up and the bubble gum
you went to bed with in your mouth
is all over the sheets and your hair.

You wear your sister's stockings to school.

Stuff your spinach into your napkin.

Peg the neighbor's house with eggs
and your mom gets a phone call.[2]

SPECIAL INTEREST POETRY

This is a form that describes a person's special interest, whether it be sports, a hobby, a favorite activity, or even school. Begin by brainstorming topics on the board: soccer, baseball, playing the piano, reading, sleeping, hanging out, jogging, rock and roll, dance, etc. Next have students select their topics and make lists of words associated with their topics. Have the students exchange papers with someone who will help them think of more words for their interest. Finally, have them begin to play with the words and thoughts, forming their poems. Some students may want to use forms such as the acrostic for their poems.

Examples:

Skiing

Sliding down hills in the snow
     going as fast as I can possibly go.
All of a sudden I fall with a plop
     and come to a very big stop.
I hop up and go
     without saying whoa
And go down the rest
     of the hill in the snow.

        Jessica Cambier
        grade four

Dancing is

A very

Nice way of expressing yourself

Coming alive with action.

Interesting art of your body and mind

Neat music and sound.

Giving all I have to this wonderful, thrilling feeling.

        Emily White
        grade four

CRYSTAL BALL POETRY

Children usually have definite ideas about what they will be like or do when they grow up. Writing crystal ball poems is a fascinating glimpse into a child's hopes and dreams. Begin by brainstorming ideas of vocations students might choose, places to live, avocations, family styles. To keep the poetry thoughtful, avoid introducing the material acquisition aspects as the students will think of this themselves.

Examples:

My Life

I will go to college and stay in school.

I will be a lawyer and not be too cool.

I will go to court and win some cases.

I will wear a dress with silk and laces.

My friends and I will go out to eat

See other lawyers and maybe we'll meet.

Tanesha Thomas
grade five

Crystal Ball

A quiet house along the shore,

Driving ten miles to the convenience store.

Only one pet, a big sweet dog

Who likes to chase sea gulls in the morning fog.

Behind my computer I sit and write

About heroes with powerful might.

Catching crabs and eating clams

Picking berries and making fresh jams.

Small room and simple in a blue house

With my dog and me there's hardly room for anything else.

My little house, by the sea,

This is a place where I can be free.

Paige Nilson
grade five

WORD PLAY

Integrating word play into the poetry lessons expands the possibilities for creativity. Each of the following devices could be taught in a separate lesson, but they are more effective if they are introduced when they fit with a particular poetic form. For example, the alphabet poem that has three A words, then three B words, etc., is a perfect introduction to the meaning of alliteration.

Become familiar with the following kinds of word play and comment upon their usage when you are writing group poems, teaching formatting, or reading poetry aloud.

Alliteration

Alliteration occurs when two or more words have the same beginning sound. It may be obvious and intentional or more subtle:

Aardvarks ate anxiously.

Bears bite badly.

Hyperbole

In a word, hyperbole is exaggeration. By their very nature, students are masters of hyperbole.

"I would die if I had to sit by him."

"I am too tired to move today."

"That assignment was a piece of _____."

Capitalize on their love of exaggeration by showing how it can be refined into an effective form of description.

Imagery

You will routinely come across phrases that effectively portray images. Point these out during your literature instruction and when you read poetry. Soon students will be commenting on the images they enjoyed in their reading.

Metaphor/Simile

Metaphor can serve as a collective term for all figurative language or as a device that shows similarity between two things:

Cleaning his room was a nightmare.

His poem was a work of art.

A simile uses a linking word such as "like" or "as" to make the comparison.

Cleaning his room was like living a nightmare.

His poem was as fine as a work of art.

Onomatopoeia

Words like "swish," "pop," and "boom" characterize onomatopoeia because they sound like their meanings. Students enjoy finding examples of these, even if they can never remember the term for the device:

Clickitat, clickitat ding, zooom, dering, dering.

Personification

Providing nonhuman beings or things with human behavior is personification. It provides variety and interest to poetry.

Repetition, Rhyme, and Rhythm

Although these elements do not need definition, they are included because we often forget that although they may seem obvious to us, students will need to learn how to recognize them. Point out effective use of each when sharing poetry with the class.

CONCLUSION

The suggestions in this chapter are intended to inspire you to risk the reading and writing of poetry with your students. They are just the beginning of what should be your own exploration and discovery. Once you have tried several of these forms or themes, you will begin to develop your own themes. During a residency in Wilmington, Delaware, Czury collected student poems which included titles such as "Morning Sounds," "Preparing for Summer," "Photo," "In My Photo," "The Best," "A Bad Day," "When There Was No Gravity," "Lost," "My Chore," "Rainy Day," and "Deep Trouble." He states that many poems were exercises he designed on the spot, by just walking in and looking at the students' faces. As you work with your students, be alert to events that you can use for writing. Soon you will find that poets live in all of us.

NOTES

[1]Ron Padgett, ed., *The Teachers and Writers Handbook of Poetic Forms* (New York: Teachers and Writers Collaborative, 1987), 106.

[2]Craig Czury and Charlestown fifth graders, Great Valley School District, Chester County, Pa., 1986-1987. *Big Trouble* was produced from an Artist In Education Residency through the Pennsylvania Council on the Arts and Great Valley School District, choreographed and staged as part of an original play, *It's Not Easy Being a Kid*, with Charlestown Elementary School fifth graders.

REFERENCES

Baylor, Byrd. *Your Own Best Secret Place*. Illustrated by Peter Parnall. New York: Charles Scribner's Sons, 1979.

Collom, Jack. *Moving Windows: Evaluating the Poetry Children Write*. New York: Teachers and Writers Collaborative, 1985.

Lipson, Greta Barclay, and Jane A. Romatowski. *Calliope: A Handbook of 47 Poetic Forms and Figures of Speech*. Carthage, Ill.: Good Apple, Inc., 1981.

Rylant, Cynthia. *When I Was Young in the Mountains*. Illustrated by Diane Goode. New York: E. P. Dutton, 1982.

OTHER RESOURCES

Adams, Adrienne, ed. and illus. *Poetry of Earth*. New York: Charles Scribner's Sons, 1972.

Amon, Aline, ed. and illus. *The Earth Is Sore: Native Americans on Nature*. New York: Atheneum, 1981.

Bodecker, N. M. *Let's Marry Said the Cherry and Other Nonsense Poems*. New York: Atheneum, 1974.

Brewton, John E., and Lorraine A. Blackburn, eds. *They've Discovered a Head in the Box for the Bread and Other Laughable Limericks*. Illustrated by Fernando Krahn. New York: Thomas Y. Crowell, 1978.

Brewton, Sara, et al., eds. *My Tang's Tungled and Other Ridiculous Situations*. New York: Thomas Y. Crowell, 1973.

Cole, William. *Poem Stew*. Illustrated by Karen Weinhaus. New York: J. B. Lippincott, 1981.

Dahl, Roald. *Revolting Rhymes*. Illustrated by Quentin Blake. New York: Alfred A. Knopf, Inc., 1982.

Dunning, Stephen, et al., eds. *Reflections on a Gift of Watermelon Pickle and Other Modern Verse*. New York: Lothrop, Lee and Shepard, 1967.

Esbensen, Barbara Juster. *Words with Wrinkled Knees: Animal Poems*. Illustrated by John Stadler. New York: Thomas Y. Crowell, 1986.

Fisher, Aileen. *Out in the Dark and the Daylight*. New York: Harper and Row, Publishers, 1980.

Fleischman, Paul. *Joyful Noise: Poems for Two Voices*. Illustrated by Eric Beddows. New York: Harper and Row, Publishers, 1988.

Fleming, Alice, ed. *America Is Not All Traffic Lights: Poems of the Midwest*. Boston: Little, Brown and Company, 1976.

Frost, Robert. *A Swinger of Birches: Poems of Robert Frost for Young People*. Owings Mill, Md.: Stemmer House, 1982.

Holman, Felice. *The Song in My Head*. Illustrated by Jim Spanfeller. New York: Charles Scribner's Sons, 1985.

Hooper, Patricia. *A Bundle of Beasts*. Illustrated by Mark Steele. Boston: Houghton Mifflin Company, 1987.

Hopkins, Lee Bennett. *The Sky Is Full of Song*. Illustrated by Dirk Zimmer. New York: Harper and Row, Publishers, 1983.

Kennedy, X. J. *The Forgetful Wishing Well: Poems for Young People*. Illustrated by David McPhail. New York: Atheneum, 1985.

Little, Lessie Jones. *Children of Long Ago*. Illustrated by Jan Spivey Gilchrist. New York: Philomel Books, 1988.

Livingston, Myra Cohn. *Celebrations*. Illustrated by Leonard Everett Fisher. New York: Holiday House, 1985.

_____. *Earth Songs*. Illustrated by Leonard Everett Fisher. New York: Holiday House, 1986.

Lowe, A. Mifflin. *Beasts by the Bunches*. Illustrated by Susan J. Harrison. Garden City, N.Y.: Doubleday and Company, Inc., 1987.

McNaughton, Colin. *There's an Awful Lot of Weirdos in Our Neighborhood and Other Wickedly Funny Verse*. New York: Simon and Schuster, Inc., 1987.

Merriam, Eve. *A Sky Full of Poems*. Illustrated by Walter Gaffney-Kessell. New York: Dell Publishing Company, Inc., 1986.

Prelutsky, Jack. *The Headless Horseman Rides Tonight: More Poems to Trouble Your Sleep*. Illustrated by Arnold Lobel. New York: Greenwillow Books, 1980.

_____. *The New Kid on the Block*. Illustrated by James Stevenson. New York: Scholastic, Inc., 1984.

_____. *Nightmares: Poems to Trouble Your Sleep*. Illustrated by Arnold Lobel. New York: Greenwillow Books, 1976.

_____, ed. *Random House Book of Poetry for Children*. Illustrated by Arnold Lobel. New York: Random House, Inc., 1983.

Rosen, Michael, ed. *Children's Library Poetry*. New York: Simon and Schuster, Inc., 1985.

Shakespeare, William. *Under the Greenwood Tree: Shakespeare for Young People*. Illustrated by Robin and Pat DeWitt. Owings Mills, Md.: Stemmer House, 1986.

Silverstein, Shel. *A Light in the Attic*. New York: Harper and Row, Publishers, 1981.

_____. *Where the Sidewalk Ends*. New York: Harper and Row, Publishers, 1974.

Viorst, Judith. *If I Were in Charge of the World and Other Worries*. New York: Atheneum, 1981.

Wallace, Daisy, ed. *Fairy Poems*. Illustrated by Trina Schart Hyman. New York: Holiday House, 1980.

_____. *Witch Poems*. Illustrated by Trina Schart Hyman. New York: Holiday House, 1976.

Wheeler, M. J. *First Came the Indians*. Illustrated by James Houston. New York: Atheneum, 1983.

Willard, Nancy. *A Visit to William Blake's Inn: Poems for Innocent and Experienced Travelers*. Illustrated by Alice Provensen and Martin Provensen. San Diego, Calif.: Harcourt Brace Jovanovich, 1981.

Chapter 11

Books to Savor
My First Choices for the
Literate Classroom

By now, you have read about ideas that will enhance your program, and you have probably recognized the need of having many books to accomplish teaching in a literate classroom. If you are new to the teaching field or to alternative programs, you may feel overwhelmed at choosing a starting point.

This chapter provides titles of the books I return to most often, the books I savor. They are suggested as a starting point for your program. This list could be used to assemble a classroom collection from your school, public, or professional library for use on a long-term basis. While you use these books, you will be able gradually to expand your list of favorites to determine which books are worth acquiring for your permanent collection.

Annotations include suggestions for usage and comments regarding the book itself. You might find folktales for art lessons and picture books for teaching music. Since there are so many different ways to use a single book, especially in a thematic study, each book will be listed under what is considered its primary category: folktale, poetry, picture book, etc. Also, there will be references to several areas of usage, as appropriate, and as you begin to use books, you will easily recognize how to utilize books in every subject.

ART, MUSIC, AND DANCE

Anno, Mitsumasa, and Masaichiro Anno. *Anno's Magical ABC: An Anamorphic Alphabet*. New York: Philomel Books, 1981.

The illustrations come into focus through using an enclosed reflective cylinder. All students are fascinated with the process and the older art students can use the directions to create their own anamorphic drawings. Use with the alphabet unit discussed in chapter 4.

Hoban, Tana. *Take Another Look*. New York: Greenwillow Books, 1981.

Hoban's photographs can be puzzling or misleading until the reader turns the cover page to reveal the true source of the photograph. Use in art to study perspective and layout, or as a class "look aloud" for prediction and critical thinking.

Jonas, Ann. *Round Trip*. New York: Greenwillow Books, 1983.

After taking a trip into town, the reader reverses the book for the trip home. The black and white drawings are intriguing examples of the use of positive/negative images.

Prokofiev, Serge. *Peter and the Wolf*. Illustrated by Barbara Cooney. New York: Viking Press, 1985.

This pop-up version is especially appealing to all ages and is well suited to the study of the music, story, Russia, and musical instruments.

Rosenberg, Jane. *Dance Me a Story: Twelve Tales from the Classic Ballets*. New York: Thames and Hudson, Inc., 1985.

The twelve stories include several fairy tales and are illustrated in the ballet theme. Use with the study of the music and the literature.

FABLES, FOLKTALES, AND FAIRY TALES

Ahlberg, Janet, and Peter Ahlberg. *The Jolly Postman or Other People's Letters*. Boston: Little Brown and Company, 1986.
Inspire elementary students to create their own missives from fairy tale characters with this charming collection of letters, advertisements, and official fairy tale communications.

Bell, Anthea. *The Wise Queen*. Illustrated by Chihiro Iwasaki. New York: Picture Book Studio, USA, 1986 (text) and 1984 (illustrations).
Use in a study of alternative fairy tales to show nonstereotypical female heroes. Iwasaki's illustrations are delicate and lovely, ideal for use with watercolor instruction.

Brown, Marcia, trans. and illus. *Shadow*. New York: Charles Scribner's Sons, 1982.
Brown's illustrations of this African folktale should inspire older art students to explore methods of illustrating traditional tales or to create their own shadow art.

Clement, Claude. *The Painter and the Wild Swans*. Illustrated by Frederic Clement. New York: Dial Books, 1986.
The Clements, who are not related, have created a stunning version of a tragic Japanese folktale. In the margins, the story is repeated in Japanese characters. Notes about the tale provide intriguing background. Use when studying Japan, art, and/or folktales.

Cole, Joanna, ed. *Best-loved Folk Tales of the World*. Illustrated by Jill Karla Schwarz. New York: Anchor Press/Doubleday, 1983.
Cole has gathered folktales from even the most remote islands of the world, making this a must for the multicultural classroom. It also has a generous representation of female heroes. Use it to show the universality of our world's stories.

Heyer, Marilee, reteller and illus. *The Weaving of a Dream*. New York: Viking Kestrel, 1986.
Heyer has created a lavish tapestry of illustrations for this haunting Chinese folktale. Use for the study of art, China, or folk literature.

Lobel, Arnold. *Fables*. New York: Harper and Row, Publishers, 1980.
Lobel's clever fables offer contemporary alternatives to the traditional collections. Use for a reading and writing unit on fables with any grade level.

McDermott, Gerald. *Arrow to the Sun*. New York: Viking Press, 1974.
Sun art is universal to all cultures. Use McDermott's version of a Pueblo tale to instigate research on sun art and to inspire artistic efforts.

McKinley, Robin. *Beauty: A Retelling of the Story of Beauty and Beast*. New York: Pocket Books, 1979.
Nearly every word in McKinley's novel-length version of *Beauty and the Beast* seems carefully selected for its beauty or power. Read aloud to mature listeners of age ten and older while studying folk literature.

Riordan, James, ed. *The Woman in the Moon and Other Tales of Forgotten Heroines*. Illustrated by Angela Barrett. New York: Dial Books for Young Readers, 1985.
Several collections of folktales about female heroes have been published (see chapter 9), but Riordan's remains a favorite for his selections and the color illustrations. Use when reading and writing traditional or alternative folktales.

Shannon, George. *Stories to Solve: Folktales from Around the World*. Illustrated by Peter Sis. New York: Greenwillow Books, 1985.

Read aloud each brief folktale and challenge students to solve the mystery or problem. Students can find other folktales that may be similarly structured. Use for critical thinking, research, creative writing, or in the study of folktales.

Zelinsky, Paul O., reteller and illus. *Rumplestiltskin*. New York: E. P. Dutton, 1986.

Oil paintings are the basis for Zelinsky's brilliant rendering of this familiar tale. His spun gold fairly shimmers on the page. Use to integrate art with folktales.

PICTURE BOOKS

Aliki. *How a Book Is Made*. New York: Thomas Y. Crowell, 1986.

No in-school publishing house should be without Aliki's description of the birth of a book. Use to inspire and inform writers in any grade.

Carle, Eric. *The Very Busy Spider*. New York: Philomel Books, 1985.

Primary students love to trace the spider's raised web in Carle's brightly illustrated picture book. Use in any art class or with primary science.

Lent, Blair. *Bayberry Bluff*. Boston: Houghton Mifflin Company, 1987.

The development of the town of Bayberry Bluff is told with simple lines and color illustrations. Use in the study of oral history or to develop a picture book of the history of your school's community. For primary students, use in the study of communities.

Müller, Jörg. *The Changing City*. New York: Atheneum, 1976.

The modernization of a composite, fictional city in Europe is demonstrated in a series of large, color tri-folds. Intermediate and older students will pore over the changes shown to occur every three years as a village becomes totally urbanized. Use with Lent's *Bayberry Bluff* to stimulate research, to develop community awareness, or as a visual timeline.

Numeroff, Laura Joffe. *If You Give a Mouse a Cookie*. Illustrated by Felicia Bond. New York: Harper and Row, Publishers, 1985.

The visual perspective of the reader changes throughout this charming tale of a rather demanding, but engaging, visiting mouse. Use in art classes or have students write about what might happen when giving other animals cookies.

Van Allsburg, Chris. *Jumanji*. Boston: Houghton Mifflin Company, 1982.

When children follow the rules of this game, it comes alive with adventure. Use with a series of lessons on games and following directions, concluding with writing about what happens when the next players of *Jumanji* do not follow the directions.

_____. *The Mysteries of Harris Burdick*. Boston: Houghton Mifflin Company, 1984.

Each set of facing pages provides a haunting illustration and one or two provocative lines of text. Use in intermediate or older writing classes to stimulate writing of the story behind the pictures.

_____. *The Z Was Zapped*. Boston: Houghton Mifflin Company, 1987.

This unique alphabet book involves listeners in guessing what has happened to each illustrated letter. It is perfect for prediction and critical thinking for all ages.

Williams, Barbara. *Little Old Lady Who Was Not Afraid of Anything*. Illustrated by Megan Lloyd. New York: Thomas Y. Crowell, 1986.

Williams's brightly illustrated tale is alive with movement and rhythm. Use with primary students for music, writing, and fun.

Wood, Audrey. *King Bidgood's in the Bathtub*. Illustrated by Don Wood. New York: Harcourt
     Brace Jovanovich, 1985.
     King Bidgood won't get out of the tub till a young page outsmarts him. This hilarious pattern
book is beloved by elementary students and is perfect as a model for student-written pattern books.

POETRY

Esbensen, Barbara Juster. *Words with Wrinkled Knees: Animal Poems*. Illustrated by John Stadler.
     New York: Thomas Y. Crowell, 1986.
     Whimsey and cleverness characterize Esbensen's animal poems. Use in the upper intermediate
through high school to inspire similar poetic forms.

Frost, Robert. *Stopping by Woods on a Snowy Evening*. Illustrated by Susan Jeffers. New York:
     E. P. Dutton, 1978.
     Use this graceful picture book as a model for illustrating single poems.

Hooper, Patricia. *A Bundle of Beasts*. Illustrated by Mark Steele. Boston: Houghton Mifflin
     Company, 1987.
     Hooper has created poems about groups of animals using terms even more rare than "gaggle of
geese." Use with upper intermediate and older students to study vocabulary, old English, or poetic
themes. Black and white illustrations. See Lowe for a companion or alternative volume.

Lowe, A. Mifflin. *Beasts by the Bunches*. Illustrated by Susan J. Harrison. Garden City, New York:
     Doubleday and Company, Inc., 1987.
     Similar to Hooper's collection, but illustrated in color, Lowe's beasts are clever and humor-
ous — especially the Boar, who is always Singular.

Prelutsky, Jack. *The New Kid on the Block*. Illustrated by James Stevenson. New York: Scholastic,
     Inc., 1984.
     Prelutsky's poems provide an irreverent look at childhood which will entertain children of all
ages. Keep this handy for spare moments when you can replace a "sponge" with a poem.

_____, ed. *Random House Book of Poetry*. Illustrated by Arnold Lobel. New York: Random
     House, Inc., 1983.
     Prelutsky has gathered together a variety of poems for all seasons, events, and emotions,
providing a useful collection.

Rosen, Michael, ed. *Children's Library Poetry*. New York: Simon and Schuster, 1985.
     Rosen has collected poems appropriate for all ages, with a variety of forms, topics, and
formats, plus occasional illustrations and plates.

WORD PLAY

Gwynne, Fred. *The King Who Rained*. New York: Simon and Schuster, Inc., 1970.
     Having a coat of arms, living in the present, and putting two coats of paint on a house are
literally interpreted in this clever picture book. Use with study of figurative language.

Juster, Norton. *Otter Nonsense*. Illustrated by Eric Carle. New York: Philomel Books, 1982.
     In this collection of animal puns, you can meet a locust and a highcust, a moose with a
mousetache and a mouse with a moosetache, a hippocrit, and a crocodull. Use with *Words with
Wrinkled Knees* to explore and create other animal word play.

Keller, Charles, ed. *News Breaks*. Illustrated by Michael Cooper. Englewood Cliffs, N.J.: Prentice-Hall, 1980.
>"The price of pigs went up and farmers went hog-wild." This is an example from Keller's collection of humorous news breaks. Although his are contrived, any newspaper will have headlines that can be interpreted both literally and figuratively. Keller has several other titles in the same vein.

TEACHER RESOURCES

Cullinan, Bernice E., ed. *Children's Literature in the Reading Program*. Newark, Del.: International Reading Association, 1987.
>Essays and "Teaching Idea(s)" on the use of children's literature provide philosophical and practical support for the classroom teacher.

Frank, Marjorie. *If You're Trying to Teach Kids How to Write, You've Gotta Have This Book*. Illustrated by Judy Howard. Nashville, Tenn.: Incentive Publications, 1979.
>In spite of an intensely busy format, Frank's book is full of wonderful idea lists for your writing program.

Fry, Edward B., Jacqueline K. Polk, and Dona Fountoukidis. *The Reading Teacher's Book of Lists*. Englewood Cliffs, N.J.: Prentice-Hall, 1984.
>Any list needed by any level teacher is found in this invaluable resource. Don't miss the report card euphemisms.

Goodman, Ken. *What's Whole in Whole Language?* Portsmouth, N.H.: Heinemann Educational Books, 1986.
>Goodman provides a quick overview of the philosophy and implementation basics of a whole language program.

Graves, Donald H. *Writing: Teachers and Children at Work*. Portsmouth, N.H.: Heinemann Educational Books, 1983.
>Graves's book is a necessity for all teachers of the writing process.

Lipson, Greta, and Jane Romatowski. *Calliope: A Handbook of 47 Poetic Forms and Figures of Speech*. Illustrated by Helen Sturges Nadler. Carthage, Ill.: Good Apple, Inc., 1981.
>Teaching poetry becomes easy with a good poetry collection and *Calliope*, described as "A Good Apple Idea and Activity Book for Grades 4-8."

Newman, Joan E. *Girls Are People Too! A Bibliography of Nontraditional Female Roles in Children's Books*. Metuchen, N.J.: The Scarecrow Press, Inc., 1982.
>The title of this resource is self-explanatory for teachers who are interested in providing a balanced literary experience.

Phillips, Kathleen C., and Barbara Steiner. *Creative Writing: A Handbook for Teaching Young People*. Illustrated by Robert B. Phillips. Littleton, Colo.: Libraries Unlimited, Inc., 1985.
>Phillips and Steiner provide an excellent resource for the teacher who needs practical ideas along with a sound philosophy of writing.

Reading is Fundamental. *Once Upon a Time*. New York: G. P. Putnam's Sons, 1986.
>Poetry, reflections, and anecdotes of authors have been collected "[c]elebrating the magic of children's books in honor of the twentieth anniversary of Reading is Fundamental." Use when studying authors and/or writing.

Smith, Frank. *Essays into Literacy*. Exeter, N.H.: Heinemann Educational Books, 1983.
Essay titles include "Learning to Read by Reading," "The Language Arts and the Learner's Mind," "Myths of Writing," and others.

Trelease, Jim. *The Read-Aloud Handbook*. New York: Penguin Books, 1985.
Trelease provides a convincing case for the merits of reading aloud, and his annotated bibliography helps teachers and parents when making read-aloud selections. It is a must for any reading teacher's bookshelf.

Veatch, Jeannette. *Reading in the Elementary School*. New York: John Wiley and Sons, 1978.
Veatch emphasizes the language experience approach in this lengthy textbook and provides outstanding lists of alternative activities for any teacher interested in breaking away from traditional basals and workbooks.

FIRST CHOICES FOR THE PRIMARY READING AND WRITING CONNECTION

The following books have obvious connections to writing opportunities. They are included to give you ideas and to inspire you to view any picture book as an opportunity to make the connection to student writing.

Alborough, Jez. *The Grass Is Always Greener*. New York: Dial Books for Young Readers, 1987.
When introducing the fable to the very youngest children, use this along with Ed Young's *The Other Bone*. Write group fables with the youngest, allowing your more competent writers the opportunity to tackle this literary form.

Balian, Lorna. *The Sweet Touch*. Nashville, Tenn.: Abingdon Press, 1976.
Peggy gets a wish and everything she touches turns to something sweet. Use when writing about wishes, sweet things, or magic.

Bang, Molly. *Ten, Nine, Eight*. New York: Greenwillow Books, 1983.
The counting book has a new direction—this one counts from ten down. Use with math and to generate ideas of other variations on a theme such as a backwards alphabet.

Barton, Byron. *Building a House*. New York: Greenwillow Books, 1981.
The steps for building a house are illustrated in full color. Use this to trigger books on directions for any child's task: building a sand castle, snow man, or mud pie.

Bauer, Caroline Feller. *My Mom Travels a Lot*. Illustrated by Nancy Winslow Parker. New York: Frederick Warne and Company, Inc., 1981.
Coping with a nontraditional lifestyle is detailed in Bauer's book. Use in discussion of how our families have different structures. Use for individual writing about families.

Blume, Judy. *The Pain and the Great One*. Illustrated by Irene Trivas. Scarsdale, N.Y.: Bradbury Press, 1974.
Each sibling thinks the other is more beloved by the parent. The younger brother is a "pain," and the older sister thinks she is just so "great." Use in having students write about their feelings about their siblings or other family members.

Carle, Eric. *The Grouchy Ladybug*. New York: Thomas Y. Crowell, 1977.
   Each hour of the day is punctuated by a grouchy ladybug's quest for a suitable fight. Use to write about a student's schedule or another fictional character's day. This will help with the learning of telling time, as well.

Crowe, Robert L. *Clyde Monster*. Illustrated by Kay Chorao. New York: E. P. Dutton, 1976.
   Clyde Monster can't sleep at night because he is afraid of "people" disturbing him in his cave. Use in writing about night fears, unwarranted fears, or resolved fears.

Flournoy, Valerie. *The Patchwork Quilt*. Illustrated by Jerry Pinkney. New York: Dial Books for Young Readers, 1985.
   The story of a child's collaboration on a quilt with an ailing grandparent provides a good basis for discussing and writing about caring for the elderly. Use to inspire a class quilt reviewing the year or based on a familiar story.

Keats, Jack. *Pet Show!* New York: Macmillan Publishing Company, Inc., 1972.
   This simple story about an exciting event can inspire similar narratives about pets.

Provenson, Alice, and Martin Provenson. *The Glorious Flight: Across the Channel with Louis Bleriot*. New York: Viking Press, 1983.
   History comes alive with the Provenson's account of this historic flight. Use to model writing historically based reports or stories.

Quackenbush, Robert. *City Trucks*. Chicago: Albert Whitman and Company, 1981.
   A boldly illustrated, yet simple book of trucks is perfect for the youngest child who is interested in creating a book about any special interest.

Rylant, Cynthia. *The Relatives Came*. Illustrated by Stephen Gammell. New York: Bradbury Press, 1985.
   It was a rollicking good time when the relatives came, with hugs, laughter, chatter, and family spilling all over the house. Use for discussion and writing about special family events.

_____. *When I Was Young in the Mountains*. Illustrated by Diane Goode. New York: E. P. Dutton, 1982.
   Rylant's personal narrative about growing up in the mountains develops an appreciation for our earliest experiences. Even the youngest school-age child will have special remembrances of being "young" which can be recorded in writing.

Turner, Ann. *Dakota Dugout*. Illustrated by Ronald Himler. New York: Macmillan Publishing Company, Inc., 1985.
   Life changes dramatically when this family settles into its dugout. Use in a study of pioneer times.

Viorst, Judith. *Alexander and the Terrible, Horrible, No Good, Very Bad Day*. Illustrated by Ray Cruz. New York: Atheneum, 1976.
   Alexander's perfectly rotten day can become the model for students to write about their own worst days.

Wood, Audrey. *The Napping House*. Illustrated by Don Wood. San Diego, Calif.: Harcourt Brace Jovanovich, 1984.
   This cumulative rhyme depicts the addition of all the sleeping household members to the bed. Use to write other cumulative rhymes.

Young, Ed. *The Other Bone*. New York: Harper and Row, Publishers, 1984.
   This wordless picture book of the dog who lost his bone to the reflection in the lake provides youngsters with opportunities to create other written or wordless fables.

Appendix A

Eighty Great Books to Share with Your Children

EARLY GRADES

Cat Walk by Mary Stolz. Harper and Row, Publishers, 1983.

A Chair for My Mother by Vera B. Williams. Greenwillow Books, 1982.

Clive Eats Alligators by Alison Lester. Houghton Mifflin Company, 1986.

Clyde Monster by Robert L. Crowe. Illustrated by Kay Chorao. E. P. Dutton, 1976.

Doctor De Soto by William Steig. Farrar, Straus & Giroux, 1982.

Frog and Toad Are Friends by Arnold Lobel. Harper and Row, Publishers, 1979.

A Garden for a Groundhog by Lorna Balian. Abingdon Press, 1985.

Goodnight Moon by Margaret Wise Brown. Harper and Row, Publishers, 1977.

Harriet and the Crocodiles by Martin Waddell. Atlantic-Little Brown, 1984.

If You Give a Mouse a Cookie by Laura Joffe Numeroff. Harper and Row, Publishers, 1985.

The Island of the Skog by Steven Kellogg. The Dial Press, 1976.

King Bidgood's in the Bathtub by Audrey Wood. Illustrated by Don Wood. Harcourt Brace Jovanovich, 1985.

The Legend of the Bluebonnet retold by Tomie dePaola. Putnam, 1984.

The Little House by Virginia Lee Burton. Houghton Mifflin Company, 1978.

Little Old Lady Who Was Not Afraid of Anything by Linda Williams. Thomas Y. Crowell, 1986.

Madeleine by Ludwig Bemelmans. Puffin Books, 1977.

Max, the Bad-Talking Parrot by Patricia Brennan Demuth. Dodd, Mead, 1986.

Miss Nelson Is Missing by Harry Allard. Illustrated by James Marshall. Scholastic, Inc., 1978.

Miss Rumphius by Barbara Cooney. Puffin Books, 1985.

The Napping House by Audrey Wood. Illustrated by Don Wood. Harcourt Brace Jovanovich, 1984.

The Pain and the Great One by Judy Blume. Illustrated by Irene Trivas. Bradbury Press, 1974.

The Paper Crane by Molly Bang. Greenwillow Books, 1985.

The Polar Express by Chris Van Allsburg. Houghton Mifflin Company, 1985.

The Rainbow-Colored Horse by Pura Belpre. Illustrated by Antonio Martorell. Frederick Warne and Company, Inc., 1978.

The Riddle of the Drum: A Tale from Tizapan, Mexico translated and retold by Verna Aardema. Illustrated by Tony Chen. Four Winds Press, 1979.

The Sweet Touch by Lorna Balian. Abingdon Press, 1976.

The Very Busy Spider by Eric Carle. Philomel Books, 1985.

Where the Wild Things Are by Maurice Sendak. Harper and Row, Publishers, 1984.

William's Doll by Charlotte Zolotow. Illustrated by William Pene Du Bois. Harper and Row, Publishers, 1985.

Folktales

Best Loved Folktales of the World selected by Joanna Cole. Doubleday, 1983.

The People Could Fly: American Black Folktales by Virginia Hamilton. Alfred A. Knopf, 1985.

The Whistling Skeleton: American Indian Tales of the Supernatural collected by George Bird Brinnell. Edited by John Birhorst. Illustrated by Robert Andrew Parker. Four Winds Press, 1982.

Poetry

Brats by X. J. Kennedy. Atheneum, 1986.

My Parents Think I'm Sleeping by Jack Prelutsky. Illustrated by Yossi Abolafia. Greenwillow Books, 1985.

Poetry selected by Michael Rosen. Kingfisher Books, Ltd., 1985.

MIDDLE GRADES

The Best Christmas Pageant Ever by Barbara Robinson. Avon, 1973.

Bridge to Terabithia by Katherine Paterson. Avon, 1979.

Call It Courage by Armstrong Sperry. Macmillan Publishing Company, Inc., 1971.

The Courage of Sarah Noble by Alice Dalgliesh. Illustrated by Leonard Weisgard. Charles Scribner's Sons, 1974.

Cricket in Times Square by George Selden. Illustrated by Garth Williams. Farrar, 1970.

Dear Mr. Henshaw by Beverly Cleary. Dell Publishing Company, Inc., 1984.

Dollhouse Murders by Betty Wright. Holiday House, 1983.

Freckle Juice by Judy Blume. Four Winds Press, 1971.

The Hundred Dresses by Eleanor Estes. Harcourt Brace Jovanovich, 1974.

In the Year of the Boar and Jackie Robinson by Bette Bao Lord. Illustrated by Marc Simont. Harper and Row, Publishers, 1984.

The Indian in the Cupboard by Lynne Reid Banks. Doubleday, 1981.

Island of the Blue Dolphins by Scott O'Dell. Houghton Mifflin Company, 1960.

James and the Giant Peach by Roald Dahl. Illustrated by Nancy Ekholm Burkert. Bantam Books, 1978.

A Lion to Guard Us by Clyde Robert Bulla. Scholastic, Inc., 1983.

Lupita Mañana by Patricia Beatty. William Morrow and Co., 1981.

The Muffin Fiend by Daniel Pinkwater. Lothrop, Lee and Shepard, 1986.

My Brother Sam Is Dead by James L. Collier and Christopher Collier. Scholastic, Inc., 1977.

My Side of the Mountain by Jean George. E. P. Dutton, 1975.

The Night of the Twisters by Ivy Ruckman. Harper and Row, Publishers, 1984.

Penny Pollard's Letters by Robin Klein. Oxford University Press, 1984.

Peppermints in the Parlor by Barbara Brooks Wallace. Atheneum, 1980.

The Pinballs by Betsy Byars. Scholastic, Inc., 1979.

Rain of Fire by Marion Dane Bauer. Clarion Books, 1983.

The Sign of the Beaver by Elizabeth George Speare. Dell Publishing Company, Inc., 1984.

Sixth Grade Can Really Kill You by Barthe DeClements. Scholastic, Inc., 1985.

Soup by Robert Newton Peck. Dell Publishing Company, Inc., 1979.

Stone Fox by John Reynolds Gardiner. Crowell, 1983.

A Taste of Blackberries by Doris B. Smith. Illustrated by Charles Robinson. Scholastic, Inc., 1976.

Tuck Everlasting by Natalie Babbitt. Bantam Books, 1976.

The Weaving of a Dream retold by Marilee Heyer. Viking Kestrel, 1986.

What Happened in Hamelin by Gloria Skurzynski. Four Winds Press, 1979.

UPPER GRADES

Dragons and Dreams edited by Jane Yolen, Martin H. Greenberg, and Charles G. Waugh. Harper and Row, Publishers, 1986.

The Facts and Fictions of Minna Pratt by Patricia MacLachlan. Harper and Row, Publishers, 1988.

The Golden Pasture by Joyce Carol Thomas. Scholastic, Inc., 1986.

The Hero and the Crown by Robin McKinley. Greenwillow Books, 1984.

In Summer Light by Zibby Oneal. Viking Kestrel, 1985.

Jump Ship to Freedom by James L. Collier and Christopher Collier. Delacorte, 1982.

One-Eyed Cat by Paula Fox. Dell Publishing Company, Inc., 1985.

A Rumor of Otters by Deborah Savage. Houghton Mifflin Company, 1986.

Short Takes selected by Elizabeth Segel. Lothrop, Lee and Shepard, 1986.

So Far from the Bamboo Grove by Yoko Kawashima Watkins. Lothrop, Lee and Shepard, 1986.

To Break the Silence edited by Peter A. Barrett. Dell Publishing Company, Inc., 1986.

Winning Kicker by Thomas J. Dygard. William Morrow and Company, 1978.

The Witch of Blackbird Pond by Elizabeth George Speare. Dell Publishing Company, Inc., 1972.

ALPHABET BOOKS

Anno, Mitsumasa. *Anno's Alphabet: An Adventure in Imagination*. New York: Thomas Y. Crowell, 1975.

Anno, Mitsumasa, and Masaichiro Anno. *Anno's Magical ABC: An Anamorphic Alphabet*. New York: Philomel Books, 1980.

Arnosky, Jim. *Mouse Numbers and Letters*. San Diego, Calif.: Harcourt Brace Jovanovich, 1982.

Azarian, Mary. *A Farmer's Alphabet*. Boston: David R. Godine, 1981.

Bridwell, Norman. *Clifford's ABC*. New York: Scholastic, Inc., 1986.

Cameron, Elizabeth. *A Wild Flower Alphabet*. New York: William Morrow and Company, Inc., 1984.

Crowther, Robert. *The Most Amazing Hide-and-Seek Alphabet Book*. New York: Viking-Penguin, Inc., 1978.

De Brunhoff, Laurent. *Babar's ABC*. New York: Random House, Inc., 1983.

Eichenberg, Fritz. *Ape in a Cape: An Alphabet of Odd Animals*. San Diego, Calif.: Harcourt Brace Jovanovich, 1952.

Elting, Mary, and Michael Folsom. *Q Is for Duck*. Illustrated by Jack Kent. New York: Clarion Books, 1980.

Emberley, Ed. *Ed Emberley's A. B. C.* Boston: Little, Brown and Company, 1978.

Fisher, Leonard B. *Alphabet Art: Thirteen ABC's from Around the World*. New York: Macmillan Publishing Company, Inc., 1978.

Fujikawa, Gyo. *Gyo Fujikawa's A to Z Picture Book*. New York: The Putnam Publishing Group, 1974.

Gag, Wanda. *The ABC Bunny*. New York: The Putnam Publishing Group, 1978.

Gretz, Susanna. *Teddy Bears ABC*. New York: Macmillan Publishing Company, Inc., 1986.

Hague, Kathleen. *Alphabears*. Illustrated by Michael Hague. New York: Holt, Rinehart & Winston, 1984.

Hoban, Tana. *A, B, See!* New York: Greenwillow Books, 1982.

Lear, Edward. *An Edward Lear Alphabet*. Illustrated by Carol Newsom. New York: Lothrop, Lee and Shepard Books, 1983.

Lobel, Arnold. *On Market Street*. Illustrated by Anita Lobel. New York: Greenwillow Books, 1981.

Mayers, Florence Casen. *ABC: Museum of Fine Arts, Boston*. New York: Harry N. Abrams, Inc., 1986.

———. *ABC: The Museum of Modern Art, New York*. New York: Harry N. Abrams, Inc., 1986.

McLean, Ruari, ed. *The Noah's Ark A. B. C. and Eight Other Victorian Alphabet Books in Color*. Facsimile edition. New York: Dover Publications, Inc., 1976.

Pienkowski, Jan. *ABC*. New York: Simon and Schuster, Inc., 1981.

Purvis, Mary E. *Animal Alphabet: Wild Animals*. New York: Simon and Schuster, Inc., 1981.

Rios, Edwin. *ABECEDARIO-ALPHABET, ABC*. Illustrated by William E. Hubbard. San Jose, Calif.: Educational Factors, 1980.

Sendak, Maurice. *Alligators All Around*. New York: Harper and Row Junior Books, 1962.

Stockham, Peter, ed. *Chapbook ABC's: Reprints of Five Rare and Charming Early Juveniles*. New York: Dover Publications, Inc., 1974.

Van Allsburg, Chris. *The Z Was Zapped*. Boston: Houghton Mifflin Company, 1987.

Appendix B

Mice Tales

This unit is the study of mice in anticipation of their acquisition as classroom pets. Mice are an appealing research topic for any grade level. Primary teachers can adapt it by eliminating the more difficult books and intermediate teachers can also adjust accordingly. The study of mice is appropriate for several reasons:

1. Throughout history, writers have used mice to reveal human foibles. Sometimes, they portray them realistically—sneaking about, stealing food, eating insects, spreading disease, and serving as food sources. They also portray them in the role of struggling against the strong, such as in the fable "The Lion and the Mouse."

2. Mice have been useful in the experimental studies, especially in the fields of medicine and the behavioral sciences.

3. Mice make pleasant, economical, affectionate, and clever pets.

4. Mice are hardy, adaptable, and prolific members of the rodent family.

When you purchase your mice, buy at least two, as they are quite sociable and love to snuggle. If you want a virtually odorless pair, buy females. Male urine is much stronger and requires more frequent changing of bedding. They are easily housed in a rodent cage or an empty aquarium with a water bottle attached. The information regarding gestation period and eating habits came from *All About Mice*, by Howard Hirschhorn, available at pet stores. (See bibliography.)

BEGINNING THE UNIT

Brainstorm with the students what they know and would like to know about mice, organizing the topics into separate lists. Possible topics include the following.

Varieties:
House
Field
Dormouse
(Rats)

Growth and Development:
Reproduction rates
Eating habits
Adaptability
Habitats
Longevity
Natural enemies

Research Usages:
Medical research
Behavioral sciences (psychology, psychiatry)

Pets:
Habitat
Food requirements
Water needs
Exercise needs
Care requirements
Disease possibilities

Literature and the Arts:
Folktales (*Pied Piper of Hamelin*, *The Cat and the Mouse*)
Stories (see references)
Fables (*Town Mouse and Country Mouse*)
Nursery rhymes ("Hickory, Dickory Dock")
Songs ("Three Blind Mice," Mickey Mouse Club song)
Plays
Cartoons (Mickey and Minnie Mouse, Mighty Mouse)
Movies (*An American Tail*, *Ben and Me*)
Illustrations (Leo Lionni, Beatrix Potter, etc.)
Dance (Nutcracker Ballet)

Fears:
Spreading disease
Biting babies
Dirty animals
Mean animals

ASSIGN RESEARCH REPORTS

Let individual students or small groups choose research topics from the above list. Be sure that a student or group studies the needs of mice to be successful classroom pets. (The pet store will be a good source of research for this portion of the study.) Students may compile a big book based on their mice reports or present individual reports. Research techniques are covered in chapter 4 and will not be repeated here. Depending on your grade level and research experience, reports may be formal, as the minireport in chapter 7, or relatively informal.

Allow several work sessions for the research. Meanwhile schedule the following activities as your schedule and resources allow.

READ ALOUD

Mrs. Frisby and the Rats of NIMH, by Robert C. O'Brien is a story about a widow, Mrs. Frisby, who must get help from a community of super rats, victims of scientific experimentation. The book is long and requires good listeners (grades three and up). Use throughout the research and reward an attentive class with seeing the movie version, *The Secret of NIMH*, comparing the two versions. Meanwhile, intersperse the reading aloud of various shorter selections from the references.

LANGUAGE ARTS

Brainstorm all the mouse words your class can generate: squeaky, "rats!," tiny, cuddly, cat's toy. Write a poem about a mouse or rat.

Example:

> Make your meanest face to
> print this dirty word R A T.
>
> Each letter nibbling, chewing
> the things in your pantry and
> leaving them dingy and tattered
> on your page. R A T.
>
> Nathan Hall
> grade five

There are several sayings using mice as a metaphor:

Poor as a church mouse.

Meek as a mouse.

Are you a man or a mouse?

Quiet as a mouse.

Explain metaphorical language and challenge students to think about the characteristics of mice and make up their own phrases about mice.

SPEAKERS

Check with parents and colleagues for possible experts on the use of mice for research. Other potential sources are veterinarians, medical center staff, medical training centers, physicians, or laboratory technicians. Invite your expert to speak to the students about the role of mice in development of medicine and the behavioral sciences. Be sure to have your students follow the visit with thank you letters.

ASSIGNED READING

Assign the reading of a mouse book or several mouse folktales from the list of references. Another exercise would be to have students find their own mouse books. If you assign book reports, designate a sharing period and compare the books' portrayals of the mice.

MATH

Present the following problem to the class in worksheet form or work on it together.

Prolific Penelope Pearl Mouse

After Penelope Pearl is three months old, she can have a litter of about ten babies every month. If she has a litter of babies every month for six months, how many babies will she have?

Mice usually stop breeding at nine months of age, but the mother's babies can start having litters after they are three months old, too.

Let's suppose that each time Penelope had babies she had five girls, who also had ten babies each. Assuming they only had one litter each, how many grandmice did Penelope have?

How many grandmice would Penelope have if each of her female babies had six litters?

Feeding and Caring
for Penelope's Offspring

A mouse eats about five grams of pellet food per day. If you had to feed Penelope's babies for one day, how much food would it take. (There are 454 grams in one pound.) How much food would it take for one month? Now figure out how much food it would take to feed Penelope's grandmice for one month.

Call the local pet store and get the price of one pound of mice pellets. Add up how much it would cost to feed Penelope's family.

Mice that are twelve weeks old need about fifteen square inches of cage space for each mouse. How much space would be needed to house Penelope's extended family?

Discuss why farmers might want to be able to poison mice, why they keep cats, the potential damage mice do to crops, etc.

SCIENCE

After the mice have been brought into the classroom, prepare forms for the students to use while observing the following details.

Weight

Length

Amount of water consumed daily

Amount of food consumed daily

Activity level (amount of time spent playing)

Response to human handling (anxiety, security)

Behavior with other mice

ART

Mouse Pins

Materials: pink felt, heavy or invisible thread, rubber bands, and walnut shells.

Use strong glue to glue felt ears, thread whiskers, a piece of rubber band tail to the walnut shell. Add eyes with a black marker. You can glue a clip or pin to the underside edge for a "Quiet as a Mouse Pin."

Mouse Prints

Materials: black ink pad, fine tipped markers, four-by-six-inch index cards.

Students press their fingerprints into the stamp pad and use markers to add ears, whiskers, and paws, turning prints into mice. See *Ed Emberley's Great Thumbprint Drawing Book* for more ideas with fingerprint art.

The-Shape-of-Mice Book

Have students create as many different mice as they can by using geometric shapes. For example, have them draw a square and make it into a mouse, continuing with other shapes. Students will discover that geometric shapes have attributes found in nature.

MUSIC

"Three Blind Mice" is the obvious mouse song. The score from the animated movie, *An American Tail*, includes several great songs, including the Grammy award-winning "Somewhere Out There."

SOCIAL STUDIES

Study the habitats of mice, the effect of mice damage on farmers' crops (see math problem, p. 178), the effects of diseases such as the bubonic plague. Gloria Skurzynski's novelized version of the Pied Piper tale, *What Happened in Hamelin*, includes notes about historical evidence of the events in Hamelin during the Middle Ages.

If you have the opportunity to schedule a special treat, rent *An American Tail* for the students to view. Though lighthearted, it provides a good introduction to the topic of immigration.

REFERENCES

Bluth, Don (producer). *The Secret of NIMH*. New York: MGM/UA Home Video, 1982.

_____. *An American Tail*. Universal City, Calif.: MCA Home Video, 1987.

Emberley, Ed. *Ed Emberley's Great Thumbprint Drawing Book*. Boston: Little Brown and Company, 1977.

Hirschhorn, Howard. *All About Mice*. Neptune City, N.J.: T. F. H. Publications, Inc., 1974.

O'Brien, Robert C. *Mrs. Frisby and the Rats of NIMH*. New York: Aladdin Books, 1971.

OTHER RESOURCES

Note: Gather as many mice books as you can find from your library sources. There are *many* more than those included in this list:

Baker, Betty. *Santa Rat*. Illustrated by Tom Huffman. New York: Greenwillow Books, 1980.

Balian, Lorna. *Mother's Mother's Day*. Nashville, Tenn.: Abingdon Press, 1982.

Barkem, Jill. *The Secret Staircase*. New York: Philomel Books, 1983.

Brown, Marcia. *Once a Mouse*. New York: Scribner's, 1961.

Carle, Eric. *Do You Want to Be My Friend?* New York: Thomas Y. Crowell, 1971.

Cleary, Beverly. *The Mouse and the Motorcycle*. New York: Morrow, 1965.

_____. *Ralph S. Mouse*. Illustrated by Paul O. Zelinsky. New York: William Morrow and Co., 1982.

_____. *Runaway Ralph*. New York: William Morrow and Co., 1970.

Emberley, Ed. *Ed Emberley's Great Thumbprint Drawing Book*. Boston: Little, Brown and Company, 1977.

Galdone, Paul. *The Town Mouse and the Country Mouse*. New York: McGraw-Hill, 1971.

Godden, Rumer. *The Mousewife*. New York: Viking press, 1951.

Hoffmann, E. T. A. *The Nutcracker*. Illustrated by Fumiko Hori. Tokyo: Gakken Company, 1971.

Ivimey, John William. *The Complete Version of the Three Blind Mice*. Illustrated by Paul Galdone. New York: Clarion, 1987.

Lawson, Robert. *Ben and Me: An Astonishing Life of Benjamin Franklin by His Good Mouse Amos*. New York: Dell Publishing Company, Inc., 1939.

Lionni, Leo. *Alexander and the Wind-up Mouse*. New York: Pantheon, 1969.

_____. *Geraldine, the Music Mouse*. New York: Pantheon Books, 1979.

_____. *The Greentail Mouse*. New York: Pantheon Books, 1973.

_____. *In the Rabbit Garden*. New York: Pantheon Books, 1975.

Lobel, Arnold. *Mouse Soup*. New York: Harper and Row, Publishers, 1977.

_____. *Mouse Tales*. New York: Harper and Row, Publishers, 1972.

Numeroff, Laura Joffe. *If You Give a Mouse a Cookie*. Illustrated by Felicia Bond. New York: Harper and Row, Publishers, 1985.

Potter, Beatrix. *The Tale of Mrs. Tittlemouse*. New York: Frederick Warne and Company, Inc., 1938.

Silverstein, Alvin, and Virginia Silverstein. *Mice All about Them*. New York: J. B. Lippincott, 1980.

Skurzynski, Gloria. *What Happened in Hamelin*. New York: Four Winds Press, 1979.

Steig, William. *Abel's Island*. New York: Farrar, Straus and Giroux, Inc., 1976.

_____. *Dr. DeSoto*. New York: Farrar, Straus and Giroux, Inc., 1982.

Titus, Eve. *Anatole*. Illustrated by Paul Galdone. New York: McGraw-Hill, 1956. See many other titles in this series.

Van Leeuwen, Jean. *The Great Christmas Kidnapping Caper*. Illustrated by Stephen Kellogg. New York: Dell Publishing Company, Inc., 1975.

White, E. B. *Stuart Little*. San Francisco, Calif.: Harper and Row, Publishers, 1945.

Yolen, Jane. *The Acorn Quest*. New York: Thomas Y. Crowell, 1981.

Note: This unit was adapted from a unit on mice by Ann Polumbus, with art suggestions from Charla Pfeffinger and help with mouse characters from Fred Eidson.

Index